EMERGENCY
WATER SOURCES

GUIDELINES FOR SELECTION AND TREATMENT

Sarah House and Bob Reed

Water, Engineering and Development Centre (WEDC)
Loughborough University UK

WEDC

Published by
WEDC
Loughborough University
Leicestershire
LE11 3TU UK

© WEDC Loughborough University 2004
(Third edition)

First edition printed in 1997

House, S.J. and Reed, R.A. (2004) *Emergency Water Sources:*

Guidelines for selection and treatment (Third edition),
Water, Engineering and Development Centre (WEDC), Loughborough.

ISBN 13 Paperback: 9781843800699
ISBN Library Ebook: 9781788532952
Book DOI: http://dx.doi.org/10.3362/9781788532952

A catalogue record for this book is available from the British Library.

This edition reprinted and distributed by Practical Action Publishing.
Since 1974, Practical Action Publishing has published and disseminated books and
information in support of international development work throughout the world.
Practical Action Publishing trades only in support of its parent charity objectives
and any profits are covenanted back to Practical Action
(Charity Reg. No. 247257, Group VAT Registration No. 880 9924 76).

Designed and produced at WEDC

Designed by Rod Shaw

Layout by Helen Batteson

Editorial support by Kimberly Clarke

Additional illustrations by Robin Borrett
and Jeremy Thistlethwaite

ABOUT THE AUTHORS

Sarah House is a civil / public health engineer who has experience of training for, and implementation of, labour-based construction for peri-urban areas of sub-Saharan Africa. She also has experience of emergency water supply and a specific interest in water and wastewater treatment process selection, design and evaluation. Her other major interests include gender and other people issues in engineering projects and the problems related to homelessness and mental health.

Bob Reed is a Programme and Project Manager at the Water, Engineering and Development Centre. He specializes in water supply and sanitation for rural areas, low-income urban communities and refugees. He has considerable experience of training, design and project implementation in the Pacific, the Caribbean, Asia and Africa. In recent years he has focused on the provision of improved and sustainable water supply and sanitation systems for displaced populations.

The authors would like to hear from anyone who uses the guidelines in the field with comments on their usefulness and areas which require adaptation or improvement. Please forward comments or suggestions to Bob Reed at the address given overleaf.

ABOUT WEDC

The Water, Engineering and Development Centre (WEDC) is one of the world's leading institutions concerned with education, training, research and consultancy for the planning, provision and management of physical infrastructure for development in low- and middle-income countries.

WEDC is devoted to activities that improve the health and well-being of people living in both rural areas and urban communities. We encourage the integration of technological, environmental, social, economic and management inputs for effective and sustainable development.

WEDC

Water, Engineering and Development Centre
Loughborough University
Leicestershire
LE11 3TU UK

Phone: +44 1509 222885
Fax: +44 1509 211079
Email: WEDC@lboro.ac.uk
http://www.lboro.ac.uk/wedc/

COLLABORATORS

The 'Rapid Assessment of Emergency Water Sources' project (R 6256A) has been funded by the Department for International Development (DFID) of the British Government.

The following organisations have acted as peer reviewers for this research contract. They have reviewed draft documents, provided access to staff for interview, provided information and have been involved in and provided support for the field trials.

Opinions noted within these documents do not necessarily represent those of DFID or the collaborators, but are solely those of the authors.

INTERNATIONAL COMMITTEE OF THE RED CROSS

International Federation
of Red Cross and Red Crescent Societies

MEDECINS
SANS FRONTIERES

OXFAM
UNITED KINGDOM AND IRELAND

RedR

unicef
United Nations Children's Fund

UNHCR
UNITED NATIONS HIGH COMMISSIONER FOR REFUGEES

Many individuals have made useful contributions and are acknowledged in Section 1.

OVERVIEW

CONTENTS

Section 4   Supporting information   101

ACRONYMS

ARRA	Administration of Refugee and Returnee Affairs (Ethiopia)
CEU	Construction Enterprise Unit
DFID	Department for International Development
GPS	Global positioning system
HCR	Shortened version of UNHCR
ICRC	International Committee of the Red Cross
IFRC	International Federation of the Red Cross and Red Crescent Societies
MSF	Médecins sans Frontières
NGO	Non-governmental organisation
NTU	Nephelometric Turbidity Units
O&M	Operation and maintenance
RAEWS	Rapid Assessment of Emergency Water Sources
REDR	Register of Engineers for Disaster Relief
RSF	Rapid sand filtration
SRS	Sanitary risk score
SSF	Slow sand filtration
THM	Trihalomethane
TU	Turbidity Units
TDS	Total dissolved solids
UNHCR	United Nations High Commissioner for Refugees
UNICEF	United Nations Children's Fund
UNPROFOR	United Nations Protection Force
UNIDO	United Nations Industrial Development Organization
UTM	Universal Transverse Mercator
WEDC	Water, Engineering and Development Centre
WHO	World Health Organization

S. House

Lungutu River, Eastern Zaire

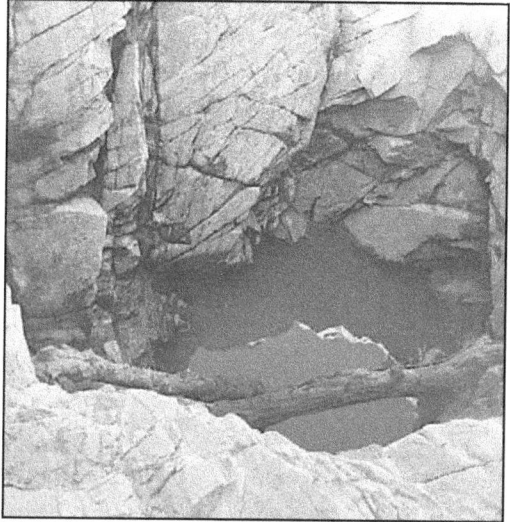

S. House

Shallow groundwater, Teferi Ber, Eastern Ethiopia

S. House

Shallow well under construction, Teferi Ber, Eastern Ethiopia

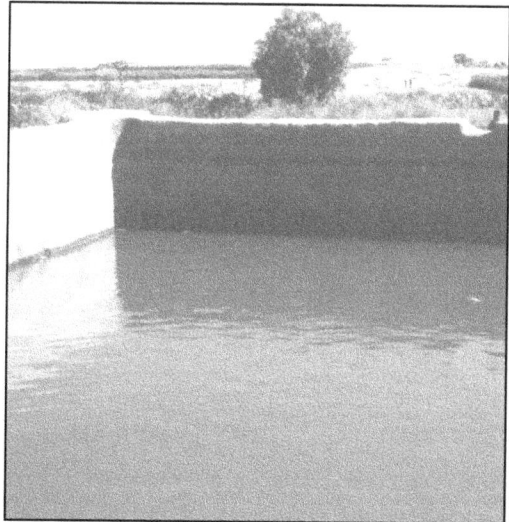

S. House

Rainwater stored in *birka*, Kebri Beyah, Eastern Ethiopia

Water sources

1

INTRODUCTION AND INSTRUCTIONS FOR USE

About these guidelines

These guidelines have been designed to help those involved in the assessment of emergency water sources to collect relevant information in a systematic way, to use this information to select a source or sources and to determine the appropriate level of treatment required to make the water suitable for drinking.

The guidelines, however, are not limited to the selection and treatment of water sources. The information collected will also be useful for:

- the design and costing of the water supply system;
- the ordering of material and equipment;
- the organization of human resources; and
- the implementation of the project.

A thorough assessment at an early stage will save valuable time later on.

Specifically, the guidelines will:

- act as an *aide-mémoire* to assessors;
- help to fill any knowledge gaps; and
- assist in the training of future assessors to undertake this occasional task, allowing them to learn from past experiences.

The selection tools and guidelines are not a replacement for experience. They should be used with engineering judgement and intuition gained from experience of emergency responses. They are not intended to make the assessor a specialist in all the skill areas but to support a basic understanding. Reference has been made where specialist help may be required (e.g. from a hydrogeologist or to interpret industrial pollution laboratory results). The assessor will need to study these documents and preferably have training in their use prior to using them in the field. A training pack has been developed to support this document and may be obtained from the authors.

What is an 'emergency'?

Perceptions of what constitutes an 'emergency' varies between personnel and between organizations. Organizations that concentrate on the initial stages of an emergency understandably consider their problems to be paramount whereas those that support affected populations for many years after the initial event consider the problems of the longer term to be equally important. These guidelines have been developed to cater for the requirements of both parties and those holding intermediate views.

Using definitions given in Davis and Lambert, (1995: p1) 'disasters' can be either natural or induced by humans. They can be slow or sudden onset and they 'result in a serious disruption of society, cause widespread human suffering and physical loss or damage, and stretch the community's normal coping mechanisms to breaking point'. *'The term 'emergency' is used to describe the crisis that arises when a community has great difficulty in coping with a disaster. External assistance is needed, sometimes lasting for many months, perhaps years'.*

Assessors may have to work in a wide variety of scenarios, which include:

- responses required immediately after the event or some years after;
- natural or man-made disasters (e.g. flooding, war or chemical disasters);
- sudden-onset or slow-onset disasters (e.g. earthquake or drought);
- operational local and national authorities or none;
- plentiful supply of surface water or an area dependant on groundwater and rainwater;
- high security risks (especially in conflict areas) or no security problem;
- serious logistical and resource problems or easy access to resources; and
- affected populations are displaced or there is limited displacement.

Each of these scenarios will require a different response and will have different constraints. The guidelines will therefore have to be adapted accordingly.

The term 'affected population' has been used to describe refugees, internally displaced persons, returnees who may be accommodated in temporary camps, and populations whose lives have been modified by the emergency but who have not been displaced. However, the documents also refer to 'local populations', which infers that the local and affected populations are different. This differentiation aims to ensure that local communities are not forgotten when there is a displacement into an area. The terms will require adaptation to suit a non-displacement situation where the affected populations and the local populations are one and the same.

Socio-political, legal, cultural and security issues

Often in emergency situations, the factors which dictate what can be undertaken to provide basic services are linked to socio-political, legal, cultural or security issues. The guidelines therefore emphasize these issues. A case study section has been included to describe some of the complex scenarios under which assessors have worked and some responses which were used.

Approach

Water source selection in an emergency situation needs a phased or upgrading approach. However, it is important to recognize that there are constraints to future upgrading, such as:

- a lack of commitment from the implementing organizations, local and affected populations;
- a lack of finances (funds are often more widely available in the acute stages of an emergency than later on); and
- political restrictions.

Therefore, decisions made in the initial phases of the emergency are likely to affect longer term options.

These guidelines use the terms 'survival' supply (the immediate response to an emergency) and 'longer term' supply (subsequent responses including improvements to survival supply and for the longer term). The survival supply requires quick assessment and decision-making and the longer term supply requires a more thorough assessment and a more holistic approach. Below are two alternative descriptions of the stages of an 'emergency' and the corresponding terminology used in these guidelines. Every emergency is different and the generalizations noted here will not fit every situation. Specific situations, for example conflicts, may require a significantly longer period at the survival level of supply, and in other emergencies survival responses may have to be re-introduced at a later date.

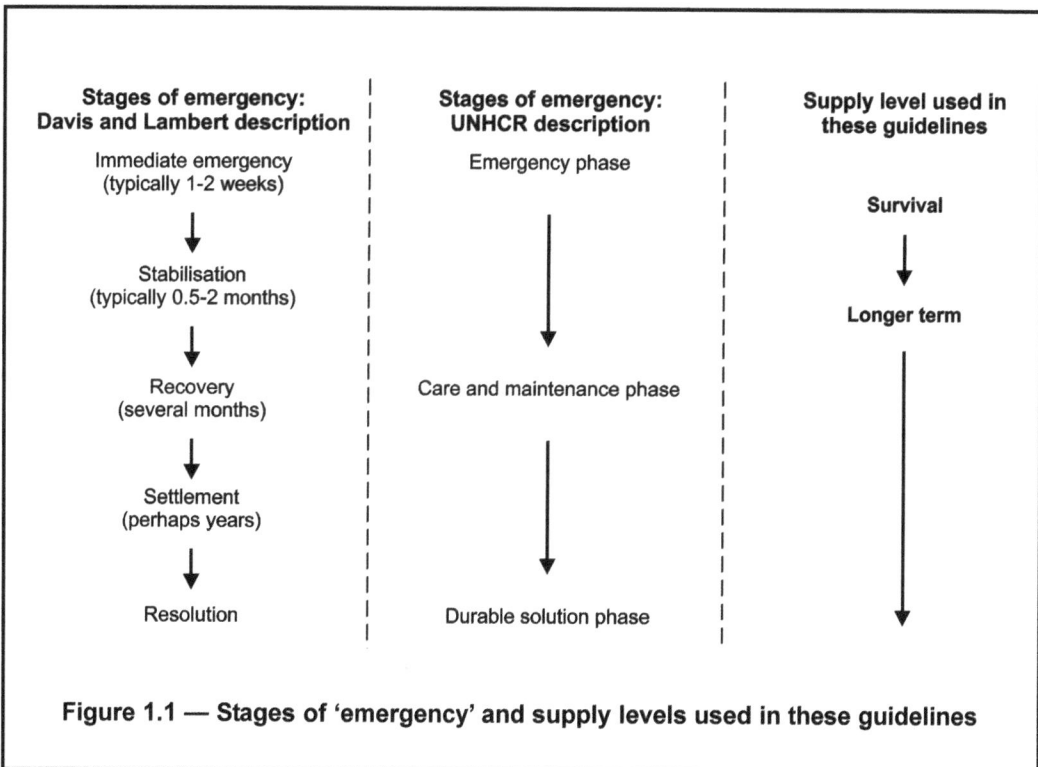

Stages of emergency: Davis and Lambert description	Stages of emergency: UNHCR description	Supply level used in these guidelines
Immediate emergency (typically 1-2 weeks) ↓	Emergency phase ↓	Survival ↓
Stabilisation (typically 0.5-2 months) ↓		Longer term
Recovery (several months) ↓	Care and maintenance phase ↓	
Settlement (perhaps years) ↓		↓
Resolution	Durable solution phase	

Figure 1.1 — Stages of 'emergency' and supply levels used in these guidelines

Application

In most emergencies there will be more than one potential water source. The options could include surface or groundwater near to the site, or tankered or bottled water brought from a distance. The guideline procedures will encourage the assessor to look at as many source options as possible, not just the most obvious ones. It may be, however, that there is only one viable option and in this case the procedures set out in these guidelines will still be useful. They will help the assessor to identify the requirements to develop the source and to highlight key considerations. Some assumptions will have to be made during the assessments, particularly in the initial stages of an emergency, but the number of assumptions should be limited by efficient and logical information gathering. Any assumptions that are made should be verified as soon as possible.

Guideline user group

The guidelines may be useful to a range of personnel involved in the selection of emergency water sources and treatment processes. These could include:

■ national or local government personnel from the affected country;

■ field staff from local or international organizations who may have limited previous experience in this task (field staff would have a basic technical understanding but this may not specifically be engineering or water related); and

■ senior staff who have significant experience in the assessment process in a range of different scenarios.

Assessors will usually work within a team comprised of either all nationals or a mixture of national and international personnel. The effective use of team members for information gathering can save time. The areas which require investigation are multi-disciplinary and cross over several fields e.g. health, social and technical. Use should be made of personnel from these disciplines where they are available.

Although assessments may be undertaken by national or international personnel, reference has been made in information gathering to the 'host country' and the 'donor country' to differentiate when this is the case. The terms will therefore have to be adapted to suit a situation where the host country and the donor country are one and the same.

Relationship between source selection with other activities

Water source and site selection are interdependent. Which is considered first will depend on the situation, particularly the political constraints. Ideally the site should be chosen on the basis of the suitability of the water source but in many cases the water source will have to be chosen in relation to a particular site.

This work focuses on the selection of water sources in relation to a particular site, but obviously the same procedures can be followed for several sites. The urgency of the decision will be a restricting factor to the thoroughness of the assessment.

Source selection for drinking water is also affected by, and related to, sanitation, hygiene practice, drainage, irrigation and similar activities. The guidelines point to the need to consider supplementary or ancillary activities where necessary.

In many cases the person evaluating the source and treatment requirements will be also producing the whole water supply project proposal. Attempts have been made in the guidelines to acknowledge this and to point out to additional information which may be required for this activity.

Completeness of surveys

It is accepted that every emergency situation will be different and the skill level and experience of the assessor will also vary. Hence, the guidelines are subdivided into sections which can be used or omitted as appropriate. Not all of the survey information will be collected on each occasion, but by highlighting its relevance the assessor can at least consider its appropriateness to his / her situation. Using information from a range of sources allows confirmation or otherwise of initial findings or assumptions.

The assessment steps as highlighted by the flowcharts S1 and L1 show only one of the many possible routes to assessment. The procedures have been represented in this way to try and make the assessor think of how logical and methodical his/her information gathering and decision-making are and as a guide to possible improvement. The procedures will have to be used with common sense and adapted to suit specific situations.

Record keeping

Good records should be kept of all gathered information and they should be stored in such a way that others can access them. Information gathering takes time and hence the assessor (or those following the assessor) should not have to repeat work because of inefficient record keeping. The survey sheets included in this document are designed to help with efficient record-keeping. They may be enlarged from A5 to A4 and further blank sheets attached where space for completion is inadequate.

Photographs and sketches

Photographs and sketches of water sources and supplies are very useful for decision-making especially for anyone referring to the survey who was not involved in the initial assessment.

Time targets for assessments

Estimated time to undertake the assessment procedure (including general orientation) starting from arrival in-country or in-field is:

- survival supply: 1 – 3 working days
- longer term supply: 3 – 7 working days

These time periods will not be possible for every scenario but are general targets.

Instructions for use

Section 2 identifies procedures and provides tools for the selection of water sources for survival supply (usually most appropriate in the initial stages of an emergency). Section 3 identifies procedures and provides tools for the selection of a water source for longer term supply (anything other than survival supply). Within these sections are procedural flowcharts, selection tools, checklists for information gathering and survey sheets.

Section 4 contains supporting information on specific issues or assessment procedures.

Section 5 contains a glossary, useful addresses, details of field equipment and a bibliography.

It is suggested that the assessor should read through and become familiar with the contents of Sections 2 and 3 and only use Sections 4 and 5 when there is a specific query. Not all assessors will want to use the total contents of Sections 2 and 3. However, specific items, for example the checklists, may be useful even to experienced assessors, and reading through these sections may still be a good revision exercise.

To use Sections 2 and 3 follow these five steps:

1. Study the flowchart which highlights the steps that need to be taken to assess water sources. It identifies how the procedure described in that section fits into the overall programme for installing an emergency water supply.

2. Study the selection tools to understand what must be considered when selecting a treatment process and water source.

3. Work through the checklists collecting as much information as possible which is appropriate to the particular scenario. Record the information on the survey sheets or in another accessible form.

4. When as much information as possible has been collected, return to the selection tools and use them as required. If some of the necessary information is not available at the time then assumptions will have to be made.

5. If additional information later becomes available, the selection should be re-assessed to see if it needs to be modified.

Acknowledgements

Thanks go to all individuals and organizations who have been involved in the study or have given permission to reproduce extracts from existing documents. It is hoped that the wide range of organizations and individuals who have contributed to the work will ensure that it is likewise useful to a wide user group and in a range of emergency situations.

All contributions are gratefully acknowledged. It should be noted, however, that the opinions in this document are solely those of the authors.

The following individuals have contributed in detail to the research either in their role as peer reviewers, or by testing the work in the field, or by providing information for specific sections of the work.

Annick Barros	*IFRC (Bukavu, Zaire)*
Barend Leuwenberg	*MSF-H (Head Office)*
Bob Elson	*WEDC, Loughborough University (UK)*
Bobby Lambert	*REDR (Head Office – peer reviewer)*
Brendan Doyle	*UNICEF (Head Office – peer reviewer)*
Daniel Mora-Castro	*UNHCR (Head Office – peer reviewer)*
Denis Heidebroek	*MSF-H (Head Office – peer reviewer)*
Dixon Chanda	*MSF-H (Head Office)*
Gary Campbell	*Independant Consultant representing UNHCR (Addis Ababa, Ethiopia)*
Koos Messelink and Bonane Cikola Rugendabanga	*MSF-H (Uvira, Zaire)*
Lila Pieters and Kalubi Misombo	*UNICEF (Bukavu, Zaire)*
Paul Larcher	*CEU, Loughborough University (UK)*
Riccardo Conti	*ICRC (Head Office – peer reviewer)*
Richard Luff	*OXFAM (Head Office – peer reviewer)*
Stuart Dale, Nina Ladner and Geoff Russell	*Public Health Laboratories, Loughborough University (UK)*
Tom de Veer	*De Veer Consultancy (The Netherlands)*
Uli Jaspers	*IFRC (Head Office – peer reviewer)*
Vincent Chordi and Antenneh Tesfaye	*UNHCR (Regional Liason Office, Addis Ababa, Ethiopia)*
Yves Chartier and Gilles Isard	*MSF-F (Head Office – peer reviewer)*

The following individuals have also contributed to the study by being involved in interviews or discussions on sub-sections of the work or providing information in the field or from head office.

Abdi Awil Hersai	*UNHCR (Jijiga, Ethiopia)*
Abebe Chekole	*Fundika Town Committee (Dimma, Ethiopia)*
Ahmed Hussein	*Water Resources Bureau (Jijiga, Ethiopia)*
Amaha Altaye	*UNHCR (Regional Liason Office, Addis Ababa, Ethiopia)*
Angelo de Bernardo	*MSF-H*
Aregawi Hagos	*OXFAM (Addis Ababa, Ethiopia)*

Antos Szkudlarek	*MSF-H*
Bedlu Wagari	*MSF-F*
Brian Skinner	*WEDC, Loughborough University (UK)*
Chris Buckley	*University of Natal (South Africa)*
Chris Preston	*OXFAM (UK)*
David Byakweli	*CARE (Chimanga near Bukavu, Zaire)*
David Lashley	*David Lashley and Partners Inc. (Barbados)*
David Parrums	*UNHCR (Uvira, Zaire)*
Dr Berhanu Dibaba	*Administration of Refugee and Returnee Affairs (Addis Ababa, Ethiopia)*
Dr Elias Mitsale Mo	*Administration of Refugee and Returnee Affairs (Teferi Ber, Ethiopia)*
Dr F. Bassani	*World Health Organization (Switzerland)*
Dr H. Galal-Gorchev	*World Health Organization (Switzerland)*
Dr John Tabayi	*UNHCR (Regional Liason Office, Addis Ababa, Ethiopia)*
Dr Sandy Cairncross	*London School of Hygiene and Tropical Medicine (UK)*
Dr S. Ben Yahmed	*World Health Organization (Switzerland)*
Dr Timothy Ama	*Administration of Refugee and Returnee Affairs (Dimma, Ethiopia)*
Erimias Goitom	*Administration of Refugee and Returnee Affairs (Dimma, Ethiopia)*
Eshetu Abate	*OXFAM (Addis Ababa, Ethiopia)*
Fouad Hikmat	*MSF-H*
Francis Mulemba	*MSF-F*
Ghidey Glegliabher	*Water Resources Bureau (Jijiga, Ethiopia)*
Gino Henry	*REDR (UK)*
Giselle Rouquie	*MSF-H (Uvira, Zaire) / MSF-F*
Habtamu Tekleab	*CARE (Teferi Ber, Ethiopia)*
Hailu Kebede	*ARRA (Dimma, Ethiopia)*
James W. Borton	*UNDP / Emergencies Unit of Ethiopia (Addis Ababa, Ethiopia)*
Jean Luc Bruno	*MSF-B (Bujumbura, Burundi)*
Jim Howard	*Independent Consultant, Water and Environmental Engineer (UK)*
John Adams	*OXFAM (Head Office)*
John Fawell	*National Centre for Environmental Toxicology, WRc (UK)*
K.S. Nair	*CARE (Jijiga, Ethiopia)*
Kim Waterhouse	*REDR (UK)*
Kristof Bosteon	*MSF-B*
Lori D. Barg	*Step by Step (USA)*
Major T. Duggleby	*British Army Water Development Team*
Manuel Jagour	*MSF-F (Bujumbura, Burundi)*
Margaret Ince	*WEDC, Loughborough University (UK)*
Mark D. Bidder	*UNDP / Emergencies Unit of Ethiopia (Addis Ababa, Ethiopia)*
Mark Graham	*Umgeni Water (South Africa)*
Mesfin Lema	*UNICEF (Addis Ababa, Ethiopia)*
Michael Smith	*WEDC, Loughborough University (UK)*
Mohammed Rafi Aziz	*MSF-B*
Mohammed Said	*Water Resources Bureau (Jijiga, Ethiopia)*
Mohammed Zaheoil Islam	*MSF-H*
Moltot Haile	*Water Resources Bureau (Jijiga, Ethiopia)*
Mr Guy	*British Army Water Development Team*
Nick Wilson	*REDR (UK)*
Paul Andre Monette	*MSF-B*

Paul Keating	*REDR (UK)*
Paul Kremers	*MSF-H (Uvira, Zaire)*
Paul Steadman	*Environmental Engineering Group, University of Newcastle upon Tyne (UK)*
Paul van Haperen	*MSF-H (Uvira, Zaire)*
Peter Stern	*Author and Civil Engineer (UK)*
Pole Kore	*Dimma Refugee Representative Committee (Dimma, Ethiopia)*
Professor H.H. Dieter	*Umweltbundesamt Institute for Water, Soil and Air Hygiene (Germany)*
Richard Jabot	*MSF-F*
Sahid Ibrahim	*Water Resources Bureau (Jijiga, Ethiopia)*
Selemani Balongelwa	*MSF-H (Uvira, Zaire)*
Shimeles Makonnen	*OXFAM (Addis Ababa, Ethiopia)*
Sobhi M. Abdel-Hai	*UNICEF (Addis Ababa, Ethiopia)*
Tim Forster	*Merlin (UK)*
Timothy David Boucher	*MSF-B*
Tudor T. Davies	*United States Environmental Protection Agency (USA)*
Waldu Muhray	*OXFAM (Head Office)*
Wies Van Bemmel	*UNHCR (Regional Liaison Office, Addis Ababa, Ethiopia)*
Yirku Adere	*Administration of Refugee and Returnee Affairs (Addis Ababa, Ethiopia)*
Yohannes Gebremedhin	*Water Supply and Sewerage Department (Addis Ababa, Ethiopia)*

Permission was given to reproduce extracts from the following publications:

· Brassington, R. (1988) *Field Hydrogeology*, John Wiley & Sons, UK.

· Cairncross, S. & Feachem, R. (1978) *Small water supplies*, Bulletin No.10, Ross Institute, London.

· Carrol, R.F. (1991) *Disposal of domestic effluents to the ground*, Overseas Building Note 195, Building Research Establishment.

· Davis, J. & Lambert, R. (1995) *Engineering in Emergencies: A practical guide for relief workers*, Intermediate Technology Publications, London.

· de Lange, E. (1994) *Manual for Simple Water Quality Analysis*, IWT Foundation, The Netherlands.

· Foerster, J. (1996) *Uvira Water Supply Project*, Internal Report, ICRC /ARC, Melbourne, Australia.

· ICRC (1994) *Water and War: Symposium on Water in Armed Conflicts*, Montreux, 21 – 23 November 1994, ICRC,

· Jordan, T.D. Jnr (1984) *A Handbook of Gravity Flow Water Systems*, Intermediate Technology Publications, London.

· Lashley, D. (1997) *Vulnerability Assessment of the Drinking Water Supply Infrastrucutre of Montserrat*, Pan American Health Organization.

· MSF (1994) *Public Health Engineering in Emergency Situations*, MSF Paris, France.

· Pacey, A. & Cullis, A. (1986) *Rainwater Harvesting: The collection of rainfall and run-off in rural areas*, Intermediate Technology Publications, London.

· Stern, P. (ed) from an original work by F. Longland (1983) *Field Engineering: An introduction to development work and construction in rural areas*, Intermediate Technology Publications, London.

· Stulz, R. & Mukerji, K. (1993) *Appropriate Building Materials: A catalogue of potential solutions*, 3rd Edn, SKAT & IT Publications,

· Viking Optical Ltd, *Suunto Clinometer Instruction Leaflet.*

· WHO (1993) *Guidelines for Drinking-Water Quality Vol.1: Recommendations*, 2nd edn, WHO, Geneva.

2

SURVIVAL SUPPLY

Steps for assessing survival supply

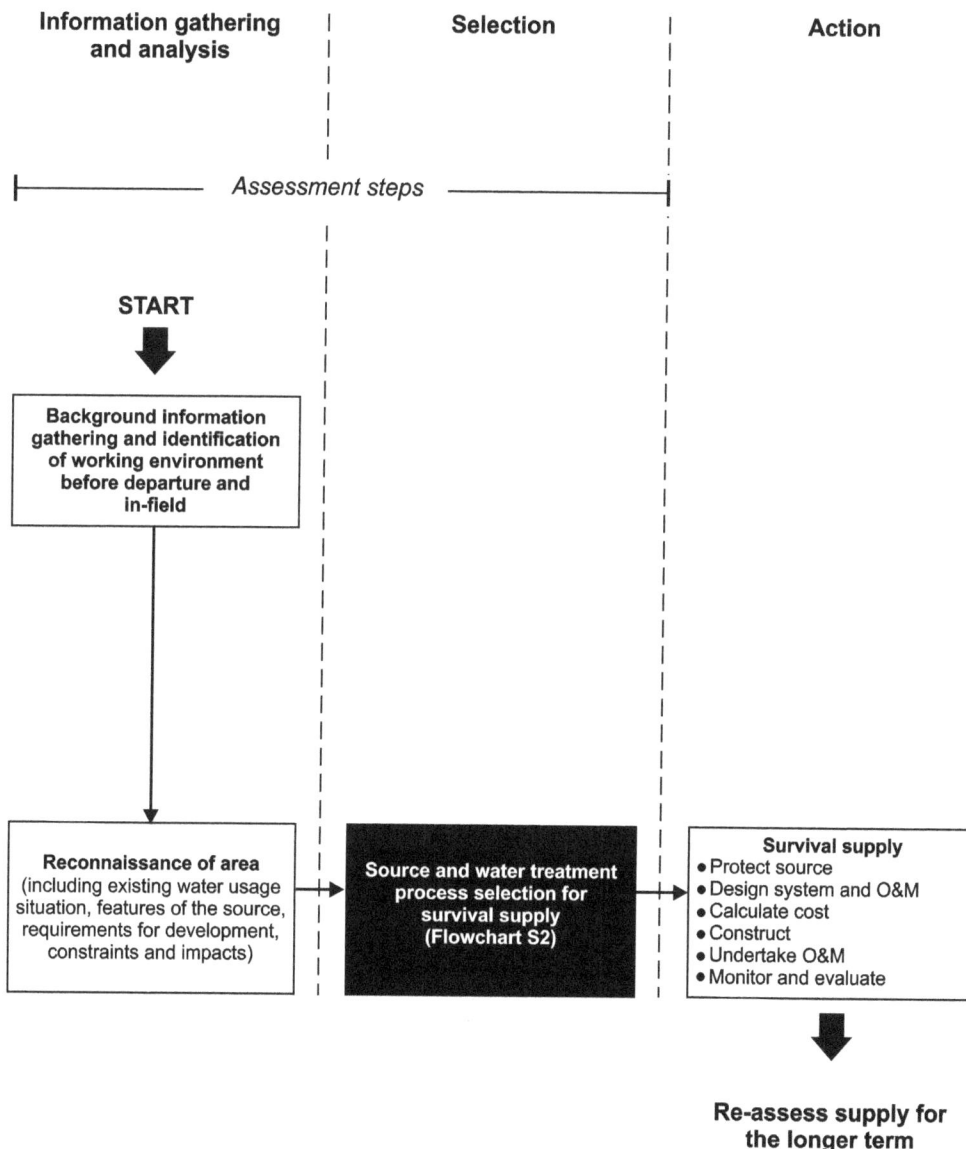

Information gathering and analysis	Selection	Action

|◄─────────────── *Assessment steps* ───────────────►|

START

▼

```
Background information
gathering and identification
of working environment
before departure and
in-field
```

│

▼

| **Reconnaissance of area**
(including existing water usage
situation, features of the source,
requirements for development,
constraints and impacts) | ──► | **Source and water treatment
process selection for
survival supply
(Flowchart S2)** | ──► | **Survival supply**
• Protect source
• Design system and O&M
• Calculate cost
• Construct
• Undertake O&M
• Monitor and evaluate |

▼

**Re-assess supply for
the longer term**

Note: For further information, also refer to Figure 3.3, p47 and the source summary table, p48

Source and water treatment process selection
for survival supply

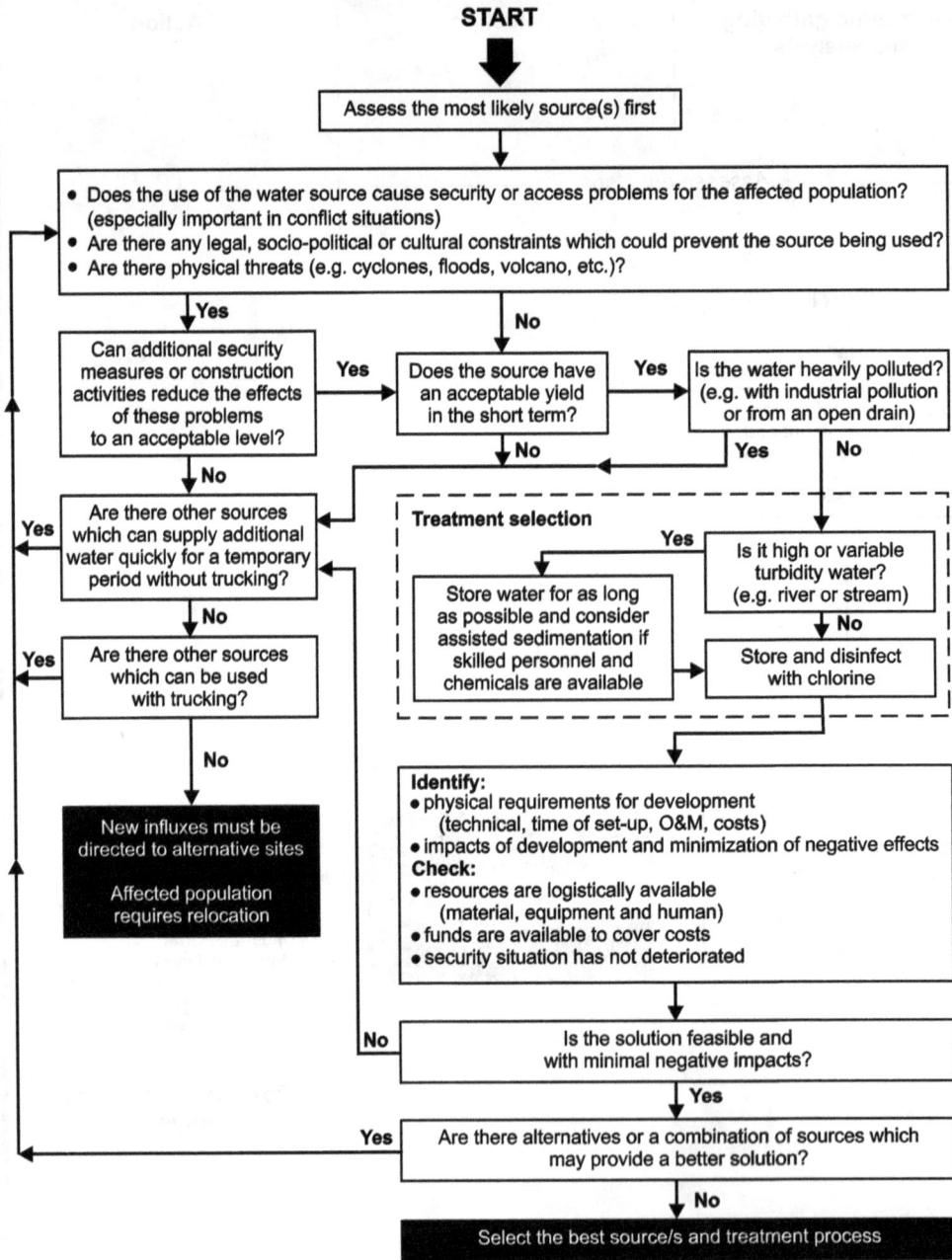

START

⬇

Assess the most likely source(s) first

- Does the use of the water source cause security or access problems for the affected population? (especially important in conflict situations)
- Are there any legal, socio-political or cultural constraints which could prevent the source being used?
- Are there physical threats (e.g. cyclones, floods, volcano, etc.)?

Yes / **No**

Can additional security measures or construction activities reduce the effects of these problems to an acceptable level?	**Yes** →	Does the source have an acceptable yield in the short term?	**Yes** →	Is the water heavily polluted? (e.g. with industrial pollution or from an open drain)

No (below yield box) / **Yes** / **No**

No (below security box)

Yes ← Are there other sources which can supply additional water quickly for a temporary period without trucking?

Treatment selection

Is it high or variable turbidity water? (e.g. river or stream)

Yes / **No**

Store water for as long as possible and consider assisted sedimentation if skilled personnel and chemicals are available

Store and disinfect with chlorine

No

Yes ← Are there other sources which can be used with trucking?

No

New influxes must be directed to alternative sites   **Affected population requires relocation**

Identify:
- physical requirements for development (technical, time of set-up, O&M, costs)
- impacts of development and minimization of negative effects

Check:
- resources are logistically available (material, equipment and human)
- funds are available to cover costs
- security situation has not deteriorated

No ← Is the solution feasible and with minimal negative impacts?

Yes

Yes ← Are there alternatives or a combination of sources which may provide a better solution?

No

Select the best source/s and treatment process

Background information gathering and identification of working environment before departure and in-field

Note: The following two checklists and the *Availability of resources / logistics* checklist (pp56-7) may be sent ahead to the field so that information gathering may begin before the arrival of the assessors.

Background information gathering before departure and in-field ■

Information

- ❑ Maps (topographic, geological, road, hydrogeological, demographic, land-use, rainfall)
- ❑ Aerial photographs / landstat images
- ❑ Regional details
    - ○ *Climate (including rainfall data)*
    - ○ *Industrial and agricultural practices*
    - ○ *Populations (culture, religion)*
    - ○ *Economy*
    - ○ *Political situation*
    - ○ *Exchange rate*
- ❑ Previous surveys / studies (organizations' database or library)
- ❑ Other agencies working in the field
- ❑ Organizational structure of employing agency and policy and mandate
- ❑ Specific job information
    - ○ *Job description*
    - ○ *Responsibilities and chain of command*
    - ○ *Other agency personnel in the field*
    - ○ *Logistical and financial constraints*
    - ○ *Communication procedures*
- ❑ Structure of government and local government (including which store information and which make decisions)
- ❑ Contacts in key departments (water and sewerage, water resources, planning, surveying, meteorological)
- ❑ National policies and development projects
- ❑ Existing national emergency plans
- ❑ Capacity of the government to cope with the water demands of the affected population
- ❑ Background to the crisis and projected developments

Sources of information

- ❑ Government departments of donor country (geological, land survey, environment, military)
- ❑ Government departments of host country (water resources, water and sewerage, surveying, meteorological, military, social, planning)
- ❑ Specialist shops (e.g. for maps: Stanfords, London, UK)
- ❑ Consulting engineers
- ❑ University departments (geography, geology, environmental science, civil engineering, mining, surveying)
- ❑ Employing organization head office (verbal from head office and returned personnel; reports from past projects)
- ❑ Organization field staff and experts in the area
- ❑ Government embassy
- ❑ Press reports
- ❑ Books, journals
- ❑ Travel guides
- ❑ The Internet
- ❑ 'District Surveys' in libraries for ex-colony countries
- ❑ Donor country briefings
- ❑ Checklist pp68-9

Identification of working environment ■

Information

- ❑ Field organizational structure of employing agency / organogram (chain of command, logistics, administration, technical, health education, medical personnel)
- ❑ Areas of responsibility for yourself and others
- ❑ Personnel from other organizations working in water or sanitation in the area (government, international and local)
- ❑ Operational structure for co-ordination between organizations and government including role of UNHCR, organization and national and local government contacts, and employment agreements
- ❑ Decision-making structure re: water source selection. Are you working for the lead organization? Which camps or populations are you responsible for supplying?
- ❑ Communication channels with affected and local populations and community structures (contacts), and role of UNHCR and governments in communication
- ❑ Organization's policy for supporting local populations
- ❑ Team members / access to local personnel (translators, surveying assistants, driver)
- ❑ Working facilities (office space, telephone / radio, fax, email, photocopying, storage space for equipment and workshops, power sources, security, vehicle)
- ❑ Methods of payment

Sources of information

- ❑ Employing organization staff
- ❑ Other organization staff (including UNHCR)
- ❑ National and local government

Reconnaissance of the area

(including existing water usage situation, features of the source, requirements for development, constraints and impacts)

Regional orientation ■

Information

❏ Physical features (high and low areas, vegetation, water sources)

❏ Location and type of water source (developed? not developed?)

❏ Human features (settlements, industry, agriculture, roads)

❏ Distances between users and water sources

❏ Distances and approximate heights between features

❏ Areas vulnerable to natural threats (cyclones, mudslides, earthquakes, etc.)

❏ Areas with high security risk (e.g. mined areas)

❏ Areas subjected to extreme weather conditions

Sources of information

❏ Observation

❏ Published and unpublished maps, aerial photographs, etc. as collected in background information gathering

❏ Simple surveying (GPS, Abney level / clinometer, altimeter)

❏ National and local government

❏ Local and affected populations

❏ Other field staff

❏ Natural threat monitoring stations

❏ *Catchment mapping: maps and symbols* pp154-60

❏ *Catchment mapping: surveying* pp161-8

Methods

❏ Mapping

❏ Panoramic photographic records

Settlement orientation ■

Information

❏ Boundaries, present subdivisions (including ethnic or clan divisions), possible areas for expansion (include distances)

❏ Population density where settlements are dispersed or mobile

❏ Slope of ground (and existing drainage channels – if any)

❏ Water sources (and areas susceptible to flooding or other physical threats)

❏ Areas with buildings / shelters, open spaces and communal areas

❏ Access roads

❏ Sanitation facilities including excreta disposal, refuse dumps / collection areas and graveyards

❏ Administration centres and feeding centres

❏ Chemical stores

❏ Lighting

❏ Security arrangements

Sources of information

❏ Observation from high ground (using binoculars) and by walking around the camp

❏ Aerial photographs

❏ Simple surveying (pacing, Abney level / clinometer, GPS)

❏ Other field staff

❏ Local government

❏ Local and affected population

❏ *Catchment mapping: maps and symbols* pp154-60

❏ *Catchment mapping: surveying* pp161-8

Methods

❏ Mapping

❏ Photographic records

2

Demographics, present water use and water demands ■

Information

- ❑ Water user numbers — affected population:
  - ○ *Individuals*
  - ○ *Livestock large and small (and average number per family)*
  - ○ *Other users / uses* **if specific supply is within remit**: *e.g. health centres (in-patient, out-patient and cholera centres); feeding centres*
- ❑ Water user numbers — local population:
  - ○ *As affected population (above)*
  - ○ *Industries and agriculture*
- ❑ Present water source (type, location, level of service, distance to collection point). Note: The populations' own coping mechanisms should be identified and potentially built upon.
- ❑ Current water consumption
- ❑ Does the affected population have adequate containers for water collection?
- ❑ Are the populations static or mobile?
- ❑ Diseases prevalent in the local and affected populations (e.g. cholera, dysentery, typhoid, malaria, fluorosis, diarrhoea to those new to the area, skin diseases)

Sources of information

- ❑ UNHCR
- ❑ Employing organization staff members
- ❑ Other field staff
- ❑ Local government (water and sewerage, social, statistical office)
- ❑ Local and affected population
- ❑ Observation
- ❑ Medical practitioners (traditional and non-traditional)
- ❑ Checklists pp70-1

Methods

- ❑ Calculation of water demand for affected and local populations using employing organization water demand figures or those given on p141

Availability of resources / logistics ■

Information

Resources

- ❑ Materials and equipment (details and availability)
- ❑ Human resources (available locally: tradespeople, water technicians, supervisors, health educators / community development personnel)
- ❑ Local construction techniques (details)
- ❑ Water treatment processes used locally (details)

Logistics

- ❑ Conditions of roads at present and in the approaching season (identify areas susceptible to flooding or other physical threats)
- ❑ Security (on access roads and within settlements)
- ❑ Access to international freight (airstrips, ports, railways, road links)
- ❑ Airport / port handling facilities
- ❑ Customs clearance procedures
- ❑ Availability and reliability of freight transporters
- ❑ Journey time for freight

Sources of information

- ❑ Observation
- ❑ National or local government (water and sewerage, building)
- ❑ Local contractors
- ❑ Local suppliers
- ❑ Head office modular kit lists
- ❑ Other field staff
- ❑ Local and affected populations
- ❑ Customs authorities
- ❑ National threat monitoring stations
- ❑ *Mobile water treatment units and modular kits* table pp283-4
- ❑ Checklist pp56-7

Physical features including yield and quality ■

COLLECT FOR EACH SOURCE

Information

- ❑ Source name / number, type and location
- ❑ Ground and water levels
- ❑ Layout / dimensions
- ❑ Yield estimation (volume / flows, variation with season, recharge capacity)
- ❑ What are the major pollution risks?
- ❑ Rough idea of present water quality and in approaching season
- ❑ Is the source heavily polluted? (e.g. an open drain or industrially polluted)
- ❑ Is the water turbid?
- ❑ Is the source affected by extreme weather conditions (e.g. below 0°C)

Sources of information

- ❑ Observation
- ❑ Local and affected populations (including users and landowner)
- ❑ National or local government (may have pumping test records)
- ❑ Water diviners
- ❑ *Measurement of yield and water levels* pp143-7
- ❑ *Water quality assessment: Assessment routines* pp148-53
- ❑ *Water quality analysis* pp169-203
- ❑ *Catchment mapping: maps and symbols* pp154-60
- ❑ *Catchment mapping: surveying* pp161-168
- ❑ Checklist pp64-5
- ❑ Checklist pp66-7

Methods

- ❑ Detailed sketch of source and abstraction point
- ❑ Flow measurement
- ❑ Catchment mapping
- ❑ Water quality analysis
- ❑ Sanitary investigation / observation

Management, legal, security, socio-political and cultural issues ■

COLLECT FOR EACH SOURCE

Information

- ❑ Present demands on the source
- ❑ Ownership of the land and source
- ❑ Present O&M arrangements (responsibility, tariff)
- ❑ Legal, security (especially important in conflict situations), socio-political or cultural constraints and accessibility
- ❑ Natural threats in the vicinity of the source (cyclones, earthquakes, mudslides, etc.)

Sources of information

- ❑ Observation
- ❑ Local and affected populations (including users and land owner)
- ❑ National and local government
- ❑ Natural threat monitoring stations
- ❑ *Management, legal, security, socio-political and cultural issues and checklists* pp108-24
- ❑ *Guidance on undertaking assessments and report writing* pp103-4
- ❑ Checklist pp68-9
- ❑ Checklist pp70-1

Requirements for development ∎

COLLECT FOR EACH SOURCE

Information

- ❏ Technical requirements (protection, abstraction, treatment, transmission, storage, distribution)
- ❏ Resources / logistics (material, equipment, human)
- ❏ Time of set up (technical requirements versus resources / logistics and other constraints)
- ❏ O&M requirements (human and material)
- ❏ Costs (materials, equipment, human, logistical)

Note: Early systems should be designed with a possibility for expansion at a later date.

Sources of information

- ❏ Past technical solutions
- ❏ Head office WATSAN division
- ❏ Agency modular kit and equipment lists
- ❏ Standard textbooks
- ❏ Local government and other organizations in-field
- ❏ *Mobile water treatment units and modular kits* table pp283-4
- ❏ *Requirements for development* pp131-5
- ❏ Checklist p61

Impacts of development ∎

COLLECT FOR EACH SOURCE

Information

- ❏ Effects of development on existing users of the source: local populations at the point of abstraction, upstream and downstream (what are the effects, how can they be minimized, what compensation can be made)
- ❏ Effects of water treatment and waste disposal (how to store and dispose of chemicals and waste)

Sources of information

- ❏ Local populations
- ❏ National or local government
- ❏ *Management, legal, security, socio-political and cultural issues with checklists* pp108-124
- ❏ *Impacts of development* pp136-40
- ❏ Checklist p62
- ❏ Checklist pp70-1

Conversations / observations log

Name / organization ■	Notes (including location and date) ■

Conversations / observations log

Name / organization ■   **Notes** (including location and date) ■

2

Addresses

Name: _____

Position: _____

Organization: _____

Address: _____

_____

_____

Phone: _____

Fax: _____

Telex: _____

Email: _____

Name: _____

Position: _____

Organization: _____

Address: _____

_____

_____

Phone: _____

Fax: _____

Telex: _____

Email: _____

Name: _____

Position: _____

Organization: _____

Address: _____

_____

_____

Phone: _____

Fax: _____

Telex: _____

Email: _____

Name: _____

Position: _____

Organization: _____

Address: _____

_____

_____

Phone: _____

Fax: _____

Telex: _____

Email: _____

Name: _____

Position: _____

Organization: _____

Address: _____

_____

_____

Phone: _____

Fax: _____

Telex: _____

Email: _____

Name: _____

Position: _____

Organization: _____

Address: _____

_____

_____

Phone: _____

Fax: _____

Telex: _____

Email: _____

Addresses (continued)

Name: _____   Name: _____

Position: _____   Position: _____

Organization: _____   Organization: _____

Address: _____   Address: _____

_____   _____

_____   _____

Phone: _____   Phone: _____

Fax: _____   Fax: _____

Telex: _____   Telex: _____

Email: _____   Email: _____

Name: _____   Name: _____

Position: _____   Position: _____

Organization: _____   Organization: _____

Address: _____   Address: _____

_____   _____

_____   _____

Phone: _____   Phone: _____

Fax: _____   Fax: _____

Telex: _____   Telex: _____

Email: _____   Email: _____

Name: _____   Name: _____

Position: _____   Position: _____

Organization: _____   Organization: _____

Address: _____   Address: _____

_____   _____

_____   _____

Phone: _____   Phone: _____

Fax: _____   Fax: _____

Telex: _____   Telex: _____

Email: _____   Email: _____

Published information log

Publication details ▪

(including title, author/s, organization, date, contents, location)

Relevance ▪

Published information log (continued)

Publication details ■

(including title, author/s, organization, date, contents, location)

Relevance ■

Resources log

Resources:

❑ Materials and equipment ❑ Human ❑ Construction techniques and water treatment processes used

Resource ■

Details (numbers, cost, quality, logistical constraints where known) ■

Resources log (continued)

Resources:
❑ Materials and equipment ❑ Human ❑ Construction techniques and water treatment processes used

Resource ■	Details (numbers, cost, quality, logistical constraints where known) ■

Reconnaissance of the area

(including existing water usage situation, features of the source, requirements for development, constraints and impacts)

Regional orientation ■

Draw a map of the area including details noted in the checklist p17.

Settlement orientation ∎

Draw a map of the settlement including details noted in the checklist p17.

Demographics, present water use and water demands ■

Water user numbers from affected population:

People: _____ Livestock: (large) _____ Livestock: (small) _____ Other users: _____

Water user numbers from local population:

People: _____ Livestock: (large) _____ Livestock: (small) _____

Other users: (e.g. industry agriculture) _____

Comment on reliability of figures: _____

Calculation of total water demand:

Present water sources in use: (type, location, level of service, distance to collection point).
Note: The populations' own coping mechanisms should be identified and potentially built upon.

Current water consumption:

Do affected population have adequate containers for water collection?

Are the populations static or mobile?

Diseases prevalent in the local and affected populations:

Logistics   (also see 'Resources log')   ■

Condition of roads and areas susceptible to flooding and other physical threats (at present and in approaching season)

Security conditions (on access roads and in settlements)

Access to international freight (airstrips, ports, railways, link roads)

Airport / port handling facilities

Customs clearance procedures

Availability and reliability of freight transporters

Journey time for freight

Other logistical issues

Physical features including yield and quality ■

Source name / number, type and location (including grid reference)

Ground and water levels

Layout / dimensions (attach sketch)

Yield estimation (volumes / flows, variation with season, recharge)

What are the major pollution risks and the present degree of protection?

Rough idea of the water quality at present and in the approaching season

Is the source heavily polluted? (e.g. an open drain or industrially polluted)

Is the water turbid?

Is the source affected by extreme weather conditions (e.g. below 0°C)

Management, legal, security, socio-political and cultural issues ■

Present demands on the source

Ownership of the land and source

Present O&M arrangements (responsibility, tariff)

Legal, security (especially important in conflict situations), **socio-political or cultural constraints and accessibility**

Natural threats in the vicinity of the source (cyclones, earthquakes, mudslides, etc.)

Requirements for development ■

Technical requirements (protection, abstraction, treatment, transmission, storage, distribution)

Resource and logistical requirements (material, equipment, human)

Time of set up (technical requirements versus resources / logistics and other constraints)

O&M requirements (human and material)

Costs (capital, O&M)

Impacts of development ■

Effects of development on existing users of the source: local populations at the point of abstraction, upstream and downstream (what are the effects?, how can they be minimized?, what compensation can be made?)

Effects of water treatment and waste disposal (how to store and dispose of chemicals and waste)

3

LONGER TERM SUPPLY

Survey sheets 79

3

Steps for assessing longer term supply

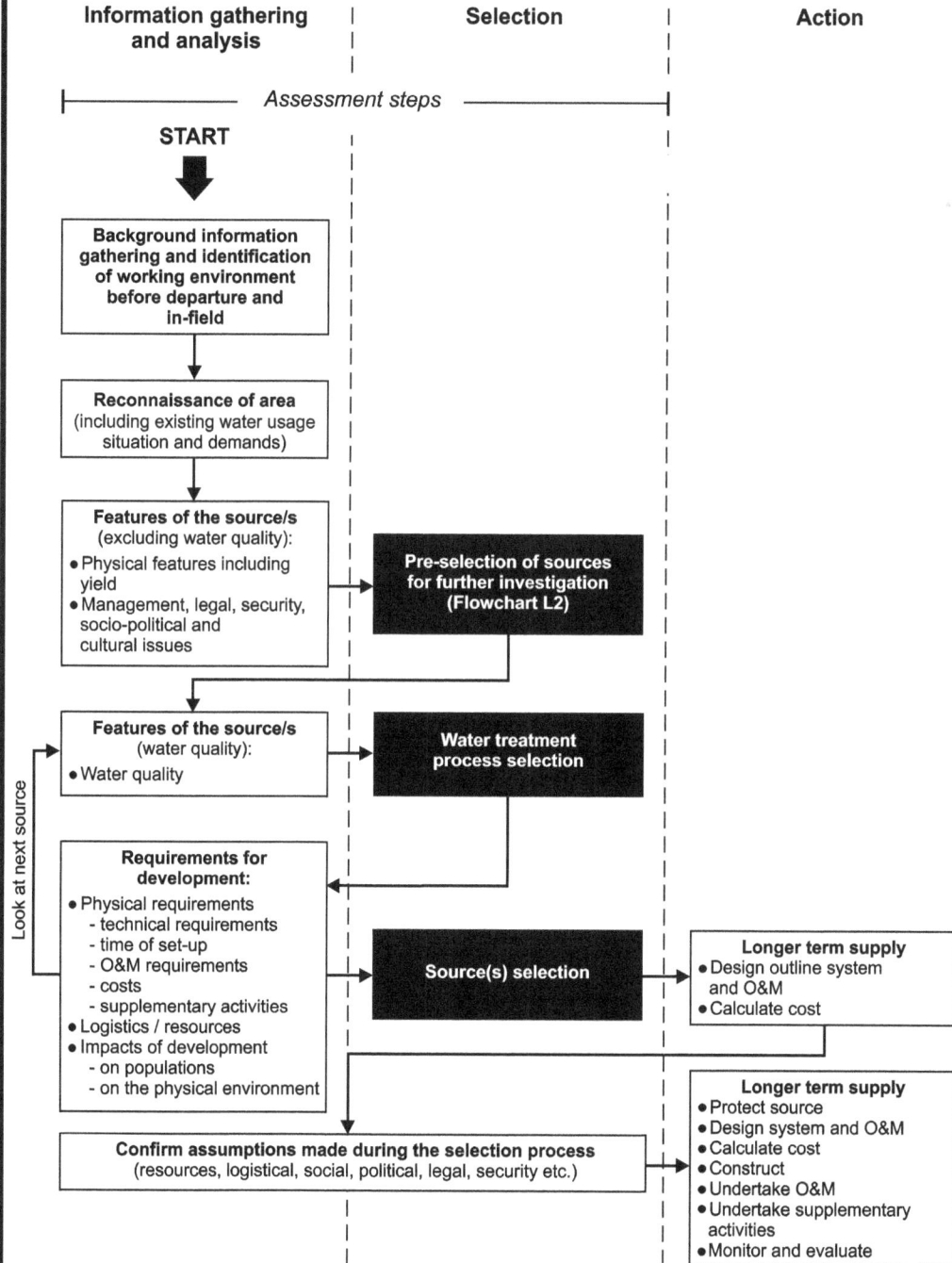

Information gathering and analysis	Selection	Action

——— *Assessment steps* ———

START

▼

Background information gathering and identification of working environment before departure and in-field

↓

Reconnaissance of area
(including existing water usage situation and demands)

↓

Features of the source/s
(excluding water quality):
- Physical features including yield
- Management, legal, security, socio-political and cultural issues

Pre-selection of sources for further investigation (Flowchart L2)

↓

Features of the source/s
(water quality):
- Water quality

Water treatment process selection

Look at next source

Requirements for development:
- Physical requirements
  - technical requirements
  - time of set-up
  - O&M requirements
  - costs
  - supplementary activities
- Logistics / resources
- Impacts of development
  - on populations
  - on the physical environment

Source(s) selection

Longer term supply
- Design outline system and O&M
- Calculate cost

Confirm assumptions made during the selection process
(resources, logistical, social, political, legal, security etc.)

Longer term supply
- Protect source
- Design system and O&M
- Calculate cost
- Construct
- Undertake O&M
- Undertake supplementary activities
- Monitor and evaluate

Pre-selection of sources for further investigation

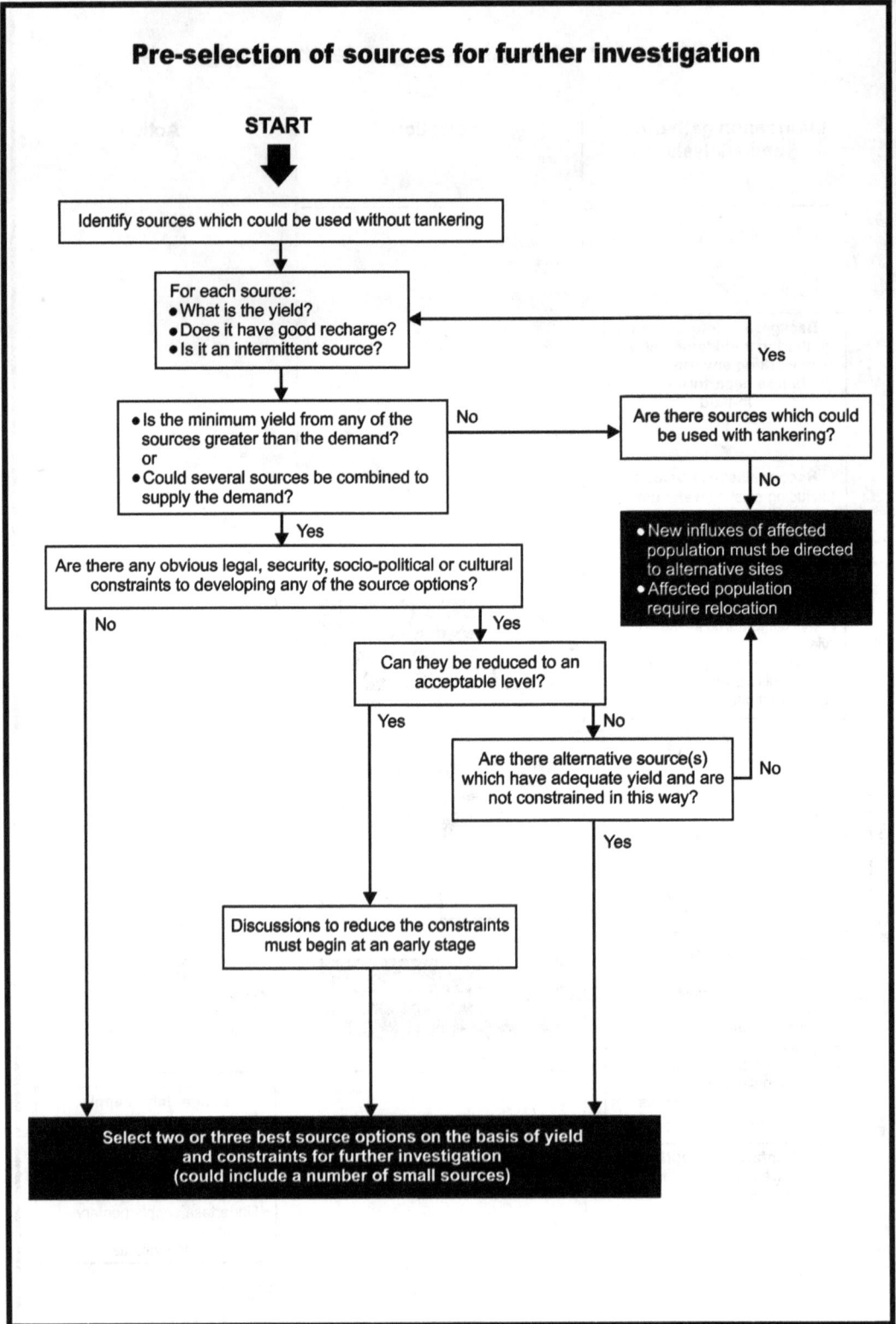

START

Identify sources which could be used without tankering

For each source:
- What is the yield?
- Does it have good recharge?
- Is it an intermittent source?

- Is the minimum yield from any of the sources greater than the demand?
or
- Could several sources be combined to supply the demand?

No →

Are there sources which could be used with tankering?

Yes

No

- New influxes of affected population must be directed to alternative sites
- Affected population require relocation

Yes

Are there any obvious legal, security, socio-political or cultural constraints to developing any of the source options?

No   **Yes**

Can they be reduced to an acceptable level?

Yes   **No**

Are there alternative source(s) which have adequate yield and are not constrained in this way?

No

Yes

Discussions to reduce the constraints must begin at an early stage

Select two or three best source options on the basis of yield and constraints for further investigation
(could include a number of small sources)

Water treatment process selection for longer term supply

Introduction ■

There is more benefit gained in terms of health and convenience from supplying large quantities of reasonable quality water than small quantities of very good quality water. However, the aim should be to provide adequate quantities of good quality water.

The main objective of water treatment for drinking water is to remove anything which is harmful to health such as pathogenic organisms, toxins, and carcinogens. Assuming high levels of toxic chemicals are not present in the water, pathogenic organisms are the most serious threat to health in the short term.

Disinfection (usually chlorination) is used to destroy the pathogenic organisms. In non-emergency situations certain waters may not require disinfection (e.g. deep groundwater, mountain streams) as the faecal contamination may be low at the point of supply. However, because of the large numbers of possibly traumatized people in confined spaces, and the fact that contamination often occurs in individual containers after distribution, disinfection should be used wherever possible in emergencies as an added precaution.

The main constraint to eliminating pathogenic organisms is high turbidity, as turbidity prevents effective disinfection and hence can allow the passage of pathogenic organisms to the user. A range of solutions are available to remove turbidity, the most common ones being storage/sedimentation, and assisted sedimentation (coagulation, flocculation, and sedimentation). It is possible that in the next few years there may also be an increase in the use of roughing filtration, as a range of institutions and organizations are working to develop such systems for use in emergency situations.

Other processes can be added depending on the water quality problems. Examples include the use of aeration, pH adjustment, and activated carbon.

In the initial stages of an emergency water must be supplied quickly, so an upgrading approach to treatment is necessary.

The availability of material resources and organizational preferences often dictate the solutions chosen for water supply. Variations include the following:

· Organizations may send in equipment before a thorough assessment has been undertaken so as to ensure a speedy implementation phase. **Several organizations have their own modular kits which simplify the process of equipment selection, installation, operation, and maintenance.** The modular items of kit include pumps, water tanks, and distribution systems including pipelines and tapstands.

· **Some organizations also have modular 'mobile' treatment units which are very expensive but useful in the immediate stages of an emergency, especially for industrially polluted waters or to supply specific units such as health centres.** See pp283-4 for details of a selection of modular kits and mobile treatment units.

Other organizations prefer to use **local materials, methods, and skills** wherever possible to benefit the local populations and to improve the effective operation and maintenance of systems over the longer term.

How to use this section ■

Study the following:

· Figure 3.1, below
· Tables pp41-2, which highlight water quality problems versus treatment options and give guideline quality levels; and
· Figure 3.2 which links the water treatment processes in a water supply scheme, p43.

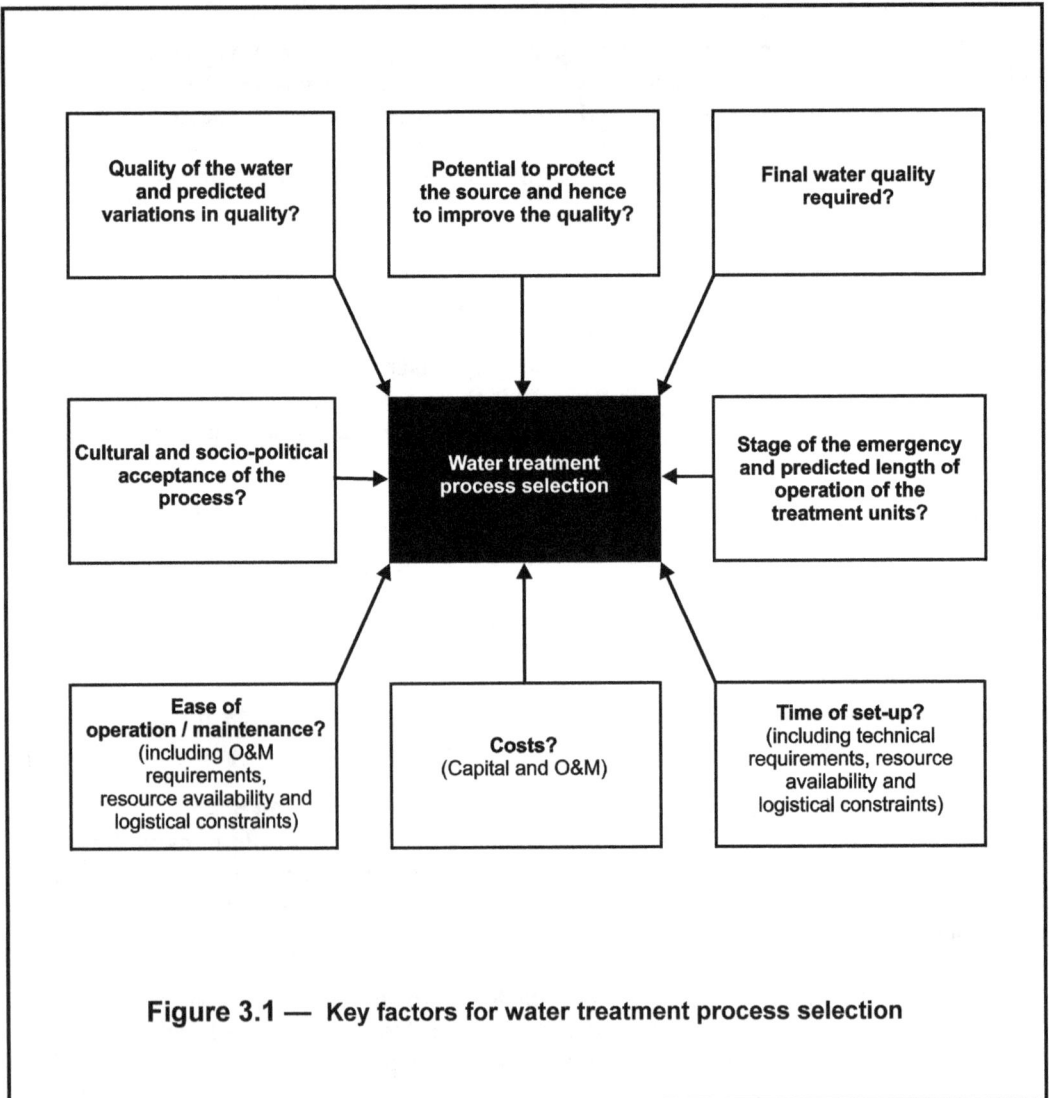

Figure 3.1 — Key factors for water treatment process selection

Complete the *Water treatment process selection tools* tables pp44-5, using the information noted on p40 and the following background information:

· *Water quality assessment routines,* section pp148-53;
· *Water quality parameter summary tables*, pp170-3;
· *Features of water treatment processes*, pp214-23; and
· *Mobile treatment units and modular kits*, section pp283-4.

Instructions on how to use Tables pp44-5 are included within the tables.

Common water quality problems versus treatment options

1A	1B	1C	1D	1E	1F
Parameter / feature	Methods of assessment	Guide levels (max.) (see tables pp170-3 for further information)			Treatment process options or avoidance activities (noted in general order of longer term preference for supply of populations in settlements rather than dispersed or for the short term)
		Survival	Longer term (min. recommended level)	Longer term (WHO)	
Floating solids	sanitary investigation / observation local knowledge	no large solids	none visible	none visible	screen water at or near to the inlet
Turbidity	sanitary investigation / observation local knowledge biological survey water quality analysis	20 NTU	10 NTU	5 NTU (1 NTU for disinfection)	infiltration
					storage and sedimentation
					roughing filtration
					assisted sedimentation
					use mobile treatment units including assisted sedimentation and / or rapid sand filtration (RSF)
Faecal pollution (*E.coli* level or sanitary risk)	catchment mapping sanitary investigation / observation local knowledge water quality analysis	<1000 *E.coli* / 100ml	<10 *E.coli* / 100ml	0 *E.coli* / 100ml	protect source, slow sand filtration (SSF) and disinfect with chlorine
		sanitary risk	sanitary risk	sanitary risk	protect the source and disinfect with chlorine
		medium - low	low	low	for very high levels of contamination (>1000 *E.coli* / 100ml) pre-chlorinate prior to, and in addition to, pre-treatment (but **not** if SSF used)
pH (needs modifying for assisted sedimentation, disinfection or corrosion purposes)	local knowledge water quality analysis	See tables p171 and p216 for specific treatment process requirements			adopt different technologies which work well within the natural pH range
					add lime to raise the pH or an acid to lower it (lower the pH only if essential)
					modify quantities of treatment chemicals to compensate for an unsuitable pH

Notes:
1. Colour, taste, conductivity, chlorine demand and permanganate value are water quality tests which can indicate the presence of the parameters noted in tables pp41-2.
2. The treatability tests (p173 and pp176-83) can help to identify the treatment process is suitable for the particular water.
3. **In all cases, if a source needs to be treated, look for alternative sources that require less or simpler treatment which may potentially be more suitable.**
4. Treatment options noted in this table are those commonly used. Local alternatives may be more suitable and should be identified in the field.
5. National water quality standards and WHO guideline values should always be aimed at all stages of an emergency. However, should this not be possible the above figures may be used as a **last resort** guide.

Occasional water quality problems versus treatment options

2A	2B	2C	2D	2E	2F
Parameter / feature	Methods of assessment	Guide levels (max.) (see table pp170-3 for further information)			Treatment process options or avoidance activities (noted in general order of longer term preference for supply of populations in settlements rather than dispersed or for the short term)
		Survival	Longer term (min. recommended level)	Longer term (WHO)	
Chloride	sanitary investigation / observation local knowledge water quality analysis	600mg/l	250mg/l	250mg/l	blend sources
					move camp
					use mobile treatment units with reverse osmosis
					distillation
Fluoride	local knowledge water quality analysis	3mg/l	1.5mg/l	1.5mg/l	blend sources
					move camp
					high dose assisted sedimentation with aluminium sulphate and lime (Nalgonda process)
					contact with activated alumina
					contact with bone char
					use mobile unit with reverse osmosis
Iron or manganese	sanitary investigation / observation local knowledge water quality analysis	Fe - Mn -	Fe 1.0mg/l Mn 0.5mg/l	Fe 0.3mg/l Mn 0.1mg/l	aerate water prior to main treatment processes including sedimentation or filtration
					pre-chlorinate prior to sedimentation or filtration (but not SSF)
Nitrate (or nitrite)	catchment mapping sanitary investigation / observation local knowledge biological survey water quality analysis	50mg/l as NO$_3^-$ 3mg/l as NO$_2^-$	50mg/l as NO$_3^-$ 3mg/l as NO$_2^-$	50mg/l as NO$_3^-$ 3mg/l as NO$_2^-$	blend water from two sources
					move the camp
					use mobile treatment units with reverse osmosis
Sulphate	catchment mapping local knowledge water quality analysis	400mg/l	400mg/l	400mg/l	blend water from two sources
					use mobile treatment units with reverse osmosis
Algae	sanitary investigation / observation	-	No visible algae		protect source from the addition of nutrients
					roughing filtration with graded media
					pre-chlorinate prior to main treatment (but not SSF)
					reduce algae with copper-based algaecide
					use mobile treatment units with microstraining capacity
Industrial or agrochemical pollutants	catchment mapping sanitary investigation / observation local knowledge biological survey water quality analysis	Refer to the section Water quality analysis; Industrial pollution and Industries and activities and associates pollutants pp181-92			protect source from inflow of pollutants
					move camp
					use mobile treatment units with activated carbon and / or reverse osmosis
Bilharzia	local knowledge	-	none present		stop people entering the water source, provide hygiene education
					storage > 24 hours
Guinea worm	local knowledge	-	none present		stop people entering the water source, provide hygiene education and filter the water before drinking

3

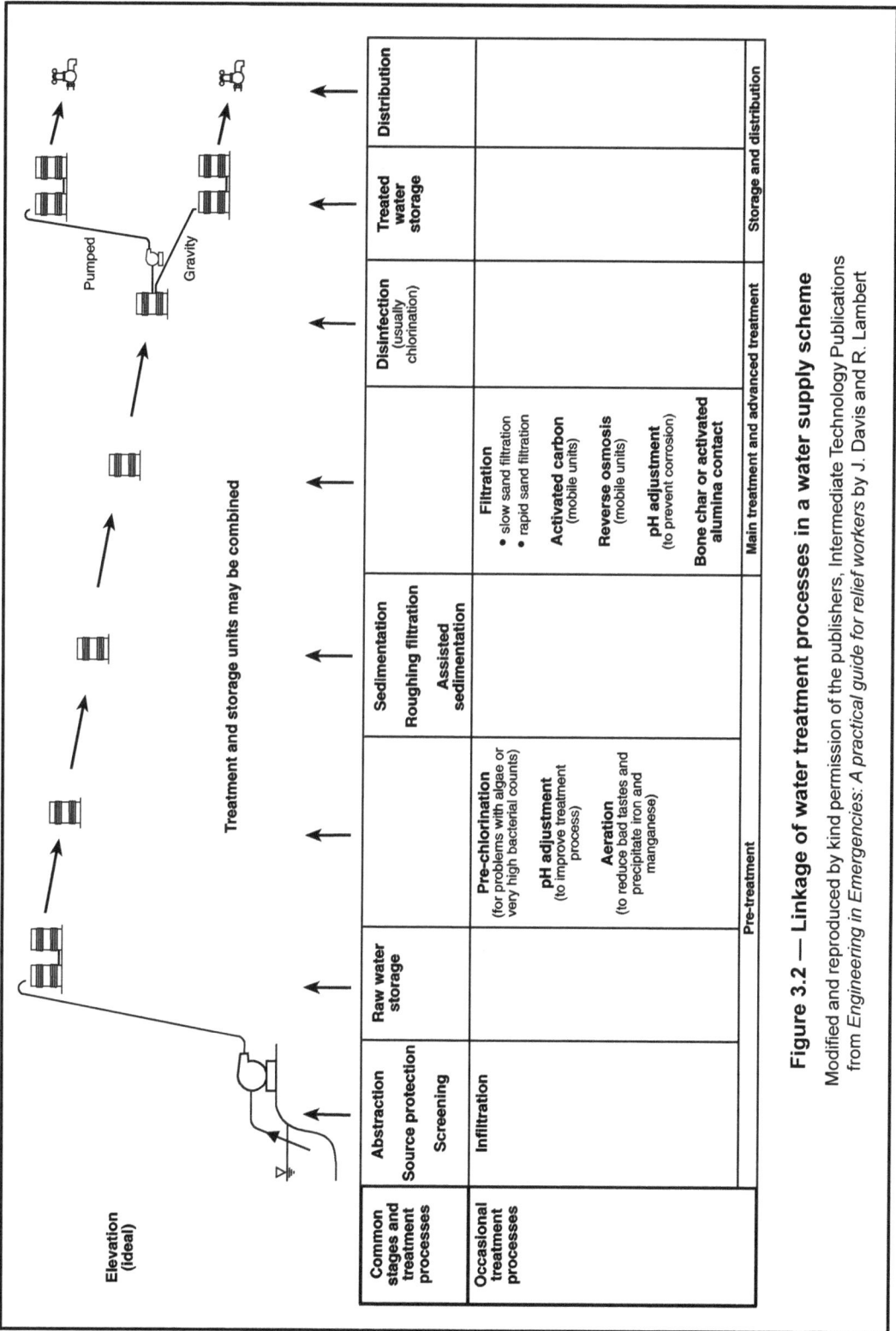

Common stages and treatment processes	Abstraction Source protection Screening	Raw water storage		Sedimentation Roughing filtration Assisted sedimentation		Disinfection (usually chlorination)	Treated water storage	Distribution
Occasional treatment processes	Infiltration		Pre-chlorination (for problems with algae or very high bacterial counts) pH adjustment (to improve treatment process) Aeration (to reduce bad tastes and precipitate iron and manganese)		Filtration • slow sand filtration • rapid sand filtration Activated carbon (mobile units) Reverse osmosis (mobile units) pH adjustment (to prevent corrosion) Bone char or activated alumina contact			
			Pre-treatment		Main treatment and advanced treatment		Storage and distribution

Figure 3.2 — Linkage of water treatment processes in a water supply scheme

Modified and reproduced by kind permission of the publishers, Intermediate Technology Publications from *Engineering in Emergencies: A practical guide for relief workers* by J. Davis and R. Lambert

Water treatment process selection tools for longer term supply ■

Complete the three tables below for each water source under investigation.

Common water quality problems treatment process selection

	(3A) Selection step	(3B) Parameter/feature	(3C) Details
1	For each parameter or feature (column 3B) note the methods of assessment which have been used in column 3C (e.g. catchment mapping, local knowledge, etc.) Refer to table p41 for details.	Floating solids: Turbidity: *E.coli* or sanitary risk: pH:	**Methods of assessment used:**
2	Columns 1C to 1E (table p41) identify the maximum guide levels for each water quality parameter or feature versus the level of supply. Note the appropriate guide levels in column 3C.		**Appropriate guide levels:**
3	In column 3C note the level or description of each parameter or feature and any variations expected in the parameter or feature (in the future or seasonally). Compare present and expected future levels with the guide levels. Note which will require treatment	Floating solids: Turbidity: *E.coli* or sanitary risk: pH:	**Level or description of each feature Variations expected Which will require treatment?**
4	Can the parameter or feature requiring treatment be improved by protecting the source? If so will the water still require treatment?		**Can it be improved by protection? Will it still require treatment?**
5	Column 1F (table p41) identifies alternative treatment / avoidance options for each parameter / feature. Consider each option in turn in relation to: · the stage of the emergency and predicted length of operation of the treatment units · its common usage in the area (and hence the likelihood of existing appropriate skills and resources to run the system effectively) · technical requirements · the availability of material, equipment and human resources · its time of set up · its cost · its ease of operation and maintenance · its acceptability to the group of concern (e.g. some groups will not drink water with 'medicines' in it and hence will not allow chlorine to be used) Select the most appropriate treatment processes.		**Treatment processes initially selected:**
6	To ensure that the treatment process will be effective check each individual process against: · the information supplied in the features of treatment processes section, tables pp214-23; and · results of the treatability tests, pp176-83		**Problems envisaged:**

Occasional water quality problems treatment process selection

	(4A) Selection step	(4B) Parameter / feature	(4C) Details		
7	Refer to table p42 for steps 7 to 12. Repeat step 1 (Table p44) but for each of the occasional water quality problems.		Methods of assessment used:		
8	Repeat step 2 (table p44) for the occasional features / parameters where a problem is expected.		Appropriate guide levels:		
9	Repeat step 3 (table p44) for the occasional features / parameters where a problem is expected.		Level or description of each feature	Variations expected	Which will require treatment?
10	Repeat step 4 (table p44) for the occasional features / parameters where a problem is expected.		Can it be improved by protection?	Will it still require treatment?	
11	Repeat step 5 (table p44) for the occasional features / parameters where a problem is expected.		Treatment processes initially selected:		
12	Repeat step 6 (table p44) for the occasional features / parameters where a problem is expected.		Problems envisaged:		

Linkage of treatment processes or avoidance activities

	(5A) Selection step	(5B) Details
13	Link all of the treatment processes using Figure 3.2, p43 as a guide.	Order of treatment:
14	Check if any of the treatment processes can be removed from the chain. Some processes will be able to deal with several parameters/ features at the same time.	Processes which can be removed:
15	Identify the final selection of treatment processes.	Order of treatment:

Key references:

- Davis and Lambert, 1995, pp317-46
- Howard, 1979
- MSF, 1994, Section I, pp16-21, 38-45
- Shulz and Okun, 1984
- Tebbutt, 1992, pp107-91
- Twort et al, 1994
- UNHCR, 1992, pp80-93
- WHO, 1971, 1989, 1993

Source selection for longer term supply

How to use this section ■

Source selection for longer term supply should only be undertaken after a thorough assessment of available information. See the checklists for suggested information to be collected and note your findings on the survey sheets provided or in another easily accessible form.

Key factors for source selection are highlighted in the schematic chart opposite.

Complete a source summary table (p48) for each source(s) option. From here the source(s) may be selected:

· by scanning the alternative summary tables and undertaking a selection based on experience;

or

· by using the source comparison tool and sample scoring chart to help analyse the variables.

Whichever method is used, experience, common sense and engineering judgement will be required to make an appropriate selection.

The source comparison tool does *not give an answer*; it is only to be used to guide the thought process, highlighting the features which are critical and those which are not so important.

Acceptable yield?

- demands
- present yield
- predicted future
  and seasonal yield

Requirements to obtain an acceptable water quality?

- existing quality (predicted
  future and seasonal)
- possibility for protection
- required quality
- treatment process required

Management, legal, security, socio-political and cultural constraints?

- management issues
- legal issues
- security issues
- socio-political issues
- cultural issues

Decision making for source selection

Impacts of development?

- on aquifers
- on existing users and
  local populations
- on vegetation and erosion
- of water treatment and
  waste disposal
- impact minimization activities,
  subsidiary or compensation
  required

Ease of O&M?

O&M requirements?

- protection
- abstraction method
  and structures
- treatment including
  raw water storage
- transmission distance
  and method
- supply storage
- distribution
- subsidiary requirements

Resource and logistical constraints?

- equipment and material
- human

Costs?
(Capital/O&M)

Time of set-up?

Technical requirements?

- protection
- abstraction method
  and structures
- treatment including
  raw water storage
- transmission distance
  and method
- supply storage
- distribution
- subsidiary requirements

Resource and logistical constraints?

- equipment and material
- human

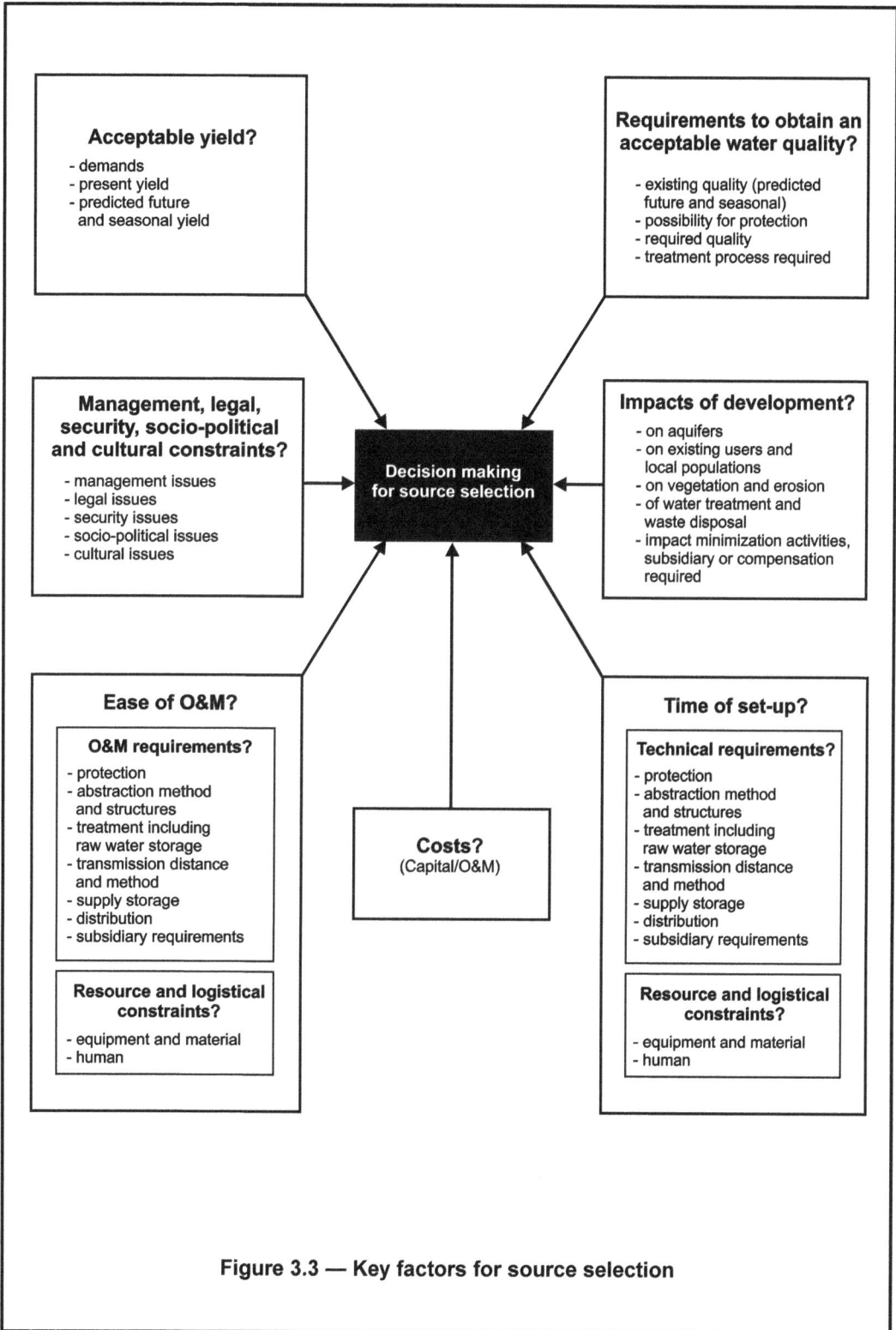

Figure 3.3 — Key factors for source selection

Source summary table

Affected population water demand = _____

Source details	Source name / number and location
	Type of source
Acceptable yield?	**Existing demand on the source** (excluding the affected population)
	Present yield
	Predicted future and seasonal yield
Requirements to obtain an acceptable water quality?	Current water quality problems
	Predicted future and seasonal water quality problems
	Treatment processes required
Management, legal, security, socio-political or cultural constraints?	Management, legal, security, socio-political or cultural constraints
Technical and O&M requirements?	Protection
	Abstraction method and structures
	Treatment (including raw water storage)
	Transmission distance and method
	Supply storage
	Distribution
	Subsidiary requirements
Resource and logistical constraints?	Material and equipment resources
	Human resources
	Logistical
Time of set-up?	Time of set-up
Ease of O&M?	Ease of O&M
Impacts of development?	On aquifers, existing users and local populations, on vegetation and erosion and on water treatment and waste disposal
	Impact minimization activities, subsidiary activities or compensation required
Costs?	Capital
	O&M

Note: This summary table may require adaption for sources for dispersed populations. A separate form could be completed for typical examples of each type of source used in the area.

Source comparison tool for longer term supply ∎

Introduction

The ranking and weighting method was chosen for source comparison as it allows several factors to be included in the comparison at the same time. It also allows for weightings to be put on the factors changing their relative importance with the stage of the emergency. For example, in the immediate emergency stage the time of set-up is critical but the level of O&M required is not so important. Over the longer term period, the O&M requirements become more important and the time of set-up less so.

It should be understood, however, that it is difficult to apply objective weightings and their identification is purely arbitrary and based on best judgement. **They should be modified to suit the particular situation**. The original weightings have been set at 10 for a high level of importance and zero for unimportant. Sometimes a veto has to be applied (Davis et al.,1995). An example of this would be where the water source is located in an area controlled by a warring faction which is in conflict with the affected population. Under this situation access to the water cannot be guaranteed. Hopefully such problems will have been identified early in the information gathering process and the source option already discarded.

Source(s) with the highest total weighted scores are more favourable, but once the numerical determinations have been completed, a **visual analysis** should be undertaken on the results. **This is the most important step in the comparison** and should identify which were the critical factors for the source selection and whether additional activities could be implemented which would modify the results.

Survival supply weightings have not been provided in the scoring table. If required the following weightings could be used (from top to bottom: 9-2-9-5-2-2-1).

If two similar options are being considered, for example trucking from two different locations or abstraction from two different points on the same river, then comparison can be made using only the critical factors. For example the following may be considered:
· costs, security and impacts of development for the trucking programmes; or
· costs, security and requirements to obtain an acceptable quality water for the water source abstraction from two points on the same river.

This method may be more suitable for sources to supply camp populations rather than those in dispersed locations or mobile.

Instructions for use

1. Collect information on the alternative source(s) options and summarize this information in the **Source summary table p48**.

2. For the first source(s) option decide on **scores** for each of the key factors using the **sample scoring chart for source comparison p52** for guidance. A high score indicates that the factor is positive and a low one that it is negative.

3. Chose the **weightings indicated in the scoring chart p51 applicable to the level of supply** (in turn related to the stage of emergency to which the assessment applies).

4. Multiply the scores by the weightings in the table p51 to obtain the **'weighted score'**.

5. Repeat steps 2 to 4 for the other source options.

6. Add all of the weighted scores for each source and insert the **'total weighted scores'** into the final row on the table p51.

7. Identify the sources in order of total weighted score.

Analysis of results

1. Which source gives the highest score and which the lowest?

2. Compare the selected source(s) with the expected result by scanning the summary table. If they are different then investigate why.

3. Which key factors have been the deciding ones in making one option's total weighted score higher than the others?

4. Could the lower scores be raised by undertaking additional activities to modify the situation in the field?

5. Would this change the final order of preference of sources?

6. Look at the source(s) with the highest total weighted score. Are any of the key factor scores tenuous or dependant on unknowns? If these scores are replaced by ones representing the worst scenario, would the order of preference change between the sources?

7. Undertake a **'sensitivity analysis'**: weightings and scores are modified slightly and the final positions compared (Reed, 1995). If there is no change in the overall positions then the results can be accepted with more confidence, but if there are variations, the results should be treated with care and further thought should be given to acceptable weightings and scores.

8. Is the order of preference sensible?

9. If so, chose the source with the highest weighted score. If not re-assess the scores and weightings for the particular scenario and repeat the process for comparison.

Key references (decision-making):
- Davis and Lambert, 1995, pp563-7
- Gosling and Edwards, 1995
- Reed, 1995, pp13-8

Key references (water source selection):
- Cairncross and Feachem, 1978, pp3-7
- UNHCR, 1992, pp30-7

Source comparison tool for longer term supply

Key factors for source selection	Weighting (supply for several months)	Weighting (supply for several years)	Source(s) 1		Source(s) 2		Source(s) 3	
			Score for source	Weighted score	Score for source	Weighted score	Score for source	Weighted score
Acceptable yield?	7	6						
Requirements to obtain an acceptable water quality?	5	5						
Time of set-up?	5	1						
Management, legal, security or socio-political and cultural constraints?	4	4						
Impacts of development?	4	5						
Costs?	3	4						
Ease of O&M?	2	5						
Total weighted score for each source(s) option								

Refer to:

· *Key factors for source selection Figure 3.2, p43*

· *Sample scoring chart for source comparison, p52*

Sample scoring chart for source comparison

Key factors for source selection	Score			
	10	**7**	**4**	**1**
Acceptable yield?	· > 50% of yield remaining after all abstraction.	· > 10% of yield remaining after all abstraction. **or** · Unknown yield but indications are that yield exceeds supply.	· Yield only meets the demand of the affected population and local residents during period of maximum yield.	· Insufficient yield to meet affected population and local demands even at period of maximum yield. **or** · Unknown yield but indications are that it would be lower than required.
Requirements to obtain an acceptable water quality?	· Only simple source protection and disinfection required.	· Protection, storage, assisted sedimentation / filtration and disinfection required.	· Protection, storage, assisted sedimentation / filtration and disinfection required plus additional treatment such as aeration or other.	· Very bad quality. · Heavy industrial / agrochemical pollution expected. · Very difficult to produce acceptable water quality using standard treatment processes.
Time of set-up?	· Time of set-up < 1 week. · Equipment and expertise already available on site.	· Time of set-up 1-4 weeks. · Some equipment and expertise already available on site. · Most additional resources can be obtained locally.	· Time of set-up 1-2 months. · Significant construction required. · Materials need to be imported. **or** · Borehole drilling required into known aquifer.	· Time of set-up > 2 months. **or** · Groundwater exploration required.
Management, legal, security, socio/ political or cultural constraints?	· No such constraints. · Local government communities and landowners are very helpful and agreeable.	· Local government, communities and owners are generally agreeable. · Some local level negotiations may be needed and local communities would need to be compensated.	· Some constraints to the development of the source. · Would require national level negotiations. **or** · Would require additional security at the source.	· Serious constraints to the development of the source. · Political interference. · Could lead to additional security problems. · Problems unlikely to be solved by negotiation.
Impacts of development?	· No obvious impacts on local users or the physical environment.	· Some negative impacts expected on the physical environment but not on local users.	· Groundwater to be used and pumping tests indicate a slow recovery of water levels and, potentially, effects on other sources. **or** · Some negative impacts expected on both local users and the physical environment.	· Groundwater source to be used from a known aquifer of limited capacity. **or** · Water sources already scarce for local communities. **or** · Negative impact expected on both the local users and the physical environment.
***Costs?**	· Low	· Lower than average	· Higher than average	· High
Ease of O&M?	· Would only require input from locally trained personnel. **and** · No fuel or power requirements.	· Would only require input from locally trained personnel **and** · Fuel or power required.	· Would require occasional input from specialist personnel. **or** · High cost of consumables.	· Would require regular input from specialist personnel and high cost of consumables. **or** · Tankering operation.

* Costs (both capital and O&M) are comparative between options. A project specific decision will be required as to the length of time considered for O&M costs. The same period must be used for all options.

Background information gathering and identification of working environment before departure and in-field

Note: The following two checklists and the *Availibility of resources / logistics checklist* pp56-7 may be sent ahead to the field so that information gathering may begin before the arrival of the assessors.

Background information gathering before departure and in-field ■

Information

- ❑ Maps (topographic, geological, road, hydrogeological, demographic, land-use, rainfall)
- ❑ Aerial photographs / landstat images
- ❑ Regional details
  - ○ *Climate (including rainfall data)*
  - ○ *Industrial and agricultural practices*
  - ○ *Populations (culture, religion)*
  - ○ *Economy*
  - ○ *Political situation*
  - ○ *Exchange rate*
- ❑ Previous surveys / studies (organizations' database or library)
- ❑ Other agencies working in the field
- ❑ Organizational structure of employing agency and policy and mandate
- ❑ Specific job information
  - ○ *Job description*
  - ○ *Responsibilities and chain of command*
  - ○ *Other agency personnel in the field*
  - ○ *Logistical and financial constraints*
  - ○ *Communication procedures*
- ❑ Structure of government and local government (including which store information and which make decisions)
- ❑ Contacts in key departments (water and sewerage, water resources, planning, surveying, meteorological)
- ❑ National policies and development projects
- ❑ Existing national emergency plans
- ❑ Capacity of the government to cope with the water demands of the affected population
- ❑ Background to the crisis and projected developments

Sources of information

- ❑ Government departments of donor country (geological, land survey, environment, military)
- ❑ Government departments of host country (water resources, water and sewerage, surveying, meteorological, military, social, planning)
- ❑ Specialist shops (e.g. for maps: Stanfords, London, UK)
- ❑ Consulting engineers
- ❑ University departments (geography, geology, environmental science, civil engineering, mining, surveying)
- ❑ Employing organization head office (verbal from head office and returned personnel; reports from past projects)
- ❑ Organization field staff and experts in the area
- ❑ Government embassy
- ❑ Press reports
- ❑ Books, journals
- ❑ Travel guides
- ❑ The Internet
- ❑ 'District Surveys' in libraries for ex-colony countries
- ❑ Donor country briefings
- ❑ Checklist pp68-9

Identification of working environment ∎

Information

- ❑ Field organizational structure of employing agency/organogram (chain of command, logistics, administration, technical, health education, medical personnel)
- ❑ Areas of responsibility for yourself and others
- ❑ Personnel from other organizations working in water or sanitation in the area (government, international and local)
- ❑ Operational structure for co-ordination between organizations, government — including role of UNHCR, organization and national and local government contacts, and employment agreements
- ❑ Decision-making structure re: water source selection. Are you working for the lead organization? Which camps or populations are you responsible for supplying?
- ❑ Communication channels with affected and local populations and community structures (contacts), and role of UNHCR and governments in communication channels
- ❑ Organization's policy for supporting local populations
- ❑ Team members / access to local personnel (translators, surveying assistants, driver)
- ❑ Working facilities (office space, telephone / radio, fax, photocopying, storage space for equipment and workshops, power sources, security, vehicle)
- ❑ Methods of payment

Sources of information

- ❑ Employing organization staff
- ❑ Other organization staff (including UNHCR)
- ❑ National and local government

Reconnaissance of the area

(including existing water usage situation, logistics and resources)

Regional orientation ■

Information

- Physical features (high and low areas, vegetation, water sources)
- Location and type of water source (developed? not developed?)
- Human features (settlements, industry, agriculture, roads)
- Distances between users and water sources
- Distances and approximate heights between features
- Areas vulnerable to natural threats (cyclones, mudslides, earthquakes, etc.)
- Areas with high security risk (e.g. mined areas)
- Areas subjected to extreme weather conditions

Sources of information

- Observation
- Published and unpublished maps, aerial photographs, etc. as collected in background information gathering
- Simple surveying (GPS, Abney level / clinometer, altimeter)
- National and local government
- Local and affected populations
- Other field staff
- Natural threat monitoring stations
- *Catchment mapping: maps and symbols* pp154-60
- *Catchment mapping: surveying* pp161-8

Methods

- Mapping
- Panoramic photographic records

Settlement orientation ■

Information

- Boundaries, present sub-divisions (including ethnic or clan divisions), possible areas for expansion (include distances)
- Population density where settlements are dispersed or mobile
- Slope of ground (and existing drainage channels if any)
- Water sources (and areas susceptible to flooding and other physical threats)
- Areas with buildings / shelters, open spaces and communal areas
- Access roads
- Sanitation facilities including excreta disposal, refuse dumps / collection areas and graveyards
- Administration centres and feeding centres
- Chemical stores
- Lighting
- Security arrangements

Sources of information

- Observation from high ground (using binoculars) and by walking around the camp
- Aerial photographs
- Simple surveying (pacing, Abney level / clinometer, GPS)
- Other field staff
- Local government
- Local and affected population
- *Catchment mapping: maps and symbols* pp154-60
- *Catchment mapping: surveying* pp161-8

Methods

- Mapping
- Photographic records

Demographics, present water usage and water demands ■

Information

- ☐ Water user numbers — affected population:
  - ○ *Individuals*
  - ○ *Livestock large and small (and average number per family)*
  - ○ *Other users / uses **if specific supply is within remit**: e.g. health centres (in-patient, out-patient and cholera centres); feeding centres*
- ☐ Water user numbers — local population:
  - ○ *As affected population (above) up and downstream*
  - ○ *Industries and agriculture*
- ☐ Present water source (type, location, level of service, distance to collection point). Note: The populations' own coping mechanisms should be identified and potentially built upon.
- ☐ Current water consumption
- ☐ Does the affected population have adequate containers for water collection?
- ☐ Are the populations static or mobile?
- ☐ Diseases prevalent in the local and affected populations (e.g. cholera, dysentery, typhoid, malaria, fluorosis, diarrhoea to those new to the area, skin diseases)

Sources of information

- ☐ UNHCR
- ☐ Employing organization staff members
- ☐ Other field staff
- ☐ Local government (water and sewerage, social, statistical office)
- ☐ Local and affected population
- ☐ Observation
- ☐ Medical practitioners (traditional and non-traditional)
- ☐ Checklist pp70-1

Methods

- ☐ Calculation of water demand for affected and local populations using employing organization's water demand figures or those given on p141

Availability of resources / logistics ■

Information

Logistics

- ☐ Condition of roads in the dry and rainy seasons (major access roads; minor access roads; internal settlement roads; road crossings)
- ☐ Flooding and other physical threats (settlement areas; access roads)
- ☐ Security (on access roads and within settlements). Which groups are causing the security problem? How common are guns in the area?
- ☐ Access to international freight (airstrips; ports; railways; road links)
- ☐ Customs clearance (import taxes, procedures, problems, delays)
- ☐ Availability and reliability of freight transporters
- ☐ Journey time for freight

Note: This survey information can be collected as the assessment procedure progresses or after the resources required for the specific engineering solution are known. Depending on the agency procedure, the initial solution may be directed by the modular kit which has been brought to the field at the assessment stage.

Sources of information

- ☐ Observation
- ☐ National or local government (water and sewerage, building)
- ☐ Local contractors
- ☐ Local suppliers
- ☐ Head office modular kit lists
- ☐ Other field staff
- ☐ Local and affected populations
- ☐ Customs authorities
- ☐ National threat monitoring systems
- ☐ *Mobile water treatment units and modular kits* Table p283-4

Availability of resources / logistics (continued) ■

Information (continued)

Resources

❑ **Material and equipment** (type; make; size; condition; capacity; power consumption; fuel requirement; cost; volume / number available; availability of drivers / operators):

- ○ *Pumps (electrical; diesel; petrol; hand pumps)*
- ○ *Generators (diesel; petrol)*
- ○ *Tanks (galvanized steel / iron; Oxfam tanks; pillow tanks)*
- ○ *Pipes (cast iron; galvanized steel / iron; asbestos cement; UPVC; MDPE; flexible hose)*
- ○ *Pipe fittings (valves, bends, air valves, couplings, etc.)*
- ○ *Mobile water treatment units*
- ○ *Construction materials and tools (cement; reinforcement steel and tying wire; gabion mesh; aggregate; sand; construction handtools; masonry hand tools; nails / screws; timber; cement mixer)*
- ○ *Drilling rigs (rotary, percussion)*
- ○ *Water tankers or trucks (tankers; flat-bed truck with sides; flat-bed truck without sides; container truck)*
- ○ *Chemicals (chlorine; aluminium sulphate; ferric chloride; ferrous sulphate; lime)*
- ○ *Fuel / power (diesel; petrol; electricity)*
- ○ *General usage transport (pick-ups; small lorries or vans)*

❑ **Human resources** (names; point of contact; employer; numbers):

- ○ *Tradespeople: plumbers; mechanics; electricians; carpenters*
- ○ *General construction personnel and supervisors*
- ○ *Water technicians / engineers*
- ○ *Health educators / community development workers*
- ○ *Logisticians*

❑ **Local construction techniques** (details):

- ○ *Well construction (hand dug well, tube well)*
- ○ *Spring tapping*
- ○ *Borehole drilling (are the drilling teams available with rigs?)*
- ○ *Pipe laying and joining*

❑ **Water treatment processes used locally:**

- ○ *Infiltration*
- ○ *Sedimentation*
- ○ *Roughing filtration*
- ○ *Assisted sedimentation*
- ○ *Slow sand filtration*
- ○ *Rapid filtration*
- ○ *Disinfection*
- ○ *Activated carbon*

Features of the source (excluding water quality)

Physical features including yield   ■

COLLECT FOR EACH SOURCE

Information

❑ Source name / number, type and location

❑ Ground and water level (note instrument used for measurement)

❑ Layout / dimensions

❑ Yield estimation: (volumes / flows, variation with season, recharge capacity)

❑ Discharges (in and out; where are they from and where do they go)

❑ Environmental features of the area surrounding the source (river bed materials; plant and tree cover; activities such as farming or industries)

❑ Is the source affected by extreme weather conditions (e.g. below 0°C)?

Sources of information

❑ Observation

❑ Local and affected populations (including users and landowner)

❑ National or local government (may have pumping test records)

❑ Water diviners

❑ *Measurement of yield and water levels* pp143-7

❑ *Catchment mapping: maps and symbols* pp154-60

❑ *Catchment mapping: surveying* pp161-8

❑ Checklist pp64-5

❑ Checklist pp66-7

Methods

❑ Detailed sketch of source and abstraction point

❑ Flow measurement

Management, legal, security, socio-political and cultural issues ■

COLLECT FOR EACH SOURCE

Information

❑ Present demands (who, what for, how much, is there competition with animals)

❑ Are there intermittent users such as nomads

❑ Who owns the land and what is the procedure to obtain permission to abstract

❑ Responsible authority for control and maintenance

❑ Is a tariff being charged for using the source (paid to whom and how much)

❑ Accessibility at present for water collection (can elderly, children, or those with disabilities gain easy access to the source?)

❑ Security problems at the source (especially consider women and children and opposing groups in conflict situations)

❑ Are any areas mined?

❑ Socio-political constraints to using the source and cultural beliefs re: water provision

❑ Consider national development objectives

❑ What are the affected populations' and local populations' priorities for water provision

❑ Natural threats within the vicinity of the source (cyclones, earthquakes, mudslides, etc.)

Sources of information

❑ Observation

❑ Local and affected populations (including local users and landowner)

❑ National or local government (may have pumping test records)

❑ Natural threat monitoring stations

❑ *Management, legal, security, socio-political and cultural issues and case studies pp108-24*

❑ *Guidance on undertaking assessments and report writing pp103-4*

❑ Checklist pp68-9

❑ Checklist pp70-1

Features of the source (water quality)

Water quality assessment　　　　　　　　　　　　■

COLLECT FOR EACH SOURCE

Information

- ❑ The quality of the water at present
- ❑ Existing protection and potential for improved protection of the source
- ❑ Predicted variations in the water quality in the future and pollution risks

Parameters commonly causing problems:
- ❑ Floating solids
- ❑ Turbidity
- ❑ Faecal contamination (thermotolerant coliforms / *E.coli* level)
- ❑ pH

Parameters occasionally causing problems:
- ❑ Algae
- ❑ Arsenic
- ❑ Chloride
- ❑ Fluoride
- ❑ Iron or manganese
- ❑ Nitrate (or nitrite)
- ❑ Sulphate
- ❑ Industrial or agrochemical pollutants

Sources of information

- ❑ Observation
- ❑ Field-testing equipment
- ❑ Local government
- ❑ Local and affected populations
- ❑ Health centres
- ❑ *Water quality assessment: Assessment routines* pp148-53
- ❑ *Water quality analysis* pp169-203
- ❑ *Biological survey* pp204-213
- ❑ *Water quality analysis and surveying equipment* pp261-82

Methods

- ❑ Catchment mapping
- ❑ Local knowledge including medical information
- ❑ Sanitary investigation / observation
- ❑ Water quality analysis
  - ○ *Core parameters (common problems)*
  - ○ *Secondary parameters (occasional problems)*
  - ○ *Treatability tests*
  - ○ *Industrial pollution assessment*
- ❑ Biological survey

Requirements for development and impacts summary

Physical requirements ∎

COLLECT FOR EACH SOURCE

Information

- ❑ **Technical requirements:**
    - ○ *Protection requirements*
    - ○ *Abstraction method*
    - ○ *Treatment requirements including storage*
    - ○ *Transmission distance and means of transmission*
    - ○ *Supply storage*
    - ○ *Distribution requirements*
    - ○ *Subsidiary requirements (e.g. road construction; threat mitigation activities)*
    - ○ *Consider standardization with existing systems in-country as support to national development objectives*

- ❑ **O&M requirements (human and consumables):**
    - ○ *O&M human resources*
    - ○ *O&M consumables*

- ❑ **Resources / logistics:**
    - ○ *Material and equipment requirements*
    - ○ *Human resource requirements*
    - ○ *Logistical requirements*

- ❑ **Costs:**
    - ○ *Costs for capital and O&M (materials, equipment, human resources, logistics)*

- ❑ **Time of set-up:**
    - ○ *Total time for system to be up and running (technical requirements versus resources / logistics and other constraints)*

- ❑ **Ease of O&M**
    - ○ *O&M requirements versus resources / logistics and other constraints*

Sources of information

- ❑ Past technical solutions
- ❑ Head office WATSAN division
- ❑ Agency modular kit and equipment lists
- ❑ Standard text books
- ❑ Local government and other organizations in field
- ❑ *Requirements for development pp131-5*
- ❑ *Mobile water treatment units and modular kits Table pp283-4*

Impacts of development   ■

COLLECT FOR EACH SOURCE

Information

- ☐ **Effects of source development on the aquifer and remote sources:**
    - ○ *Location and capacity of aquifers*
    - ○ *Which sources are fed from the same aquifers*
- ☐ **Effects of development on existing users of the source and local populations at the point of abstraction and downstream:**
    - ○ *Determine: yield of source at present, existing demands, new abstraction demand, remaining yield (dry season) and the effects on existing users*
    - ○ *Possible compensation for local communities up and downstream for the loss of yield or inconvenience. Also compare local and affected populations' supplies and consider upgrading local supplies to prevent friction*
    - ○ *Consider migration of people and animals / livestock to improved water sources (may be pronounced with nomadic populations)*
    - ○ *Effects on community structures / management capacity of organizations and populations*
    - ○ *What subsidiary / ancillary activities are required (training, road construction, sanitation, agricultural extension, hygiene promotion, etc.)?*
- ☐ **Effects on vegetation and erosion:**
    - ○ *Change in yield*
    - ○ *Effects of abstraction on vegetation and erosion and potential actions to minimize effects*
    - ○ *Effects of migration to improved water sources on vegetation and erosion*
- ☐ **Effects of water treatment and waste disposal:**
    - ○ *Increase in waste water — how will it affect levels of standing water*
    - ○ *How will chemicals and fuel for water treatment be stored (location, security)?*
    - ○ *How will waste chemicals be disposed of?*
    - ○ *How will the sludge produced during treatment be disposed of?*

Sources of information

- ☐ Observation
- ☐ National or local government
- ☐ Local and affected populations
- ☐ *Impacts of development section pp136-8*
- ☐ *Management, legal, security, socio-political and cultural issues with case studies pp108-24*
- ☐ *Groundwater investigation pp249-52*
- ☐ Checklist p64-5
- ☐ Checklist pp70-1

Confirmation of assumptions made during the selection process

Resources, logistics, legal, security, socio-political, and cultural issues ■

COLLECT FOR THE SELECTED SOURCE

Information

❏ **Resources**
- ○ *Can the required resources be made available within a suitable time-scale?*
- ○ *Are the costs within the available budget?*

❏ **Logistics**
- ○ *Will logistical constraints prevent the solution being implemented?*

❏ **Legal, security, socio-political, and cultural issues**
- ○ *Have there been any developments in these areas which could prevent implementation? (physical developments could be due to natural threats or human activities)*
- ○ *Have the selected options been discussed with the local and affected populations and accepted as culturally appropriate?*

Sources of information

❏ See previous checklists

Groundwater investigation

The use of groundwater is limited in the initial stages of an emergency because:

❑ It is difficult to locate;

❑ It is difficult to assess the capacity of the aquifer in a short time period; and

❑ Access to equipment and an experienced drilling team is often limited.

If groundwater is available, however, it is an excellent source of water, often with limited requirements for treatment, and if the conditions are right can supply large quantities of potable water. Development of new groundwater sources is limited in the initial stages of the emergency because of time restrictions. However a general overview of the groundwater situation in the area is an important addition to the initial assessment of emergency water sources. The information gathered can be used to identify whether further studies should be undertaken by a hydrogeologist and can be a useful start to his / her investigation.

Situations where groundwater could be used in the early stages:

❑ Spring sources;

❑ Existing developed groundwater sources such as shallow wells and boreholes which have reliable yields and additional capacity;

❑ Sub-surface flow abstracted from sandy / gravel river beds of rivers which flow intermittently and can be rapidly and easily abstracted; and

❑ New boreholes in areas where drilling equipment is readily available and the aquifer is already located and known to be reliable.

Information

Level 1 (possible to collect some of this information as part of the initial assessment of emergency water sources):

❑ Locations and details of all natural and man-made features including topography (can indicate potential recharge routes, pollution sources and location of populations who could supply information on water sources)

❑ Details of existing water sources including types, water levels, seasonal variations, present yields and reliability (can indicate locations, depths and reliability of aquifers)

❑ Existing borehole logs and testing results (indicates geology and hence possible aquifer characteristics, such as yield, water quality, drawdown during pumping, seasonal fluctuations)

❑ Climatic data (indicates potential for recharge)

❑ Soil and rock types (indicates potential aquifer characteristics)

❑ Vegetation (indicates potential locations of springs and shallow groundwater)

❑ Investigation of river beds, erosion channels and nearby hills for rock outcrops (identification of the rocks and angle of outcrops provide further information in the assessment of aquifer capacity)

❑ Use of aerial photographs (highlights topographical, vegetational and geomorphological features which can be interpreted by an experienced hydrogeologist. Aerial photographs can also highlight drainage patterns and land use)

Level 2 (unlikely to be collected as part of an initial assessment, but may be recommended in the RAEWS conclusions):

❑ Use of remote sensing images (1:12,500 to 1:25,000) (highlights topographical, vegetational and geomorphological features which can be interpreted by an experienced hydrogeologist)

❑ Geomorphological analysis and hydroclimatic monitoring

❑ Geophysical surveying assessment (electrical resistivity, seismic refraction, electromagnetic profiling, VLF profiling)

❑ Exploratory drilling (hand drilling, machine drilling, geological logging, test pumping)

Sources of information

❑ Local well drilling team

❑ Observation

❑ Local populations

❑ National and local government (water resources, agriculture, geological survey and water supply departments)

❑ Other organizations working in the provision of water supply (consultants, NGOs, etc.)

❑ University departments of host country (geography, geology, environmental science, civil engineering, mining, surveying)

❑ Certain organizations such as the British Geological Survey can provide interpretations of information based on satellite imagery and their vast data information banks for a fee (See *Useful addresses* pp289-90)

❑ Other sources of information as indicated in the checklist p53

❑ Hand drilling — See reference Oxfam (1991)

❑ *Measurement of yield and water levels* pp143-7

❑ See *Background to groundwater and aquifers* pp230-5

❑ *Rock and soil identification* pp235-48

❑ *Groundwater investigation* pp249-52

Methods

❑ Catchment mapping

❑ Cross section drawing of topography and water levels using details from existing sources

❑ *Pumping tests on existing boreholes

❑ Interpretation of the information identified under Level 1 using table *Indicators of the presence of groundwaters* p252

* Note: Difficult to do in the field but useful if possible.

Rainwater investigation

The use of rainwater in emergencies is limited because:
- ❏ It requires significant time and capital to set up large schemes;
- ❏ It may only be available for short periods of the year; and
- ❏ It is unpredictable.

However, rainfall can be a useful source of water as a supplement to individual household supplies if simple catchment structures can be constructed, or for small centres such as clinics or health centres where other sources are limited. Consideration should only be given for mid to long term projects where there is time to investigate yields and develop appropriate catchment structures and storage systems or for the short term if the emergency begins in the rainy season.

Rainwater can be collected on corrugated sheeting or plastic roofs, on other artificial material, or on the ground surface if it is relatively impermeable.

Techniques for storage include:
- ❏ Ponds (do not tend to have isolated abstraction point)
- ❏ *Birkas* (cement-lined ponds)
- ❏ *Hafir* dam (artificial pond with isolated inlet and outlet structures)
- ❏ Sand or sub-surface dams
- ❏ Household tanks (ferrocement, bamboo reinforced cement, concrete, steel, etc.)

Different geographical areas may have differing names for rainwater harvesting or storage techniques.

Information

- ❏ Is rainwater harvesting a common technique in the area?
- ❏ In which months of the year does it rain?
- ❏ Does the amount of rain vary each year?
- ❏ What technologies are used?
- ❏ Can the technologies be improved to prevent contamination (e.g. add isolated abstraction structures)?
- ❏ Are the storage units publicly or privately owned?
- ❏ Is there a tariff?
- ❏ What capacity of storage already exists in the area?
- ❏ How long does the stored water last taking into account existing demands prior to the emergency?
- ❏ Is there a possibility of increasing storage capacity?
- ❏ Who owns the land on which the catchment and storage units are located?

To estimate potential yields:

- ❏ Annual rainfall
- ❏ Temperature variations
- ❏ Permeability of the ground or catchment surface / run-off coefficient
- ❏ Size of catchment area
- ❏ Current position in rainfall cycle

Source of information

- ❏ Owners of storage units and catchment land
- ❏ Local populations
- ❏ Observation
- ❏ National and local government

Methods

- ❏ Calculate storage potential, run-off capacity, evaporation and seepage. See *Rainwater harvesting* pp253-4

National government / local government / NGO / international organization

This checklist may be used when collecting information from government departments or other organizations working in the field. It contains information included in the main checklists but which is brought together for ease of access during interview.

National or local government (includes organizations managing utilities)   ■

Note that **caution is required in conflict situations when gathering information** especially from government departments. Requests for aerial photographs and similar items may be misinterpreted. Employer organization and co-ordinating organization (e.g. UNHCR) guidance should be followed in these circumstances. If you are a government employee of the host country or you are working alongside government counterparts this information may be easier to access.

Some of the information may have already been requested by the employing organization, country or regional co-ordinator. Organizational procedures for communicating with official personnel set down by the employing organization should be followed.

Reasons for contacting the host government:

❏ You are guests working in their area of responsibility

❏ It is necessary for gaining government approvals

❏ They will be responsible for looking after the facilities when the outside organizations leave

❏ They may be able to provide or loan resources (both human and material)

❏ They could be useful sources of information

❏ They know the area and probably the location, size and quality of water sources

❏ It can provide links with local populations

❏ A good relationship with the local authorities can reduce possible frictions

❏ It is courteous

Departments which may be useful to contact:

❏ National or regional government: administration of refugee or returnee affairs, water resources, environment, geological survey, health, military

❏ Local government: administration, water and sewerage, surveying, social, planning, engineering, public works

When meeting with government departments it may be useful to take with you:

❏ Information showing who you are and your areas of expertise

❏ Documents proving permission to act and letters of support

❏ Photographs of past emergency work for subsequent meetings (if requested)

Can the government department give you, or provide information on any of the following?:

❑ Logistical constraints

❑ Security situation and local clearance procedures

❑ Maps of the area (topographic, geological or road)

❑ Aerial photographs

❑ Aquifer details

❑ Numbers and water demands of local populations

❑ Water demands and effluent details of local industries and agriculture

❑ Government resources which could be made available (possibly for exchange or payment)

❑ Personnel assistance (engineers, technicians)

❑ Introductions to local leaders

❑ Contacts for local contractors and specialists

❑ Availability of local resources and supplier contacts

❑ Standard specifications for materials and equipment which they usually use (especially pumps)

❑ Where to find further information

❑ Local staff recruitment policy

❑ Method of payment for affected population if included in construction work

❑ Environmental problems in the area

❑ Main concerns of the government and local populations

On specific water sources:

❑ Details of land rights and who permission for abstraction should be sought from

❑ Construction drawings of sources already used

❑ Borehole logs

❑ Pumping or yield records

❑ Details of operating procedures or problems with existing systems

❑ Water quality records

❑ Socio-political or cultural issues to be considered when dealing with water

❑ River basin studies

Additional for national government:

❑ Permission to become active

❑ Procedures for importing goods

❑ Letters of introduction

❑ Line of government responsibility

❑ Policy and level of support to the affected populations

❑ Designated agency responsible for co-ordination of the interventions (often UNHCR)

Non-governmental organizations and international organizations ■

Much of the information noted above may also be requested from non-governmental organizations and international organizations working in the field. Requesting information from more than one source can verify or dispute information already collected. In conflict situations or where governments are inoperational, other field organizations may be the best source of information.

Affected population / local population issues

The person undertaking the rapid assessment of emergency water sources in the early stages of an emergency will often have to act within a short time frame. There are key factors which he / she must assess in order to select a water supply and treatment process to provide potable water.

In the initial stages of an emergency, the questioning of the affected population may be mostly superficial with questions used to confirm observations on existing water sources, pollution risks, availability of containers, etc. However, as soon as possible further questioning of greater depth should be undertaken to help the assessor gain an understanding of the populations he / she is supporting. This will help to ensure that the technological solutions are appropriate to the users. Care must be taken to question as many different groups as possible including those who are vulnerable (consider vulnerability on the basis of gender, age, ethnicity and culture). One method of involving the affected population at an early stage is to request that existing community groups come forward (e.g. women's groups or people who have previously been on water committees) when calls are made for workers. Representatives of these groups can then be consulted on subjects such as the suitability of chosen locations for standposts and the cultural acceptability of proposed sources.

Refer to *Guidance undertaking assessments and report writing* pp103-7 for guidance on avoiding assessment pitfalls. **Record answers to questions in the *Conversations / observations* log** pp79-80

Population / community structure and skills

❑ How is the population divided?

❑ Who are the population's representatives or acting representatives? (initial contacts for questions)

❑ What are the social hierarchies and which are the most vulnerable groups?

❑ Are there personnel with the following skills: tradespeople, construction personnel, supervisors, health educators, water technicians, engineers?

❑ How are food and other resources presently being distributed?

❑ What is the balance of males and females? (if high percentage of single men it may imply that both men and women may have lead responsibility for water usage in different family groups)

Cultural practices

❑ Which days are religious / cultural festivals or days of rest?

❑ General gender and age roles (before and after being affected by the emergency): who collects water, is responsible for family hygiene, cooks? (can indicate which groups have greatest responsibility for water use and hence who should be consulted)

❑ Are there any restrictions for a particular group (e.g. Muslim women in *purdah* may have to collect water in the dark)?

❑ Where do people bathe and wash clothes? (potential source of pollution)

❑ What forms of sanitation are used? (potential source of pollution)

❑ What are the requirements for sanitation: cleaning materials; segregation; level of privacy; water for hand washing? (can indicate level of hygiene practice and hence potential for post-supply contamination)

❑ Are there any particular attitudes to water treatment (e.g. are they worried about the use of chemicals)? (could lead to rejection of water supply)

❑ Do women have any particular needs or concerns (for example over water and privacy needs during periods of menstruation)?

❑ Are there any other cultural beliefs related to water not included above?

Past and present sources of water and, the populations needs and concerns

❑ What types of water source did they use before affected by the emergency (well, spring, stream)?

❑ Was it chlorinated?

❑ What was the level of service (piped supply, direct from source, etc.)?

❑ How much water did they use?

❑ Details of the water used at present (what does it taste like, does it look muddy or clear and does the taste or appearance change with the seasons)?

❑ Are the water collection containers adequate in number, quality and size?

❑ What are their priorities in the supply of water and sanitation?

❑ What are their needs and concerns?

Security of water collection points

❑ Are there any problems with the location of the water collection points in terms of security or accessibility (especially for women, children, the elderly, those physically impaired, those vulnerable due to their ethnicity, those vulnerable due to conflicts)?

Key references:

- Anderson et al, 1992
- Davis and Lambert ,1995, pp55-77
- Gosling and Edwards, 1995

Water treatment works and urban water supply systems

The following checklists are to be used for the assessment of existing water treatment works in urban environments in addition to the general checklists provided previously:

❑ Urban water supply system inventory

❑ Resources / spares checklist

❑ Water treatment works operational checklist

Sources of information: Local government water and sewerage departments; existing works staff; local and international consulting and contracting firms.

Urban water supply system inventory ■

General

❑ Are there maps / plans already available of the supply network?

❑ Does a contingency plan for emergencies already exist?

❑ Are recent test data results available and inventories of age and condition of pipes and other equipment?

❑ Identify damaged sections / items and potential causes of pollution: vandalism; war damage; cross-connections; back-syphonage; pipe near sewer; illegal tapping; fire (Hodgson and Tannock, undated)

❑ Who is responsible for operation and maintenance of each section of the supply system

❑ Identify and map location of:

  ○ *Sources*

  ○ *Treatment works*

  ○ *Pumping stations*

  ○ *Trunk mains*

  ○ *Distribution mains*

  ○ *Raw and clear water reservoirs*

  ○ *Location of consumers (domestic and industrial, including power plants)*

  ○ *Heights of all features*

  ○ *Power stations or fuel suppliers (e.g. electricity, diesel or petrol)*

  ○ *Workshop / storage facilities*

  ○ *Laboratories for water quality testing*

  ○ *Areas susceptible to physical threats (landslides, floods etc.)*

Sources (UNHCR, 1996)

❑ **Springs**

Identify: expected yield at design and date of design; actual yield and date; description and condition of spring box; description and effectiveness of protection above and around spring; potential sources of contamination

❑ **Hand dug well**

Identify: yield; draw down; lining type and condition; height and number of rings; parapet height and material; apron width and material; depth to bottom of well and to static water level; water drawing mechanism and condition; geology if known; potential sources of contamination

❏ **Borehole**

Identify: drilling company, technique used and date; diameter; pumping test results: date, duration, static water level, drawdown and safe yield; gravel packing type and volume; casing details: type, diameter, length, screen length, percentage of openings

❏ **Hand pump**

Identify: make; model; date of installation; number of strokes required to deliver output — note initial 5 litres and then subsequent 5 litres; borehole details (as above); sand presence in water

Pump units and power supply (UNHCR, 1996)

❏ **Pumps**

Identify: type; make; model; serial number; condition; rated yield and head; actual yield and head; power supply; stockage of fuel for how long; flood protection; motor house condition

❏ **Power unit (engine)**

Identify: type; make; model; serial number; condition; hp; r.p.m.; fuel use (l/hour); cooling system

❏ **Power (generator)**

Identify: type; make; model; serial number; power (KVA); power factor; phase; voltage; amperage; r.p.m.; frequency; condition

❏ **Electrical supply panel**

Identify: type; make; model; serial number; voltage; Hz; hp

Pipelines (UNHCR, 1996)

❏ Identify: materials; sizes; working pressures; isolation valves on pipelines; water hydrants; standpipes; air valves; corrosion protection; invert levels

Treatment works (see *Water treatment works operational checklist* for detailed assessment pp74-8)

❏ Process operation; process control; hydraulic operation; structural soundness

❏ Operation and maintenance: maintenance programme; chemicals and fuels; disposal of wastes; operational management and availability of skilled personnel; record keeping; budget; health and safety

Distribution

❏ Identify: details and condition of distribution units; wastewater drainage arrangements

Workshop / storage facilities

❏ Identify: capacity of staff; availability of spares; capacity for storage; management capability and systems

Sewage treatment works and sewerage system

❏ As water supply system and treatment work

❏ Identify possible areas of contamination to the water supply

Solid waste disposal

❏ What are the existing facilities and are they working?

❏ Does solid waste pose any potential hazards to the water supply?

Resources / spares checklist ▪

See checklist pp56-7

Also:
- ❑ Locations of factories which make equipment
- ❑ What supplies does local government have?
- ❑ Who supplies the local government?
- ❑ What equipment do NGOs and international organizations have in stock; are the parts compatible, and if not what adapters are required?

Skilled personnel
- ❑ Who is still available from existing staff?
- ❑ Which skills are lacking?
- ❑ Is additional training required to run new or modified equipment?

Water treatment works operational checklist ▪

Produce a process diagram and layout map of the operational treatment works including numbers and sizes of units and any spare land available for expansion.

Works details:

- ❑ Built in (and upgraded in) year _____
- ❑ Design capacity _____
- ❑ Operating capacity (usual) _____
- ❑ Operating capacity (at present) _____
- ❑ Area of supply _____
- ❑ Is the access to the works OK? _____
- ❑ Are there any natural threats to the system? (earthquakes, hurricanes, volcanoes, mudslides, etc) _____
- ❑ Which sections of the system are most vulnerable? _____
- ❑ Can mitigation measures be put in place to prevent further damage? (include details) _____

Process operation:

Screening / intake:
❑ Is screening in place and adequate?
❑ Are the screens being cleaned?
❑ Is the intake protected, such as by a fence?
❑ Is it located away from major pollution sources?
❑ Can the intake cope adequately with change in water levels?
❑ Is the point of abstraction susceptible to erosion?

Raw water storage:
❑ What is the turbidity at the inlet and outlet?
❑ What is the retention time?
❑ What is the size of the reservoir and its effective capacity?

Sedimentation:
❑ Are settled solids prevented from being disturbed to the outlet?
❑ Does the settlement tank have baffles?
❑ Is the retention time > 1 hour?
❑ How often are the tanks desludged?
❑ What is the turbidity at the inlet and outlet?

Assisted sedimentation (coagulation, flocculation, sedimentation):
❑ Is the coagulant mixed immediately?
❑ How is the coagulant being flocculated?
❑ Is the coagulant dose controlled?
❑ Is the turbidity at the outlet to the sedimentation tank < 10 TU?

Chlorination or other disinfection process:
❑ Is the contact time > 30 min?
❑ Are chlorine residuals checked regularly?
❑ Are chemicals weighed or measured accurately?
❑ Is the free residual entering the distribution system > 0.4mg/l?
❑ Are there no interruptions to disinfection?
❑ What is the method of dosage?
❑ In what form is the chlorine dosed?
❑ Is there safety equipment for handling the chlorine?

Slow sand filtration:
❑ Are the filters blocked or being bypassed?
❑ Is the top layer of the *schmutzdecke* being removed when required?
❑ What is the run time between subsequent removals of the top layer of *schmutzdecke*?
❑ Does the plant have facilities for washing filter sand?
❑ Is the turbidity on leaving the filter < 5TU?

❑ What is the media?

❑ Is the depth of sand > 600 mm?

❑ How long does the filter run before the removed sand needs replacing?

Rapid gravity filtration:

❑ Is the filter being regularly backwashed?

❑ What is the run time between backwashes?

❑ What is the backwash rate?

❑ Is air scour used?

❑ Where does the washwater go?

❑ Does the washwater contaminate the clean water?

❑ What is the media?

Clear water storage:

❑ Is the capacity > 1 day for demand?

❑ Is the tank clean, undamaged and covered?

❑ Are vents and overflow pipes protected by screens?

Other:

Consider the process operation of any additional processes:

❑ Grit chamber

❑ Oil / grease trap

❑ Aeration

❑ Pre-chlorination

❑ Activated carbon

❑ Fluoridation

Process control:

Are the following being checked on a regular basis:

❑ Turbidity?

❑ pH?

❑ Chlorine residuals?

❑ Jar test for assisted sedimentation?

❑ Microbiological (*E.coli* / total coliform)?

Hydraulic operation:

❑ Is the flow control equipment present and functional?

❑ Are the process units being operated at designed flow rates?

❑ Are overflows being used on a regular basis?

Structural soundness:

❑ Is there any point of leakage in the treatment system?

❑ Are any of the units cracked, broken or otherwise damaged?

❑ Are any of the units dirty?

❑ Is the drainage in the treatment works area adequate?

Operation and maintenance:

Maintenance programme:

❑ Is there an accepted and implemented programme of maintenance?

❑ What does it consist of?; check off each treatment process structure and equipment (pumps, dosing equipment, etc.); are the items of equipment and structures calibrated, oiled, greased, and any damage repaired?

Chemicals and fuels:

❑ Note usual dosages of all chemicals

❑ How are the treatment process chemicals and fuels stored?

❑ How are the chemicals handled?

❑ Are the chemicals delivered on a regular basis?

❑ Are there likely to be interruptions to deliveries?

Disposal of spoilt chemicals and sludges:

❑ How are spoilt chemicals disposed of?

❑ How are sludges produced during treatment disposed of?

Workshop / storage facilities

❑ What is the capacity of workshop staff?

❑ How available are spare items of equipment?

❑ How quick are systems for obtaining additional spares?

❑ What is the capacity of storage facilities?

❑ How effective are stock control systems?

Operational management and personnel:

❑ Names and duties of responsible personnel; also position, training, period in job, total experience in water treatment

❑ How much time is spent on tasks?

❑ Are there enough skilled personnel to keep the plant running?

Record keeping:

Are records kept of the following:

❑ Process control results (especially bacteriological and residual chlorine)?

❑ Chemical consumption?

❑ Problems with the treatment processes?

❑ Maintenance?

Health and safety:

❑ Are there obvious health and safety problems on the site?

❑ Are there facilities to cope with chemical spillage or injury to personnel? What are they?

Budget:

❑ Who pays?

❑ How much money is available? Is it adequate?

❑ How long does it take to get funds?

Assessment of potential for increase in capacity:

❑ Could the treatment works cope with further flow? How much?

❑ Could the works be expanded to cope with extra flow? How much? How could this be achieved?

Key references:

·   Hodgson and Tannock (undated)

·   Lloyd and Helmer, 1991

·   Jagour, 1996

·   Schulz and Okun, 1984

·   Siru, 1992

·   UNHCR, 1996

·   Youde, 1996

·   PAHO, 1997

Conversations / observations log

Name/organization ■ | **Notes** (including location and date) ■

Conversations / observations log

Name/organization ■   **Notes** (including location and date) ■

Addresses

Name: _____

Position: _____

Organization: _____

Address: _____

_____

_____

Phone: _____

Fax: _____

Telex: _____

Email: _____

Name: _____

Position: _____

Organization: _____

Address: _____

_____

_____

Phone: _____

Fax: _____

Telex: _____

Email: _____

Name: _____

Position: _____

Organization: _____

Address: _____

_____

_____

Phone: _____

Fax: _____

Telex: _____

Email: _____

Name: _____

Position: _____

Organization: _____

Address: _____

_____

_____

Phone: _____

Fax: _____

Telex: _____

Email: _____

Name: _____

Position: _____

Organization: _____

Address: _____

_____

_____

Phone: _____

Fax: _____

Telex: _____

Email: _____

Name: _____

Position: _____

Organization: _____

Address: _____

_____

_____

Phone: _____

Fax: _____

Telex: _____

Email: _____

Addresses (continued)

Name: _____

Position: _____

Organization: _____

Address: _____

_____

_____

Phone: _____

Fax: _____

Telex: _____

Email: _____

Name: _____

Position: _____

Organization: _____

Address: _____

_____

_____

Phone: _____

Fax: _____

Telex: _____

Email: _____

Name: _____

Position: _____

Organization: _____

Address: _____

_____

_____

Phone: _____

Fax: _____

Telex: _____

Email: _____

Name: _____

Position: _____

Organization: _____

Address: _____

_____

_____

Phone: _____

Fax: _____

Telex: _____

Email: _____

Name: _____

Position: _____

Organization: _____

Address: _____

_____

_____

Phone: _____

Fax: _____

Telex: _____

Email: _____

Name: _____

Position: _____

Organization: _____

Address: _____

_____

_____

Phone: _____

Fax: _____

Telex: _____

Email: _____

Published information log

Publication details ■	Relevance ■
(including title, author/s, organization, date, contents, location)	

Published information log (continued)

Publication details ■

(including title, author/s, organization, date, contents, location)

Relevance ■

Resources log

Resources:

❑ Materials and equipment   ❑ Human   ❑ Construction techniques and water treatment processes used

Resource ■	**Details** (numbers, cost, quality, logistical constraints where available) ■

Resources log (continued)

Resources:
❏ Materials and equipment   ❏ Human   ❏ Construction techniques and water treatment processes used

Resource ■	Details (numbers, cost, quality, logistical constraints where available) ■

Reconnaissance of area

(including existing water usage situation, resources and logistics)

Regional orientation ▪

Draw a map of the area including details noted in the checklist p55.

Settlement orientation ■

Draw a map of the settlement including details noted in the checklist p55.

Demographics, present water usage and water demands ■

Water user numbers from affected population:

People: _____ Livestock: (large) _____ Livestock: (small) _____ Other users: _____

Water user numbers from local population:

People: _____ Livestock: (large) _____ Livestock: (small) _____

Other users: (e.g. industry agriculture) _____

Comment on reliability of figures: _____

Calculation of total water demand:

Present water sources in use: (type, location, level of service, distance to collection point). Note: The populations' own coping mechanisms should be identified and potentially built upon.

Current water consumption:

Do affected population have adequate containers for water collection?

Are the populations static or mobile?

Diseases prevalent in the local and affected populations:

Logistics (see also 'Resources log') ■

Condition of roads and areas susceptible to flooding and other physical threats (at present and throughout the seasons)

_____

Security conditions (on access roads and in settlements)

_____

Access to international freight (airstrips, ports, railways, link roads)

_____

Airport / port handling facilities

_____

Customs clearance procedures

_____

Availability and reliability of freight transporters

_____

Journey time for freight

_____

Other logistical issues

_____

Features of the source (excluding water quality)

Physical features including yield ■

Source name/ number and location and type (including grid reference)

Ground and water levels (note instrument for measurement)

Layout / dimensions (attach sketch, see p93)

Yield estimation
· **volumes / flows**
· **variation with season**
· **recharge capacity**

Discharges in and out (where from, where to)

Environmental features of catchment area (farming, industry, settlements, tree cover, etc.)

Is the source affected by extreme weather conditions (e.g. below 0ºC)

For groundwater sources

	Date	Date
Test reference number		
Constant yield or step drawdown test		
Pump details		
Method of flow measurement used		
Reference point / level		
Static water level		
Drawdown		
Specific capacity		
Safe yield		
Observations		

Note: If a supply system already exists then refer to the *Urban water treatment works and supply system checklist pp72-8*

Draw a sketch of the source and the surrounding area

Include:

❑ Layout / dimensions

❑ Ground level and water level

❑ Discharges (in and out; where do they come from and where do they go)

❑ Environmental features (river bed materials; plant and tree cover, activities in catchment area)

❑ Water collection points

❑ Current structures and source protection activities

Management, legal, security, socio-political and cultural issues ■

Present demands (who, what for and how much, is there competition with animals?)

Are there intermittent users such as nomads?

Who owns the land and what is the procedure to obtain permission to abstract?

Who is responsible authority for control and maintenance?

Is a tariff being charged for the water? (how much and paid to whom?)

Is the source accessible for all? (elderly, children, disabled)

Are there security problems at the source? (especially for women and children and other vulnerable groups such as opposing groups in conflicts)

Are any areas mined?

Socio - political constraints to using the source and cultural beliefs re- water provision

---

What are the local and affected populations' priorities for water provision?

Are there natural threats in the vicinity of the source? (cyclones, earthquakes, mudslides, etc.) **What are they and what is the risk?**

Features of the source (water quality)

For further information refer to:

❑ *Water quality assessment routines* pp148-53;   ❑ *Catchment mapping: maps and symbols* pp154-60;

❑ *Catchment mapping: surveying* pp161-7;   ❑ *Water quality analysis* pp169-203;

❑ *Biological survey* pp204-13

❑ *Water quality analysis and surveying equipment* pp261-92;

Water quality assessment summary ■

Water quality assessment method	Water quality inferences for
	source name/ number and location _____
Catchment mapping	Observations:
	Inference:
Local knowledge including medical information	Observations:
	Inference:
Sanitary investigation & observation	**Sanitary risk:** high - medium - low - very low
	Improved sanitary risk: high - medium - low - very low
	Specific risks which can potentially be improved:
	1.
	2.
	3.
	4.
	5.
	Observations of the water source:
	Inference:
Water quality analysis (see following page for details)	**Key findings:**
	❑ Core parameters:
	❑ Secondary parameters:
	❑ Treatability tests:
	Inference:
Biological survey	**Species found:** Yes No
	❑ intolerant
	❑ slightly intolerant
	❑ moderately tolerant
	❑ tolerant
	Inference: Clean water / some minor pollution / moderate pollution / some major pollution / severe pollution
	Type of pollution expected:
Overall conclusions	**Present quality:**
	Predicted variations in quality:

Water quality analysis ■

	Measured value / description	Prediction of variation	Date of assessment	Test kit / method used
Core tests				
Turbidity (TU)				
Odour				
Colour				
Conductivity (µS/cm)				
pH				
E.coli / 100 ml				
Secondary tests (only test if there is an indication that there may be a problem)				
Chloride mg/l				
Fluoride mg/l				
Iron mg/l				
Manganese mg/l				
Nitrate mg/l				
Nitrite mg/l				
Sulphate mg/l				
Taste				
Arsenic mg/l *				
Permanganate Value				
Chlorine demand (of raw water) mg/l				

* Suitable field equipment may not be available for this parameter

Treatability tests ■

	Dosage required / time	Date of assessment	Test kit / method used
Treatability tests			
Sedimentation			
Assisted sedimentation			
pH adjustment			
Chlorination (chlorine demand of treated water)			
Other			

Industrial pollution laboratory analysis ■

Date sample sent to the laboratory

Address of laboratory

Details:

❑ chemicals added for stabilization

❑ storage conditions in transit

❑ time from sampling to laboratory analyses

Key results (attach data sheet)

Requirements for development and impacts summary

Source name, location and reference:

Technical and O&M requirements and time of set up ■

Technical and O&M requirements	Details	Predicted time for set-up	Potential time delays for set up / problems for set up and O&M
Protection			
Abstraction method and equipment structures			
Treatment (including raw water storage)			
Transmission distance and means of transmission			
Supply storage (if additional to raw water storage for treatment)			
Distribution			
Other (subsiduary)			
Estimated total time of set-up (items can be implemented in parallel)			

Resources and costs ■

	Key resources (capital and O&M)		Capital cost	O&M costs
	Material	Human		
Protection				
Abstraction				
Treatment system (including raw water storage)				
Transmission				
Supply storage (if additional to raw water storage for treatment)				
Distribution				
Other (subsiduary)				
Total costs				

Impacts of development ■

Potential effects of source development on the aquifer and remote sources

❏ Potential effects on aquifer

Effects of development on existing users of the source and local populations at the point of abstraction and downstream

❏ Determine: yield of source at present,
new abstraction demand, existing demands,
remaining yield (dry season)
and the effects on existing users

❏ Possible compensation for local
communities for the loss of yield
or inconvenience

❏ Consider migration of people and
animals / livestock to improved water
sources (may be pronounced with
nomadic populations) and the effects

❏ What are the effects on community
structures / management capacity of
organisations and populations?

❏ What subsidiary / ancillary activities are
required? (training, road construction,
sanitation, agricultural extension,
hygiene promotion etc.)

Effects on vegetation and erosion

❏ What are the effects of abstraction
on vegetation and erosion?

❏ What are the effects of migration to
improved water sources on
vegetationand erosion?

Effects of water treatment and waste disposal

❏ Increase in waste water - how will it affect
levels of standing water?

❏ How will chemicals and fuel for water
treatment be stored ?(location, security)

❏ How will waste chemicals be disposed of?

❏ How will the sludge produced during
treatment be disposed of?

4

SUPPORTING INFORMATION

102

4

Guidance on undertaking assessments and report writing

Assessments ■

Davis and Lambert, 1995, Chapter 4, 'Assessment and planning' provides background ideas on carrying out assessments and planning in emergencies. Gosling, 1995, is also a useful source of background reading on undertaking assessments / surveys.

Key points to remember about undertaking assessments / surveys are:

- In an emergency you will not be able to collect as much substantive information as you would in a period of non-emergency. **Information should therefore be collected from as many different people and sources as possible** to corroborate findings. Be aware of bias and inaccuracies. Additional data may be collected after decisions have been made, for confirmation.

- 'It is essential to **understand local political and social structures** and to be aware of conflicting interests within communities when collecting information. It is best to cross-check information using different sources. It is also important to discuss the purpose of the assessment with communities to avoid raising expectations unrealistically' (Gosling, 1995 p135).

- In conflict situations it is important to be seen as non-partisan.

- 'In carrying out an assessment, the principle should be to collect *enough* data to implement an *effective* response. Time spent collecting unnecessary information is time wasted. On the other hand, not doing an adequate assessment may lead to much more effort, time and money wasted on an ineffective response. Focus on the most relevant factors (**the question 'so what?' is a useful test of relevance** — ask it frequently.' (Davis and Lambert, 1995 p56).

- **Identify key information required** prior to undertaking the survey.

- **Keep good records** of any gathered information and store them in such a way that others can access them. Information gathering takes time and hence the assessor (or those following the assessor) should not have to repeat work due to inefficient record keeping.

- **Photographs and sketches of water sources and supplies are often very useful** for decision-making, especially for anyone referring to the survey who was not involved in the initial assessment.

- **Local women are often good sources of information on water sources** as they are often the main users and managers of community supplies. **The refugee women, as well as the men, should be questioned on locations of potential standposts, latrines and other facilities.** The security of women and children when collecting water and undertaking their other duties such as clothes washing should be a priority. Female translators should be used where possible in interviewing women, especially in cultures where women's contact with men is restricted.

- 'It is important to remember that in some situations interviewers and observers may pose a threat to the people, interpreters and authorities concerned. Rapid assessment teams can compromise these groups by asking the wrong questions, quoting their answers to the wrong person, or being seen to notice the wrong thing' (Gosling, 1995 p135).

- Co-ordination meetings should be arranged regularly for all team members involved in the collection of information and care must be taken to ensure that everyone knows the objectives and boundaries of the work and the final results.

Report writing ∎

The style and length of a report on the assessment of water sources will depend on:

- preferences of the organization you are working for;
- the scope of the assessment you are undertaking;
- the stage of the emergency at which you are undertaking your assessment; and
- other variations.

The guidelines of the employing agency should be followed were applicable. Below are some examples of report formats which could be used where there is flexibility for report writing.

An **outline of an assessment report** is suggested in Davis and Lambert, 1995, p60. It has been slightly modified and reproduced with the kind permission of Intermediate Technology Publications from *Engineering in Emergencies: A Practical Guide for Relief Workers* by Jan Davis and Robert Lambert:

- Title, authors, location, date
- Acknowledgements
- Executive summary, 1 page: key recommendations, proposals, main budget and staffing requirements, responsibilities for implementation
- Action plan, 1–2 pages
- Introduction, 1–2 pages: objectives of assessment, background work, methodology used
- Presentation of key results, 1–2 pages
- Detailed recommendations, 1–2 pages
- Resource implications (human, financial, institutional, etc.), 1–2 pages
- Terms of reference (if they have been specified)
- Appendices: relevant analyses of data collected, maps, design drawings, etc.

Suggested *appendices for a source and water treatment selection assessment* would be:

Maps:
- Regional catchment
- Local catchment
- Settlement or area where affected populations are located
- Detail of source to be used (and scheme to be implemented if this is part of the assessors remit)

Summary survey sheets:
- Reconnaissance of the area survey sheet
- Source details summary sheet (for all sources)
- Decision-making sheets (if used) for source and water treatment selection
- Features of the source survey sheets (excluding water quality and water quality)
- Requirements for development and impacts summary
- Resources log

Other:
- Notes of meetings with key personnel (from local government departments, other organizations etc.)
- Conversations / observations log (if kept)
- Any other relevant survey information

It is possible that the person selecting the water source will also be the same person who designs the entire system. In this case a more thorough report may be necessary.

The format outlined on the following pages is recommended by, and reproduced with the kind permission of D. Mora-Castro of UNHCR, 1996, and could be followed for a comprehensive report on a proposed scheme.

Comprehensive scheme report

'A correct technical project description is an important tool for both the funding and the executing agency. It should provide — in clear, concise terms — enough information to justify the need for the project, to assess its cost-effectiveness, to be the basis for the preparation of budgets, implementation and monitoring plans, and to facilitate the fundraising exercise.'

Ideally, the assessor and designer's report should contain:

Introduction:
- reasons for the project
- background information on water supply and sanitation sectors
- situation / status of existing infrastructure
- socio-economic and cultural background of beneficiaries
- self-help activities
- if relevant, long-term development plans for the 'project' site

Location map:
- showing project site and overall layout of the proposed system

Institutional background:
- description of all government and non-government institutions which impact on water supply, sanitation and public health at the project site and vicinities
- information on the implementing agency's goals, operational responsibilities, managerial capacity, staffing, location of headquarters and regional and local facilities

Sector policies:
- targets for service and standards
- financial arrangements
- institutional development
- beneficiary community participation
- administrative and technical support

Beneficiaries:
- description of social, cultural and economic background
- criteria for the selection of target groups including identification of vulnerable groups
- water demand estimates (including livestock, gardening and other purposes)

Public health aspects:
- presence of waterborne diseases and other existing health conditions
- curative and preventive health practices
- health education and hygiene training programmes
- institutional arrangements, etc.

Water resources:
- overview of available surface and groundwater resources
- available geological, meteorological and hydrological data, their reliability, and the results of analyses in terms of water balances and budgets
- present and future demand and patterns (in space and time)
- water quality and pollution problems

Existing water supply services (if any):
- type
- coverage
- standards
- reliability
- water quality
- user charges
- operating and maintenance status

Need for the project:
- why existing water arrangements cannot cope with present or projected demands
- consequences the lack of better services will have on beneficiaries
- outline of priorities and comments on urgency of project implementation

The project:
- technical description
- definition of the project and outline of its components, including maps, photos, sketches, and bills of quantities, as appropriate
- description of additional project preparation work requirements (studies and surveys, further design work required, and related projects such as opening of access roads, borehole drilling, etc.) and necessary support activities, such as logistics, training of local operators, health education, etc.

Implementation arrangements:
- identification of all involved
- need for consultants or contractors (if applicable)
- description of their functions and responsibilities
- co-ordination and monitoring mechanisms
- needs for assistance and support (staff, training, financial)
- implementation schedule, complete with chronogramme depicting the tasks of each group involved
- critical paths and necessary administrative steps (provision of budget, preparation of tender documents, procurement of land and water rights, etc.)

Operation and maintenance arrangements:
- future arrangements for O&M, including self-help
- technical assistance required
- annual costs and any other requirement

Environmental impact:
- description of the various impacts to be expected, including those in public health, sanitation and water resources themselves

Cost estimates:
- summary of project costs, taking into account a realistic provision for unexpected costs for each budget item. These costs are to be estimated on the proposed bills of quantities and on unit prices for each element
- breakdown of costs into foreign exchange and local currency may be desirable, along with full explanation on how costs were estimated and a list of basic assumptions (particularly those for unit prices, contingencies, price increases, etc.)
- breakdown of 'in kind' and 'in cash' costs should is be desirable

Financial plan:
- final budget summary will be presented in this section and, if relevant, all possible sources of funding should be identified, both for project implementation and for the long-term O&M of the system to be constructed
- discussion on arrangements for future accounting and reporting should also be included

Technical annexes:
- map of the camp / village / settlement / site, including all project-related buildings and installations (existing or to be constructed)
- assessment of water source productivity (pumping test analyses, flow measurements hydrographs, etc.)
- chemical and bacteriological assessment of water quality
- planimetric details and hydraulic profile of conduction and distribution lines
- technical details, specifications and plans ('blue prints') of all structures
- system components and their interconnections
- terms of reference
- technical specifications for additional inputs

Key references:
· Davis and Lambert, 1995, pp55–77
· Gosling and Edwards, 1995
· Mora-Castro, 1996

Management, legal, security, socio-political and cultural issues with case studies

Management, legal, security, socio-political and cultural issues ■

Emergencies come in many forms, from slow-onset droughts to quick-onset earthquakes. They may be caused by an industrial accident, a natural disaster, conflict or political or ethnic persecution. Whatever form an emergency takes it is often characterized by confusion, problems with logistics and resources, and the need for outside assistance. Water is required for life itself and hence is an inherently political and social issue. In a conflict situation it becomes more so. The ability to provide adequate water in emergency situations is therefore much more complicated than the purely technical solution. The person selecting a water source therefore has to be aware of these issues, and negotiation may be an essential part of any decision.

Water and security in conflict situations

The problems of water provision in conflict situations were identified by the working groups of the 'Water and War Symposium on Water in Armed Conflicts' held in Montreux in November 1994 (ICRC, 1994), and include the:

- deliberate cutting off of the water to a region, community or suburb, with the aim of depriving the civilian population;
- deliberate destruction of water installations (water treatment plants, pumping stations, storage reservoirs, water distribution networks, irrigation works, and so on);
- deliberate destruction of the power supply, leading to complete stoppage of water, sewage and irrigation installations;
- destruction of, and damage to, water installations as a result of indiscriminate shelling;
- hindrance of access, made difficult because of mines, booby traps or shelling, thus preventing any repair or maintenance;
- restriction of the delivery of equipment, spare parts, power generators, pipes, fuel needed to operate generators and pumps, and chemicals (particularly chlorine and fertilizers) required to treat water, by classifying them as 'strategic material';
- use of personnel from water treatment plants for other tasks, forcing them to leave an area or not allowing them to carry out their work;
- destruction of water installations as part of a 'scorched earth' policy when leaving an area;
- overuse of resources, leading directly or indirectly to long-term and irreversible effects on the quality of the water;
- looting of equipment, documents and so on; and
- deliberate or unintended poisoning of water supplies as a direct or indirect consequence of war.

Conflict situations can limit the supply of water to survival level for long periods of time. In conflict situations it is also important to be seen as non partisan.

Water and security in natural disasters

The following information has been identified from Campbell, 1996, Lashley, 1997, PAHO, 1997 and the United Nations Department of Humanitarian Affairs, 1996.

Natural threats which can lead to disasters include earthquakes, volcanoes, hurricanes, floods and droughts. They may occur on their own or several may occur at the same time. Each threat will have its own direct impacts on infrastructure and the water supply system but additional damage may also be caused by secondary effects. These include mudslides, liquefaction, tsunamis, strong water currents, strong winds and fault movements.

Effects on water supply systems may include structural damage and modification to, and pollution of, catchment areas and water sources. Water quality can be modified by gases from volcanic eruptions, landslides, direct pollution and changes in aquifer characteristics due to modified fault systems.

In addition to the water supply being damaged directly, other impacts may be indirect and include damage to energy supplies, communication networks and access roads which may affect the operation of systems. Trained personnel may leave the areas or be evacuated. Security due to impending threats may limit access to sources and supply systems. See the case study on Montserrat, p124 for examples of some of these occurrences.

Populations and governments in hazard prone areas often have experience of appropriate interventions. They should be consulted at an early stage.

Social and cultural issues

The water supply facilities provided must be suitable to the needs of the populations concerned and to sub-sets of those populations. Communities and especially groups of people forced together by an emergency are not a coherent whole and people within the overall group often have differing needs and priorities. People from one ethnic group may be more vulnerable than those of another, and hence additional security considerations may be needed when selecting water sources and siting water points. Similarly, women may have additional security needs and requirements for privacy. Locating water where women may be vulnerable to assault should be proactively avoided. In some cultural and religious groups privacy is even more important (for example Muslim women) and special considerations should be given to the needs of such groups. In all such circumstances consultation with the groups concerned is very important as it is always difficult for outsiders to judge the needs of people from different social and cultural backgrounds.

Legal issues

Legal considerations are often interlinked with political ones. Before water sources are used the owners' permission will be required, whether it is private or government land. Only where such people or organizations no longer exist may permission to abstract be bypassed.

Management

All systems which are put into place for the abstraction, transmission, treatment and distribution of water will need to be managed. Appropriate resources (material, financial and human) must be available for the whole period that the system is in place. Training may be required for staff and effective management systems should be implemented. Systems should be designed so that operation and maintenance is appropriate to the resources and personnel available. The Hartisheik case study (p112) highlights some of the difficulties of implementing a system of supply which requires a high level of operation and maintenance.

Political issues, conflicts of interest and the needs of local populations, affected populations and the organizations working to provide relief

In emergency situations populations often require outside assistance, whether from their government, national non-government organizations or from international relief organizations. Vast sums of money are directed to the affected populations, whether they are refugees or internally displaced. The resources provided for the affected populations may be superior to those used by the local populations who have been affected by an influx. The presence of the new population is also likely to have negative impacts on local communities. The pollution of locally used water sources, destruction of the environment and devaluation of the local currency are common. On the other hand they may bring business and new ideas, and hence benefit the few who are able to make use of these resources. Those involved in decision-making, including those who are selecting a water source in emergencies, should be aware of these imbalances and problems. There is a general consensus that more consideration must be given to the needs of local populations but the issue is complicated by the risk of creating dependency. The Uvira case study on p119 (Foerster, 1996) shows how different approaches can be applied to different groups of people at the same time.

As well as the local and affected populations having differing needs and priorities, so do the organizations working in the provision of relief. The national government may, for example, want to prevent further unrest in the region, or limit any construction work which may imply permanence and hence discourage displaced populations from returning home. They may, on the other hand, have more complicated or sinister motives, and their actions may make the provision of relief for an opposing side during conflict very difficult. Governments will have a significant influence on camp locations. Often areas allocated for camps are lacking in natural resources and hence not used by local populations.

International relief organizations also have their own agendas. As well as aiming to help those affected, they also have their own mandates and needs for fundraising, and hence may need to be 'seen' to be in the correct places at the correct times. This can lead to competition between the organizations and an environment in which information is not always readily shared. Communication between participating organizations is often lacking, because of the demands put on relief personnel in the complex arena of the emergency and due to inter-agency rivalry. Communication is especially important when sources of water are being considered and systems to treat and supply the water are being chosen. After the initial survival supply has been provided, time should be taken to reassess the situation, to seek out additional information and to modify earlier decisions if necessary.

Funding may be available only for donor identified areas.

Developmental versus traditional relief responses

Relief responses have often been based on the short term. The aim has been to supply basic resources (usually by external organizations) until the 'emergency' is over and the populations can return home or support themselves. However emergencies are often lengthy and simple short- term solutions may not be suitable. At what point should a relief response become a developmental one? The relief situation is a highly dependant situation, whereas the developmental one tries to support self-reliance. The two approaches are often conflicting and opinions vary within and between relief organizations as to the appropriateness of the developmental versus traditional relief responses. The selection of water sources will have impacts on the longer term, so it is important that both the short and longer term should be considered. In emergencies, planning for, or even considering the longer term can be very difficult, but it is not impossible and is very important where water resources are concerned.

Andrew Chalinder discusses some of these issues and others in his publication 'Water and Sanitation in Emergencies. Good Practice Review 1' which is a useful reference for further information.

Case studies ■

The following case studies highlight some of the management, legal, security, socio-political and cultural aspects discussed above.

Dimma refugee camp, Ethiopia

the Cross Mandate Initiative, considering local and affected populations, internal migration of populations, surface water

{case study noted during fieldwork with information supplied by, and reproduced with kind permission of UNHCR, Ethiopia and ARRA, Ethiopia}

Dimma is an isolated refugee camp in South Western Ethiopia. The refugees are primarily Sudanese from the Nuer tribe, although a range of other tribes and a few Ugandans are also present. Dimma camp is situated in the centre of a large uninhabited area which was once a game reserve. There is a scattered population of Surma nomads and gold miners, but the nearest established town is 70km away. The camp was established in 1986, closed in 1991, and re-opened in 1992 in a village / settlement format. The refugees (estimated population 12,333 in 1996) have a high level of support including water, food, schools, clinics and vocational training. Attempts have been made to encourage each family to construct a pit latrine but there has been some resistance to their use.

S. House

Dimma Refugee Camp, South Western Ethiopia

Fundika town (estimated population 11,000 in 1996), developed next to Dimma camp when the camp was established. Initially it provided labour for the camp construction and established business links with the refugees, but it now acts as a trading centre for the refugees, nomads and gold miners. The town is growing rapidly and is poorly served with utilities, particularly water. The people of the town wash clothes and vehicles and bathe in a tributary of the Akobo river upstream of the abstraction point for the refugee camp water supply. The town people have been paying water carriers for water to be collected from the tributary and carried up hill to the town. There is no sanitation in the town, with defecation occurring in the adjoining fields and along the river banks.

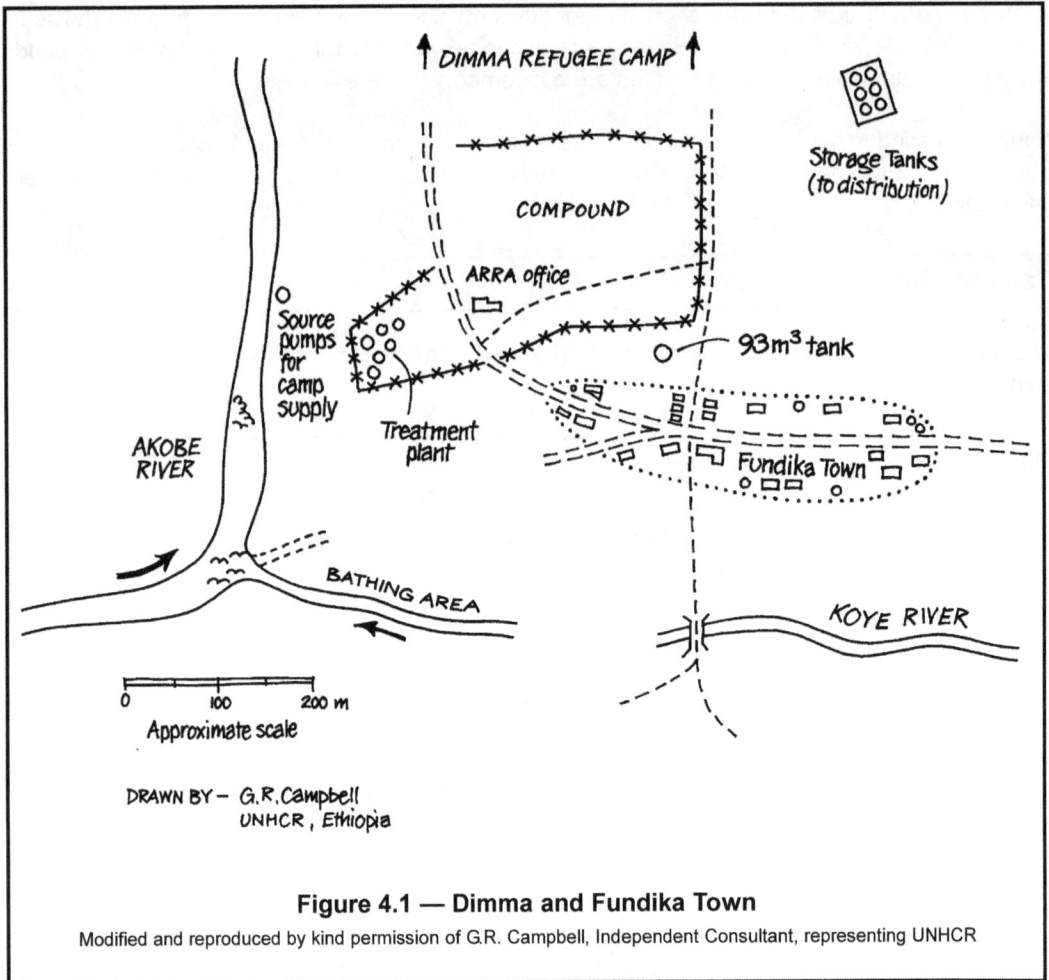

Figure 4.1 — Dimma and Fundika Town

Modified and reproduced by kind permission of G.R. Campbell, Independent Consultant, representing UNHCR

In Ethiopia the 'Cross Mandate Initiative' exists, where local communities become the focus of development activity alongside the refugees, who are entitled to support from the United Nations High Commissioner for Refugees (UNHCR). UNHCR and the Administration of Refugee and Returnee Affairs (ARRA) (the Ethiopian Government department responsible for refugees and returnees) have provided water tapstands and drainage curtains in Fundika town. The arrangement is that UNHCR and ARRA would construct and maintain the tapstands and pipelines initially, and after a period of three months the maintenance would be handed over to the town. A nominal fee was agreed to be charged for a jerrycan of water. At present the tapstands in the town can only be supplied with water when there is spare capacity after supplying the refugees. If UNHCR want to supply the town on a full-time basis the capacity of the treatment system will have to be increased.

Many discussions arise from this case study and the questions and ethical / political issues are endless:

- The town is relatively rich from the gold trade but the residents still appear to be reluctant to pay for a clean water supply because the refugees are being supplied with water free. The townspeople were prepared to pay for water from the polluted river but were not so happy to pay for clean water from a tap! The politics of supplying refugees but not surrounding communities is a complicated one.

- Can UNHCR afford to supply a rapidly growing town with clean water? The town did not exist before the arrival of the camp and soon it will be bigger than the camp. If UNHCR / ARRA does not supply the town, the refugees are also at risk from drinking water supplied to them in the town and both the townspeople and the refugees are served by the ARRA / UNHCR clinic.
- The town is still growing and does not have a formal structure. Would it be able to manage and run its own water system? Could it be organized on a commercial basis?

Lessons:

- When dealing with the provision of resources to refugees, displaced persons and others, decisions are never simple and usually political.
- Refugees are nearly always supported by external organizations. Their water supply cannot be ignored but differences in supplies with local populations can cause conflict.

Hartisheik refugee camp, Ethiopia

water source decision-making for short and long term, moving camps, socio-political constraints, finances, tankering, boreholes, rainwater catchment, changes in migration patterns of nomadic people and livestock

{case study noted during fieldwork with information supplied by, and reproduced with kind permission of UNHCR, Ethiopia}

S. House

Birka for storage of rainwater, Hartisheik, Eastern Ethiopia

The Hartisheik camps were formed in 1988 when over 200,000 refugees arrived from Somalia. The location of the camps was determined by clan boundaries. Today the Hartisheik camps have approximately 60,000 residents and Hartisheik town, which expanded after the arrival of the refugees, a similar number.

The geology of the area around the Hartisheik camps means that there are high levels of run-off and poor percolation. Water that does percolate through the soil travels great depths below the surface through the permeable Jessoma sandstone. Drilling to over 300m in the Hartisheik area has failed to find water. The high runoff, however, means that rainwater catchment is possible using the ground surface. Ponds and *birkas* (simple ponds or tanks, often with a cement lining) are used for storage (see left). However, rainfall is seasonal and erratic.

The initial assessment of the area recommended that the camp be moved due to the non-availability of water. However, the Somali region is complicated and due to restrictions placed by the Ethiopian

Government and the existence of clan boundaries it was not possible to move the camp. Hence, as an initial survival level response, water was trucked from the nearest reliable borehole source located in the town of Jijiga, 70km away. This resulted in a cost of $US14 per 1000 litres of water. With the continued civil unrest in Somalia, the rapid repatriation of refugees seemed less likely and alternatives were investigated to reduce the cost of water supply to the camps. As there are few surface water sources in the region and those that do exist are seasonal, groundwater was investigated. Two exploratory boreholes and three production boreholes were drilled in the Jerrer Valley, approximately 40km from Hartisheik, and the trucking operation costs were reduced to $US8 per 1000 litres of water. The location of the boreholes in the Jerrer Valley has been, and continues to be, a complicated affair. Clan fighting over the boreholes has cost several lives. The trucking operation is undertaken under careful negotiation with the local clans, and water is provided to local villages en route and to the towns, as well as to the camps at Kebri Beyah and Hartisheik.

Groundwater borehole, Jerrer Valley

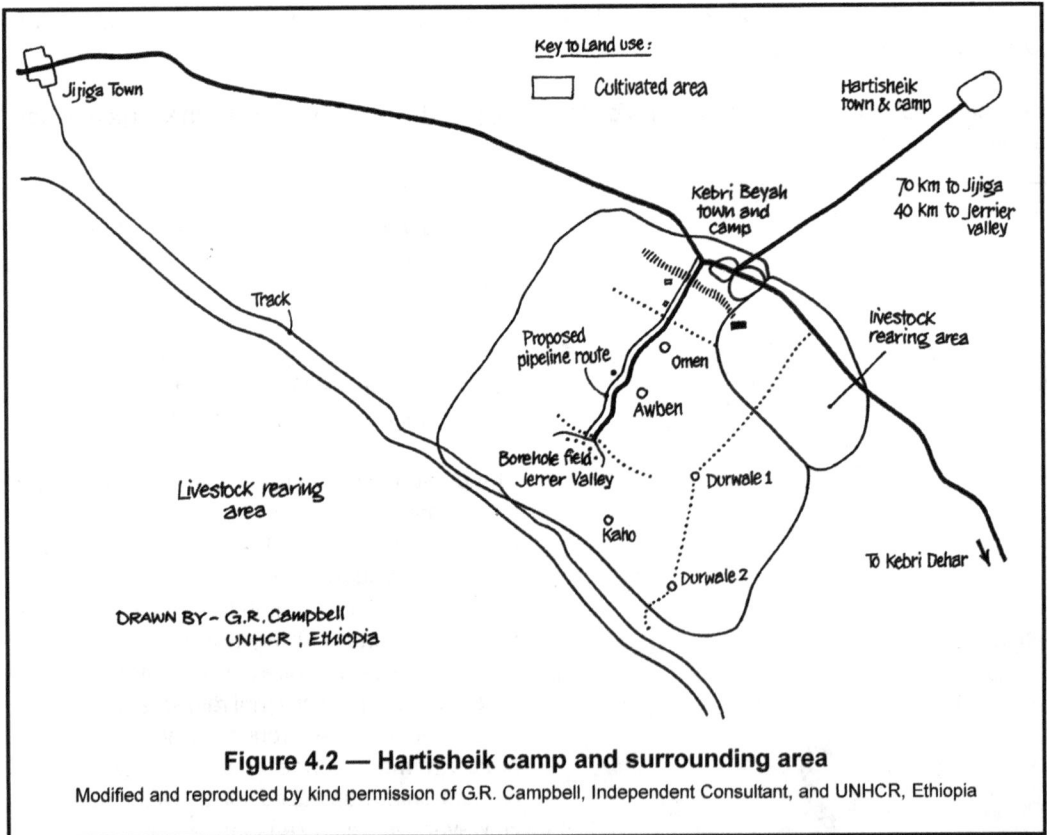

Figure 4.2 — Hartisheik camp and surrounding area

Modified and reproduced by kind permission of G.R. Campbell, Independent Consultant, and UNHCR, Ethiopia

Early disagreements between the local communities and the manage-ment of the water trucking operation led to the water tankers being shot at as they passed en route to the camps. The operation suffers not only from being in a technically difficult area for the provision of water supply but also, more seriously, from social, political and security constraints.

The water is being trucked under a programme managed by CARE and financed by UNHCR, the annual budget totalling approximately $US2 million per year. The costs include road maintenance, an essential part of the operation. To reduce the difficulties of the tankering operation and the costs there have been plans for several years to build a pipeline from the Jerrer Valley to Kebri Beyah. However, political, security and financial constraints have severely delayed its construction. The capital cost of the pipeline to Kebri Beyah could be recovered in a few years by reducing and subsequently phasing out the tankering programme but the budget for the refugee programme is continually being cut. The pressure to find an alternative to tankering remains and sustaining such a high-cost maintenance system in preference to developing a high capital cost but lower maintenance system is a false economy.

Hartisheik Refugee Camp

Trucking programme, Jerrer Valley to Hartisheik

There are various ponds and *birkas* fed by rainwater catchment around the towns of Hartisheik and Kebri Beyah from which water is sold on a private basis while it is available. UNHCR is constructing a series of *hafir* dams in the area with large scale collection of rainwater to try and supplement water from the tankering operation. The *hafir* dams consist of large excavated ponds with bunds to prevent entry by people and animals and hence limit contamination. They have inlet structures to funnel in rainwater and to act as a silt trap, and outlet structures to facilitate the drawing of water without contaminating the main storage area. One of the boreholes in the Jerrer Valley is used to supply livestock. The construction of the boreholes in the Jerrer Valley is also having impacts on the environment in that the pattern of migration of animals and nomads has been altered over a large land area. This could also lead to problems in the future between rival clans and resource use.

Lessons:
- The most obvious and ideal options, such as moving a camp from a location such as Hartisheik, are not always possible for political, social or security reasons.
- The siting of new boreholes or rainwater catchment structures can be complicated, especially if the 'owners' of the land are different from the recipients of the water.
- Financial planning for relief projects should consider the pay-back period and should account over periods longer than one financial year to realize the benefits of capital investments.
- The provision of new permanent water sources or other services can attract human and livestock migrants to an area and significantly change patterns of land use.
- Rainwater can be a useful supplementary source of water for refugee and displaced persons.

Teferi Ber and Darwanaji, Ethiopia

water source decision-making, land and water rights, communication with refugees and local communities, tankering, shallow wells

{case study noted during fieldwork with information supplied by, and reproduced with kind permission of UNHCR, Ethiopia}

The camps in Teferi Ber and Darwanaji have been supplied with water from a tankering operation for some years. The initial decision to tanker from a borehole in a neighbouring town was taken as the refugees were not expected to remain for a long period of time. Initial attempts to reduce the tankering operation and replace it with shallow wells was met with disapproval from the communities concerned, who had all been happy with the tankering operation. This resulted in the first wells, which were constructed by Oxfam, being destroyed. After significant discussion at local and regional level, the tankering operation is being run down and wells are being constructed alongside a river bed and are now accepted by the communities.

The contractual arrangements for construction of the wells has differed in the two locations. In one, the local community has provided its own labour under UNHCR supervision, and in the other the wells have been constructed by contractors. Careful negotiation was required prior to construction of the wells with regard to the issue of ownership of land and water rights. Written agreements have been formed, allowing the refugee population access to private wells, in exchange for upgrading works being completed by UNHCR.

The two areas concerned have refugee camps, local communities, and reintegration areas for returnees. The well construction programme has been financed using money from the reintegration programmes due to the limited funds available in the refugee programmes budget.

Lessons:
- Land and water rights are important issues which must be considered at the source selection decision-making stages.
- Effective communication and agreement with both local and displaced populations is essential if programmes are to be effective.
- Funding is not always available for improvements to supply systems in the longer term.

Bangladesh, Rohingya refugees from Burma

water source decision-making, upgrading of supplies, surface water sources, treatment processes

{case study provided and reproduced by kind permission of G.R. Campbell}

When G. Campbell and M. Gambrill (engineers seconded to Oxfam) arrived on site they found that the initial suggestions in an earlier assessment made inadequate provision for survival level of supply. They looked at all of the possible sources: springs, hand dug wells, a river and a pond. For the immediate period it was decided to continue using the pond (which was already being used by the refugees) whilst setting up an alternative point of abstraction on the river. The hand dug wells were dry at the time of the assessment and the spring sources were very small in yield and hence not suitable for the needs of the populations.

G.R. Campbell

Water supply for Rohingya refugees, Dumdumia, Bangladesh

Survival response:
- Used an existing source which was being used by the local population. This was pond water which was being treated in a small slow sand filter. The team turned the filter into a rapid sand filter, passing by mechanical means, a greater volume of water, and increasing the storage capacity.
- Thereafter, as the pond began to run dry, water was transferred to the pond from the nearby river, allowing recharge and some settlement to occur.
- Prevented people washing in the pond by using national guards who were previously the main users of the pond (i.e. the existing local population). The guards agreed to protect the source as they were unhappy that the refugees were using the pond. The guards were allowed to continue washing in the pond.

Subsequent response:
- Used the turbid river water. An infiltration gallery was constructed using ranging sizes of stones and the resulting water was pumped into an Oxfam slow sand filter.
- A tapstand was given to the local residents (national guards) when the supply was developed for the refugees.
- Bathing ponds were constructed around the camps.

Lessons:
- A phased response is often most suitable for the water supply to displaced populations.
- By compensating the local populations, understanding can be possible and everyone can benefit.

Bathing pond, Bangladesh

Infiltration gallery pump, Dumdumia, Bangladesh

Uvira, Zaire

local population water supplies, logistical difficulties

{case study noted during fieldwork and with information supplied by, and reproduced by kind permission of the International Committee of the Red Cross; Ref: Foerster, 1996}

For this case study, refer to the map on page 155.

The following extracts are from a report written by Foerster (1996):

'Since 1994, conflicts in Rwanda and Burundi have forced Hutus to flee for Zaire, Uganda and Tanzania. The Kivu region (Zaire) has received over 1 million refugees. International organizations have set up camps all along the border. The distribution of food and non-food essentials have helped the refugees to survive. Water, cooking and heating fuel are derived from the immediate environment whilst sheeting and food are brought in from other countries.'

'The effect of this sudden increase in population in the Kivu region on natural resources (water and fuel in particular) is becoming increasingly threatening. Refugees have benefited from international humanitarian aid, unlike neighbouring villages which have been overlooked. This unbalanced access to natural resources (in particular clean water) could create antagonism between the refugees and the local population. In August 1996, the new camp of Kahunda was set up by HCR in the north of the Ruzizi Plain. The water supply for the camp was derived from an irrigation canal from the Kitemesho river. This canal was used by the local population prior to the arrival of the refugees. When the UNHCR engineers installed their treatment plant, the local population sabotaged the canal by constructing a dam further up stream to prevent water from reaching the treatment plant.'

'Most of the village population from the Ruzizi Plain gets its daily water requirements from the numerous canals and rivers which feed into the Ruzizi River. For the refugees, this water is treated whilst the locals use it untreated. Incidences of water borne diseases are high amongst the local population (diarrhoea, malaria, billharzia). During the dry season many rivers dry up completely and the concentration of pollutants in the remaining water bodies increases. During the wet season, erosion in the steep hills and mountains immediately west of the Ruzizi Plain increases the turbidity and suspended matter content of the water. It is estimated that 100% of the refugees have access to clean water whilst only 30% of the locals have this luxury.'

'The water supply infrastructure in the region is practically non-existent. The objective of the Uvira Water Supply Project (UWSP) is to give the local population increased access to clean water by developing ground water resources.'

The UWSP was structured to ensure that in the future it could continue without the financial or technical input of the International Committee of the Red Cross (ICRC) and Australian Red Cross (ARC). The organization was developing the skills to build wells to ensure future supply, and the communities were contributing to the provision of clean water, which indicated the demand and will help in the longer term.

Extremely restricted access to Uvira caused severe logistical problems for this project and for the support to the refugee settlements. Uvira is situated to the south of the Zone d'Uvira on the north-western shores of Lake Tanganyika in Zaire. During the latter part of the project period (before the project was forced to close due to unforeseen events in the region), access was limited to a small airstrip at Kiliba. The only asphalt road was from Bukavu, but this escarpment road was off limits because of anti-personnel mines and guerrilla activities around Kamanyola which threaten the security of convoys. Instead of the escarpment road to Bukavu, one can cross the border to Rwanda via Kamembe, but this road was also closed due to security incidents between Rwanda and Zaire. South of Uvira, there is a dirt track leading to Fizi which only 4WD vehicles can use and only during the dry season. The road is slow with many river crossings and military check points. West of Uvira, there are no roads at all. The mountains are scattered with villages connected by walking tracks. East of Uvira, the border to Burundi is closed and Bujumbura and its airport have been inaccessible since April 1996. The only way into Uvira is by air using the Kiliba airfield. This airfield is owned by the sugar factory in Kiliba and was closed for the first four months of the project. The airfield re-opened in late September 1996 after long negotiations with the Zairean authorities.

Lessons:
- Local populations are often ignored when displaced people are supplied with water. Separate organizations to those working with the refugees can work in a more developmental fashion with local populations in the vicinity of refugee camps to try and reduce the negative impacts on the locals and to prevent frictions between the two groups.
- Logistics can be extremely problematic in areas where displacements occur, especially in areas of conflict.

Lebanon

complexity of urban emergencies, security and politics in armed conflicts

{case study reproduced by kind permission of the International Committee of the Red Cross; Ref: ICRC, 1994}

The following extracts highlight the complications of supplying water during the Lebanon 1989 and 1990 wars.

'By 14 May [1989], the situation was described as increasingly alarming by all the press releases issued at the time, as most of the suburbs lacked water, both in the western sector of the city, under Muslim control, and in the hills on the eastern side... The southern Muslim suburbs were particularly short of water owing to poor coverage and lack of resources, coupled with rapid demographic growth in recent years. The complex distribution schemes and the interconnection of the pumping and distribution networks made the western sector dependent on the eastern side.'

'Several wells and pumping stations were connected to the network in the southern outskirts ... Two other wells were ready to be connected to the network but were too close to the front line to be equipped. The Damour well, which had a capacity of about 5000 m³/day, could not be put in use for political reasons (the Druze and Shiite conflicts). It was decided immediately to install a 420KVA backup generator to operate the Borj el Brajneh pumping station and to equip two boreholes at Haj el Selloum in order to give to the southern suburbs (mainly Hezbollah) at least a minimum supply of water, independent from the supply systems on the eastern side, which were politically very vulnerable and likely to suffer damage in the event of hostilities. The 420 KVA generator was purchased in east Beirut and taken over to the western side by the ICRC convoy, with agreement of all factions... Access to the site had to be negotiated constantly and specific details submitted on the number of workers, trucks and special engines involved in the operation, which was expected to take many months.'

'In the Upper Metn, between Bikfaya and the coast, 45 villages were severely affected by water shortages [1990]. The installation of back-up generators to drive the pumps... which normally fed the main distribution reservoir in Bikfaya, was considered too difficult. The only solution was to repair the gravity line running from the artificial lake of Ballout. A 400m stretch had been completely damaged... in the no man's land between the Christian and Syrian sectors. UNICEF supplied the 8-inch and 4-inch pipes, and the ICRC was in charge of the repair work. The work started in early May but was delayed because of sporadic shelling in the Bikfaya area. The most dangerous section of the line was between the front lines of the Lebanese and the Syrian armies. Access was difficult and the area strewn with mines. Information on the mined areas was provided by the Syrian army.'

Lessons:
- Urban areas in conflicts have the added complication that water supply routes may cross boundaries between warring groups and hence are open to attack and sabotage.
- Negotiation is an essential skill when seeking to gain access to water sources in complex socio-political environments.
- Water installations are often mined in conflict situations and therefore pose serious security risks to personnel.

Iraq

---

interdependence of water and power, armed conflicts, and needs assessment

{case study reproduced by kind permission of the International Committee of the Red Cross; Ref: ICRC, 1994}

The following extracts highlight water supply issues and problems encountered during the Gulf War in 1991.

'When armed conflict breaks out, power stations are often put out of action. The high tension power lines are also very vulnerable to bombardment and sabotage. Emergency generators moreover need diesel and this is likely to be in short supply or severely rationed in view of its strategic importance. Water shortages resulting from lack of electricity are common in today's conflicts: Mostar, Sarajevo, Aden, Monrovia, Mogadishu and Kigali are just a few examples of cities that had to face this problem.' 'Surgical strikes launched against power stations often lead to a complete breakdown of water supply systems. During August and September 1991, an independent international team carried out a study on the question of water in Iraq... The study showed that, by the beginning of September 1991, production had returned to 37 percent of the 1990 capacity and over 75 percent of transmission lines were operational. The shortage of spare parts meant, however, that it was impossible to improve the situation further. A considerable deterioration in the electricity and water production systems was foreseeable, with serious consequences on public health (supply of drinking water and disposal of wastewater) and manufacturing output. Although the coalition forces respected Protocol I additional to the 1949 Geneva Conventions by not targeting or attacking drinking water installations, virtually all of these were put out of action by the shortage of electricity. Thus the end result was the same.' (Nembrini, in ICRC, 1994)

'As regards the quality of water in Baghdad, untreated sewage was dumped directly into the river — the source of water supply — and all the drinking water plants were therefore using water with high sewage contamination. Most of the sewage lifting stations were shut down and blockages occurred, causing flooding from manholes and sewer outlets. Many pipes broke under the excessive water pressure on the weakened sewer bedding, increasing the risk of cross contamination.'

'In these areas [of the Shiite uprising in the south and the Kurdish uprising in the north] the situation was aggravated by looting in March and April, which further amplified existing problems. Some of the installations, vehicles and maintenance equipment were targeted as facilities belonging to the Iraqi state.'

'Problems varied in urgency according to the region and over time in each of the regions, which made it very difficult to gain an overall view of the situation, especially in the initial stages of the water and sanitation programme. Priorities were therefore constantly reassessed during the first part of the operation.'

'Excellent co-operation with the Iraqi engineers and permanent co-ordination with the other humanitarian organizations (in particular UNICEF) were instrumental in ensuring the success of the programme and avoiding any overlapping with other projects.'

'Some of the Iraqi water treatment stations were fitted with the latest technology and were therefore complicated to operate, whereas in rural areas facilities were more rudimentary. Field staff had to be experienced enough to deal with both highly technical issues and more simple problems.'

Lessons:

- Water abstraction, treatment and supply facilities are dependant on power sources, especially in urban areas. Power plants and fuel are often the focus of attacks in conflicts, thereby complicating the provision of water.
- Inadequate maintenance of sewerage systems can have serious public health impacts and may pollute water sources.
- In conflicts, water supply facilities can be targeted as items belonging to the state.
- Needs assessment requires continual revision as the emergency progresses.

Former Yugoslavia

armed conflict, industrial pollution

{case study reproduced by kind permission of the International Committee of the Red Cross; Ref: ICRC, 1994}

The following extracts highlight complications to the supply of water to Sarajevo and Srebrenica in the former Yugoslavia during 1992 and 1993.

'Early in April, the water coming [to Srebrenica] from the Zeleni Jadar water source, where the water catchment and the treatment plant were located, was cut off. Consequently there was no more running water in town and not enough water could be delivered to the standposts connected to small springs. The queues in front of the taps were longer than 50m day and night. Médecins sans Frontières started to organize the distribution of water with an old fireman's truck collecting water from a spring not far from the town; 15 rounds a day, corresponding to the total capacity available, were insufficient to fill the collapsible tanks installed, which were regularly emptied in less than half an hour. A total of 15 springs were protected but this was barely enough as some started to dry up with the arrival of the summer. People could not wash themselves and more than 20 percent of the population had scabies.'

'With the help of local workers, the river flowing through Srebrenica was diverted and the water brought into town through a pipeline of about 10km, where the ICRC and Médecins sans Frontières installed 50 public standposts. The need for water was so great that people started to drill holes in this emergency pipeline.'

'At the beginning of June 1993, Médecins sans Frontières and UNPROFOR were allowed to carry out some cleaning work at the Zeleni Jadar station, which could only be reached by the use of armoured carriers. The station was restarted but four days later the permission was cancelled. For more than a month MSF, the ICRC and UNPROFOR tried to get access to the plant, but were always sent back at the checkpoint or denied authorization. As the situation became more and more critical, the issue was taken up by General Morillon in his discussions with the Bosnian Serb military leadership. The latter finally provided written authorisation to inspect the water installations.

But, a couple of days before the humanitarian organizations again gained access, the Bosnian Serbs blew up the plant entirely.'

'A recent UNIDO study involved the inspection of fifty destroyed Croatian electrical transformers, refineries, ammunition dumps and other installations, where large quantities of noxious and polluting materials were found to have been released. In at least two cases substances were released directly into tributaries of the Danube, a major source of drinking water, including polyaromatic hydrocarbons not normally tested for by downstream authorities monitoring water quality. In addition, heavy metals leaching from an ammunition dump near Zagreb are likely to migrate through the carboniferous limestone strata and emerge in wells used for drinking water near the Croatian coast' (Plant in ICRC, 1994).

'During the war, supply from gravity sources [to Sarajevo] was interrupted. Lack of electricity and damage to many of the pumps has significantly reduced the supply from the Bacevo field and war damage to other system facilities has been severe. Sniping and shelling prevented leak repairs and leakage now consumes an estimated 70 percent of the limited supply. The watershed has deteriorated because of farming and dumping, and blockage of the river channels threatens to allow toxic chemicals and other waste to enter the Bacevo aquifer.'

Lessons:
- Armed conflicts can place serious restrictions on movements, logistics and access to resources, dramatically limiting the options for provision of water.
- The threat of industrial pollution to water sources is high in industrialized countries such as Eastern Europe and the former Yugoslavia.

Caribbean Island of Montserrat

natural disasters, vulnerability assessments

{Case study provided and reproduced by kind permission of David A. Lashley of David Lashley & Partners Inc., Barbados; Ref: Lashley, 1997}

Montserrat is an Island located in the Leeward Islands of the Eastern Caribbean. It is 11 miles long and 7 miles wide with a population of 10,000 (prior to the events of 1997). The island is volcanic in origin and is also subjected to low intensity earthquakes and hurricanes during certain periods of the year. The Soufriere Hills Volcano in the southern part of the island, rises to 3,000 foot above sea level. The volcano slopes to the sea from it's peak down towards the west, south and east and in the north to the Belham Valley where the land again rises into the Centre Hills.

A period of volcanic activity began in 1995 with a small eruption and was followed by a series of heavy ash falls. In August 1995, 6,000 of the population were evacuated from the southern part of the island to the north of the Belham Valley. The evacuation order was lifted in the following months but minor activity continued until major eruptions occurred during June 1997.

Montserrat's water supply is mainly reliant on springs with 16 springs, supplying 90% of the islands water. Seismic activity related to the volcano had not been of sufficient magnitude to produce major surface movement at the time of vulnerability assessments in early 1997. However there was some concern that movement of the joints in the rock formation could lead to changes in spring location and water quality. Hurricanes periodically affect the water supplies by directly damaging facilities and, over the longer term, by reducing vegetation cover and hence impacting on the stability of the spring sources with increased erosion and slope failures. Water catchments are also subjected to acid rain and ash falls due to the volcanic activity, and to flood flows in the rainy season. Recommendations were made that a broader range of water quality sampling and analysis should be undertaken on a more regular basis to monitor any trends in changing quality which may require early mitigation actions. Access to the springs is by foot with no vehicular access, making maintenance and repairs difficult.

Two of the main spring sources, which supplied 35% of the total demand, were located on the southern face of the Centre Hills, the face most exposed to the volcano. Access to these sources was also within the 'unsafe zone'. Therefore, as the volcanic conditions worsened, reliance had to be switched to alternative sources in the north west of the island. Mass migration of over 50% of the islands population to the north following the heaviest volcanic activity has also affected the location of demand. Existing reservoir locations indicated the supply system would need to be adapted to meet the new locations of demand and sources. Modifications proposed included reversing the flow in a section of the supply system and adding additional pumping and storage facilities. Vulnerability assessments and the emergency response to provide drinking water had to be continually modified as the volcanic threat worsened. By August 1997 it was estimated that over half of the islands population had left the island.

Lessons:
- Vulnerability assessments of water sources and supply systems during natural emergencies is a complex task and requires continual revaluation to respond to the latest information on the scale and impact of the threat.
- In areas vulnerable to natural threats, water sources may be impacted or damaged by several different threats and secondary impacts (e.g. hurricanes, seismic activity, floods, landslides, volcanic activity).
- Mass migration during natural emergencies also affects decisions over source use and supply systems.

Key references:
- Bell, 1992
- Campbell, 1996
- Chalinder, 1994
- Foerster, 1996
- ICRC, 1994
- Lashey, 1997

Typical water source features

The following table summarizes the most common features of water sources (i to vii) and their development. There will always be exceptions and this should be borne in mind when reading the table. It does, however, allow some degree of comparison.

Source: Surface water

Type of source	(i) Lakes and ponds	(ii) Lowland rivers and streams	(iii) Highland streams
Features of yield	· Depends on size of and level of recharge · Yield can reduce during the dry season	· Large river flows generally stable · Some rivers dry up completely in the dry season	· Can be seasonal · Some streams dry up completely in the dry season
Features of quality	· Bacteriologically poor to good in large ponds and lakes, poor to fair in smaller water bodies · Can have high mineral levels · Turbidity can be good but can also be variable	· Generally bacteriologically poor · Often high turbidity, especially in the rainy season	· Often bacteriologically better than lowland streams · Turbidity depends on the geology and soil conditions
Possible treatment requirements	· Sedimentation, assisted sedimentation, filtration, disinfection and / or other · Only disinfection required for low turbidity water · Will vary with location	· Sedimentation, assisted sedimentation, filtration, disinfection and / or other · Will vary with location	· Only disinfection required for low turbidity mountain streams · Sedimentation, assisted sedimentation, filtration, disinfection and / or other for high turbidity streams
Accessibility	· Generally accessible · There can be large changes in water level which can make access difficult	· Generally accessible · There can be large changes in water level which can make access difficult	· Topography may make access difficult
Protection requirements	· Difficult to protect, especially if large perimeter · Need to fence off the area and use guards to restrict contact with water to certain areas · Must provide alternative access to water for existing users	· Difficult to protect, especially to control upstream usage · Need to fence off the area and use guards to restrict contact with water to certain areas · Must provide alternative access to water for existing users	· Difficult to protect, especially to control upstream usage · Need to fence off the area and use guards to restrict contact with water to certain areas · Must provide alternative access to water for existing users · Protection also required from moving boulders
Abstraction equipment and structures	· Intake structure and pumping facilities	· Intake structure and probably pumping facilities	· Intake structure and pumping facilities if gravity flow is not possible
Storage requirements	· Storage required for treatment and supply	· Storage required for treatment and supply	· Storage required for treatment and supply
Capital cost per person served	· Moderate to high · Pumping and treatment equipment costs high	· Moderate to high depending on method used · Pumping and treatment equipment costs high	· Moderate to high depending on method used · Pumping and treatment equipment costs high
O&M physical requirements	· Maintenance of abstraction filters, structures and pumps and for treatment systems · Treatment operation and monitoring	· Maintenance for abstraction filters, structures and pumps and for treatment systems · Treatment operation and monitoring	· Maintenance for abstraction filters, structures and pumps and for treatment systems · Treatment operation and monitoring
O&M consumable requirements	· Fuel or electricity to power pumps · Pump spare parts · Treatment chemicals	· Fuel or electricity to power pumps. · Pump spare parts · Treatment chemicals	· Fuel or electricity to power pumps if required · Pump spare parts · Treatment chemicals
Time of set up	· Temporary facilities can be set up quickly	· Temporary facilities can be set up quickly	· Temporary facilities can be set up quickly
Impacts of development	· Problems will be caused if the source is protected but no alternative is provided for local users (domestic, farmers and animals) · Reducing water levels may reduce local groundwater table · Care must be taken with disposal of sludges	· Care must be taken to ensure sufficient yield remains for downstream users (domestic, farmers and animals) · Care must be taken with disposal of sludges	· Care must be taken to ensure sufficient yield remains for downstream users (domestic, farmers and animals) · Care must be taken with disposal of sludges

Source: Groundwater and rainwater

Type of source	(iv) Deep borehole	(v) Dug well	(vi) Spring catchment	(vii) Rainwater catchment
Features of yield	· Yield depends on aquifer type, wet surface area and quality of borehole development. · Can be high · Generally stable if not overpumped	· Yield will depend on aquifer type, depth of well, height of water table and wet surface area · Can be high but generally not as high as deep boreholes · Can be seasonal	· Steady for artesian flow. · Some springs dry up in the dry season · Springs sometimes move location	· Variable · New supplies unavailable during the dry season · More appropriate for small users such as medical centres or institutions
Features of quality	· Generally good quality bacteriologically · Can taste bad from iron, manganese and low levels of dissolved oxygen · Low turbidity	· If well lining is adequately sealed, the well is capped and a pump issued then quality can be good · If unprotected then microbiological quality is likely to be poor · Also can have chemical problems, e.g. nitrates · Low-medium turbidity	· Good quality · Exception to this could be springs in areas of highly fissured rock · Generally low turbidity	· Depends on cleanliness of catchment structures · Low in minerals · Low turbidity if collection system is clean · Heavy air pollution and volcanic activity can modify the water quality
Common treatment requirements	· Disinfection · Possibly aeration and sedimentation or filtration if removing iron or manganese	· Disinfection · If pumped and unacceptable turbidity then assisted sedimentation or filtration could also be used	· Disinfection	· Sedimentation (for solids introduced from catchment structures) and disinfection.
Accessibility	· Can be difficult to locate groundwater and access initially	· Can be difficult to locate groundwater and access initially	· Generally requires piped transmission from high areas · Often difficult to reach spring and to protect without damage	· Good for small users · Difficult to access large volumes
Protection requirements	· Lining, capping and drainage around the borehole	· Well headwall, lining, cover and drainage around well	· Requires a spring box at the eye of the spring and appropriate cut off drainage upstream · Farming or similar activities should be limited uphill of the spring	· Catchment structures, covered tanks and protection from contaminated runoff
Abstraction equipment and structures	· Pumps with drive unit and ideally a pump house	· Windlass and bucket, handpump, or pumps with drive units and, ideally, a pump house	· Natural abstraction · Often can be transmitted to communities by gravity pipeline but requires pump if the source is located below the populations	· Requires catchment structure such as a roof or other smooth and sloping area
Storage requirements	· May require storage for treatment and supply	· Additional storage not commonly used when users draw directly from the well · Disinfection takes place in the well in this situation · If pumping occurs then storage may be required for treatment and supply	· Requires storage for treatment and supply	· Requires storage for treatment and supply · Additional storage is needed if rainwater is required during the dry season
Capital cost per person served	· High	· Low to moderate depending on water-lifting device and excavation method	· Fairly low · Costs increase with pipe distances	· Low-moderate for roof catchments (if roof cost is not included) · Moderate to high for ground catchments
O&M physical requirements	· Maintenance of pumping equipment and protection structures · Treatment operation and monitoring	· Maintenance of pumping or other water-lifting equipment and structural repair · Treatment operation and monitoring	· Maintenance limited to structural repair of spring box and pipelines and cleaning of spring box and surroundings · If the spring is located below the populations then maintenance of pumping equipment · Treatment operation and monitoring	· Catchment structures require cleaning · Treatment operation and monitoring
O&M consumable requirements	· Fuel or electricity to power pumps · Pump spare parts · Disinfectants	· Handpower only or same as deep borehole · Pump spare parts · Disinfectants	· Fuel or power for transmission if gravity cannot be used · Disinfectants	· Disinfectants
Time of set up	· Time consuming to locate water sources, get equipment to site and drill boreholes	· Time consuming to locate water sources and dig new wells · Can be quicker than surface water if time to import equipment is included in the equation	· Protection at the eye of the spring and piped transmission take some time	· Depends on existing structures available for water catchment
Impacts of abstraction	· Depletion of aquifers can affect other water supplies	· Depletion of aquifers can affect other water supplies · Care must be taken with disposal of sludges	· Care must be taken to ensure all users (including those downstream) have access to the supply · Will need to limit farming activities up hill	· Care must be taken with disposal of sludges

4

S.House

Surface water   Above: River, Eastern Zaire   Below: River, Kurdistan, Southern Turkey

R.A.Reed

P.A. Larcher

Surface water   Above: Lake abstraction, Rwanda   Below: Stream abstraction, Nyamirangwe Camp, Eastern Zaire

S. House

S. House

Groundwater　　　　　　　Above: Spring protection, Eastern Zaire　　　Below: Drilling for water, Eastern Ethiopia

S. House

Groundwater   Above: Local shallow well, Teferi Ber, Ethiopia   Below: Shallow well, Teferi Ber Refugee Camp, Ethiopia

S. House

S. House

4

Requirements for development

Technical ◼

When developing a source and supply system, technical solutions will be required for:
- protection
- abstraction (method and equipment structures)
- treatment (including raw water storage)
- means of transmission
- supply storage
- distribution
- other subsidiary activities (e.g. road maintenance, supply systems for local populations, information dissemination programmes, environmental protection, threat mitigation activities).

Care must be taken to ensure designs meet the needs of extreme conditions e.g. burying pipes and tanks in very cold weather, and designing roofs to withstand snow.

This document does not cover the design of systems for abstraction and supply. Standard texts can be used as support for this task. Examples include Davis and Lambert, 1995, UNHCR, 1995, MSF,1994, and a wide range of technical publications devoted to water supply.

Checklist and survey sheets have been included for the summary of technical requirements within these documents.

Resources / logistics ◼

Logistics and resources are often key constraints and therefore factors to consider when selecting water sources and designing supply systems. For example, it would not be appropriate to rely on a system of tankering from a source at a distance if diesel is in short supply and the security situation defines that it is not logistically possible to improve the situation.

Logistical and resource considerations can be particularly crucial when selecting water sources and systems in areas where there are conflicts or in very remote areas were logistics are difficult and likely to be variable.

For further information on logistics refer to Davis and Lambert, 1995, p106–27.

Checklist and survey sheets have been included for resources and logistics within these documents.

Time of set-up ◼

Time of set-up can also be a crucial factor for decision-making, especially in the initial stages of an emergency. For example, there would be no point in choosing a groundwater source for survival supply if the borehole needs to be drilled first.

To evaluate the time of set-up the technical solution for source development and supply will need to be chosen and the availability of resources and logistics for putting the system into place assessed. The urgency and scale of the situation will also affect the relative importance of the time of set-up versus other considerations.

Operation and maintenance (O&M) ■

Operation and maintenance requirements are an important consideration when selecting a water source and its supply system. They become increasingly more important as the emergency period lengthens. Over the longer term the operation and maintenance costs may even become higher than the capital costs (see below for further discussion).

For effective operation and maintenance of systems there should be staff trained in the task; an adequate supply of spare parts, chemicals and fuels; and sufficient technical backup to respond should there be a problem. Finances should therefore be available for these items. The supply of fuel is essential for a pumping system and stockpiles should be kept in areas where fuel shortages are common. Training may be required for staff, and record keeping systems introduced and followed. Records must be kept of chemicals used, water quality levels and problems in operation to help with re-ordering, checking the process efficiency of the system and in fault-finding.

Difficulties encountered with systems which require mechanical plant or vehicles include their total breakdown. Competent mechanics must be available and wherever possible dual systems should be operated (e.g. pumps) so that the supply can continue working if one item is out of order.

Management of systems is also an important part of operation and maintenance. See table pp135 for an example of percentage costs spent on management and administration on a large tankering programme in Ethiopia.

For further discussion on operation and maintenance of water supply systems refer to UNHCR, 1995, pp111–20.

The sections *Features of treatment processes* pp214–23 and *Typical water source features* pp125-6 include some comments on the operation and maintenance requirements of developing specific sources and selecting specific treatment processes. Summary sheets for operation and maintenance requirements have also been included as part of these documents.

Costs ■

Costs of developing a source and the respective supply system will vary depending on the location. Higher costs are likely in remote areas with severe logistical problems and low availability of material resources. It has been suggested that when working in landlocked countries that approximately 50% should be added to the estimated price of materials and equipment (Conti, 1997).

Costs may include:

Capital costs
- Equipment and material for the system
- Personnel for installation
- Transportation
- Import taxes
- Accommodation for management / workforce
- Workshops / plant buildings

Water supply systems

Tankering, Jerrer Valley to Hartisheik, Eastern Ethiopia

Pump, Luvungi Camp, Eastern Zaire

Storage tanks, Dumdumia, Bangladesh

Water supply systems

S. House

Waiting for water, Hartisheik, Eastern Ethiopia

R.A. Reed

Fighting for water, Kurdistan, Southern Turkey

S. House

Water tapstand, Luvungi Bridge, Eastern Zaire

Operation and maintenance costs

- Equipment and material spare parts
- Fuels and lubricants
- Operational personnel
- Management / administration

For many solutions there may also be hidden costs. See the following table for a breakdown of costs of the tankering programme which transports water from boreholes in the Jerrer Valley to the Hartisheik refugee camps in the Somali National Regional State of Ethiopia. A hidden cost for this supply system may have been that of the road maintenance unit. Other hidden costs for systems may include: the provision of additional facilities for local communities to compensate them for loss of water supply; costs for environmental damage mitigation activities; or hygiene mobilization programmes.

Breakdown of costs for Jerrer Valley – Hartisheik tankering programme

(information kindly supplied by K.S. Nair, CARE, Jijiga, Ethiopia)

Item	Percentage of total cost
Capital costs	
30 water tankers	61%
30 water trailers	22%
7 light vehicles	6%
Buildings (office / residence)	3%
Workshop	3%
Workshop equipment and tools	5%
Operation and maintenance costs (1996)	
Management / administration	60%
Spare parts and lubricants	20%
Fuel	13%
Road unit expense (to maintain the roads on the tankering route)	7%

Note: The tanker programme in the above table delivers 625m^3 per day over a 90km return journey. The tankers could deliver a greater volume.

Emergencies which last for a short period of time are likely to have capital costs which are higher than those for operation and maintenance. However as the length of the emergency increases, the relative importance of each set of costs will change. Comparison of sources and systems of supply may yield significantly different results when estimating costs over short rather than long periods of time. This point is particularly relevant when comparing the costs of a system which involves tankering with one that does not. Difficulties in determining the period of time to use for estimation include that the length of emergencies are difficult to predict and that funding organizations may specify a time period. Reducing costs in the short term may however be a false economy.

Summary sheets for costs have been included as part of these documents.

Impacts of development

The development of a new water supply scheme will have impacts on those who use it, on those who live in the vicinity and on the environment.

Often, impacts of the development of emergency water sources and of other aspects of refugee and displaced persons' camps are ignored. Assessment of impacts is difficult enough in times of stability but in an emergency situation it is even more problematic. The early stages of an emergency are often chaotic and there are many constraints to overcome when developing a water supply system. Both of these are an added hindrance.

However, the earlier that problems are identified and efforts made to mitigate them, the more likely the negative impacts can be reduced. This is especially important when considering the impacts on other users of the source or local populations in the vicinity. Consideration of the needs of local populations is not only important ethically, but may also reduce friction between the local and affected populations.

Although environmental damage may seem a secondary problem, the international community is often confronted with local authorities demanding remedial action for environmental damage, (Mora-Castro, 1996).

The impacts of development checklists in Sections 2 and 3 have been developed to encourage assessors to think about the impacts of their decisions and actions at an early stage. They do not provide answers. Even if the considerations cannot be made as part of the initial response, they should be considered as soon as possible.

The following notes may be used with the checklist p62 (items noted in boxes are sub-sections of the checklist).

I   **Effects of source development on the aquifer and remote sources:**

> • Location and capacity of aquifers (see *Groundwater investigation* p249–52)
> • Which sources are fed from the same aquifers

- Evaluation of the effects of the development of a source on remote sources will be very difficult for assessors who have little knowledge of hydrogeology.
- Existing (or new) pumping tests can give an indication of the aquifer's capacity and its effects on remote sources. Pumping tests are time consuming, need the agreement of the borehole owners, and require a high level of monitoring. They also require interpretation by experienced personnel.
- Borehole logs and water quality data may give an indication of whether sources are fed from the same aquifer.
- If a large population is to be supplied from a borehole source it is recommended that a hydrogeologist should assess the situation. Camps can last for many years and the effects of damaging an aquifer can be devastating to an area which is reliant on it.
- As soon as possible all nearby wells should be monitored for changes in water level.

II **Effects of development on existing users of the source and local populations at the point of abstraction and downstream:**

> • Determine: yield of source at present, existing demands, new abstraction demand, remaining yield (dry season) and the effects on existing users.
> • Consider compensation for local communities at the point of abstraction or downstream for the loss of yield or inconvenience. Also compare local and affected populations' supplies and consider upgrading local supplies to prevent friction.
> • Consider possible migration of people and animals / livestock to improved water sources (may be pronounced with nomadic populations).
> • Consider the effects on community structures / management capacity of organizations and populations.
> • What subsidiary / ancillary activities are required (training, road construction, sanitation, agricultural extension, hygiene promotion, etc.)?

• If assessment of yield is being made outside the dry season, then the assessor will have to rely on local knowledge, existing records of water levels and observation to estimate the dry season yields.
• If the source has greater than 50% yield remaining during the period of minimum yield after all deductions then any negative impacts should be minimal.
• If the source has less than 50% remaining during the period of minimum yield after all deductions, then other sources should be identified and assessed. The other sources can be used in conjunction with the first during periods of minimum yield, or as an alternative. Water rationing may be required during the dry season.
• **Impacts on local populations should be assessed as a priority in all circumstances.** Compensation for local populations should be considered, and could include improvement of their water supplies, although care should be taken to limit dependency. Care must be taken to consider the long-term effects on populations of both development of the source and the effects of compensation. A separate organization may be involved in responding to the needs of the local populations.
• It is essential that the assessor is aware of the complex socio-political environment in which the emergency exists. See the *Case studies* pp111–24 for example scenarios.
• Special care should be made where local populations pay for their water. Supplying water free to affected populations but not to local populations could result in friction between the two groups.
• Improved water sources may attract new users, such as nomadic populations and their animals. See the *Case studies* pp111–24.

III **Effects on vegetation and erosion:**

> • Change in yield
> • Effects of abstraction on vegetation and erosion and potential actions to minimize effects
> • Effects of migration to improved water sources on vegetation and erosion

• Evaluation of the effects of abstraction on vegetation and erosion will be based on judgements made about the effects of change in yield.
• Changes to migration patterns of nomadic people and animals to improved sources in areas where there is water scarcity can be dramatic. Local populations can be affected by subsequent erosion and destruction of vegetation.

IV Effects of water treatment and waste disposal:

- Increase in waste water — how will it affect levels of standing water?
- How will chemicals and fuel for water treatment be stored (location, security)?
- How will waste chemicals be disposed of?
- How will the sludge produced during treatment be disposed of?

- Assess drainage options for spillage / waste water. Can it easily be moved away from the camp by correct siting of distribution points? If not what actions can be identified to improve the situation (drainage channels, soakpits, raised platforms, concrete drainage curtains, etc.)
- Can the source be adequately protected from the spilled water?
- Waste chemicals are dangerous, especially if children get hold of them or animals feed on the waste. A plan of action is required for disposal. Burying with hospital wastes is a potential solution. See *Water treatment: Treatment processes and health and safety* pp224–29 for further details of health and safety considerations.
- Sludge may contain high numbers of pathogens and therefore thought must be given to the final disposal of the sludge. Try to identify a suitable area for burial which is near enough to the treatment works to prevent excessive haulage but will not damage local agriculture or contaminate the water source.

Camps

Nyamirangwe Camp, Eastern Zaire

Noyapara Camp, Bangladesh

Hartisheik Camp, Eastern Ethiopia

Camps

Kurdistan, Northern Iraq

Kibogoye Camp, South West Ethiopia

Wat Cowley Camp, Western Sudan

Water quantities

Some organisations currently have their own recommendations for water quantity provision. The figures here are provided for those who may not already have organisational recommendations.

It is recommended that in the initial stages of an emergency demand should be calculated:

$$\text{demand} \quad = \quad (\text{individual demand} + \text{livestock demand}) \times 110\%$$

When determining numbers of users (people and livestock) consideration should be given to future increases. These may be due to new arrivals of displaced population or from internal migration for trade and other purposes. Population numbers can be roughly estimated by counting the number on a measured area and multiplying out to the entire area.

Water demands (figures are l/head/day unless otherwise stated)

	'Survival' level	'Longer term' level
Individual/ family demands		
Individual	· 3 - 5 · 3 min cold weather · 5 min hot weather	· 15 - 20
Livestock	· large / medium animals 5 · small animals 1	· large / medium animals 20-30 · small animals 5

The figures given below should be used to assess sources to supply individual centres if this is part of the assessors remit.

Individual/ family demands		
Family latrines		· 2 - 8 l/cubicle/day for cleaning latrine · 1 - 2 l/user/day for handwashing
Aid staff	· 30	· 80
Communal demands		
Defecation fields		· 1 - 2 l/user/day for hand washing
Communal trench latrines		· 2 - 8 l/cubicle/day for cleaning latrine · 2 - 8 l/m of trench/day for cleaning latrine · 1 - 2 l/user/day for hand washing
Health centres and hospitals	· out patients 5 · in patients 40 - 60	· out patients 5 · in patients 40 - 60 · larger volumes up to 300 l/user/day may be used by hospitals in some circumstances especially where there are laundry facilities
Cholera centres	· 60 l/patient/day	· 60 l/patient/day
Feeding centres		· 15 supplementary feeding · 30 therapeutic feeding · Variations will depend on the activities at the feeding centres
Schools		· 10 - 15 l/cubicle/day for cleaning the latrine · 1 - 2 l/user/day for handwashing
Mosques		· 5
Other communal units		· 5
Offices		· 5

Notes:

1. Demands for communal centres such as health centres and schools do not include 'individual demands' of users. These should be added where appropriate.

2. The values stated here are applicable to low-income, middle-income and high-income situations. If the emergency is resolved, the quantities will begin to diverge to the levels that the communities have been accustomed to prior to the emergency.

3. To assess the water demands of local populations, try first to measure the usage or obtain information from local government or other organizations. If this information is not available then use the longer term figures for individuals and livestock and add on for other large users such as industries or agriculture.

4. The feeding centre values have been determined from a number of sources. A range of values have been noted (from 4 l/day for first 500 people, 3 l/day for second 500 and 1 l/day for other people to up 20 – 30 l/person/day).

Measurement of yield and water levels

Groundwater — wells and boreholes

Step-drawdown test (USAID, 1982b)

1. **Measure the static level** in the well before any pumping has taken place. Use a measuring tape with a weighted end.
   - The tape should be covered in chalk along the lower part of its length.
   - The tape should then be lowered into the well until approximately 1m of the tape is below the water level.
   - A reading should then be taken against a reference point at the top of the well (e.g. the top of the well casing) = (a).
   - Withdraw the tape from the well and take the reading at the start of the wet portion of the tape = (b).
   - Subtract (b) from (a) and this is water level 1 (the 'static water level').

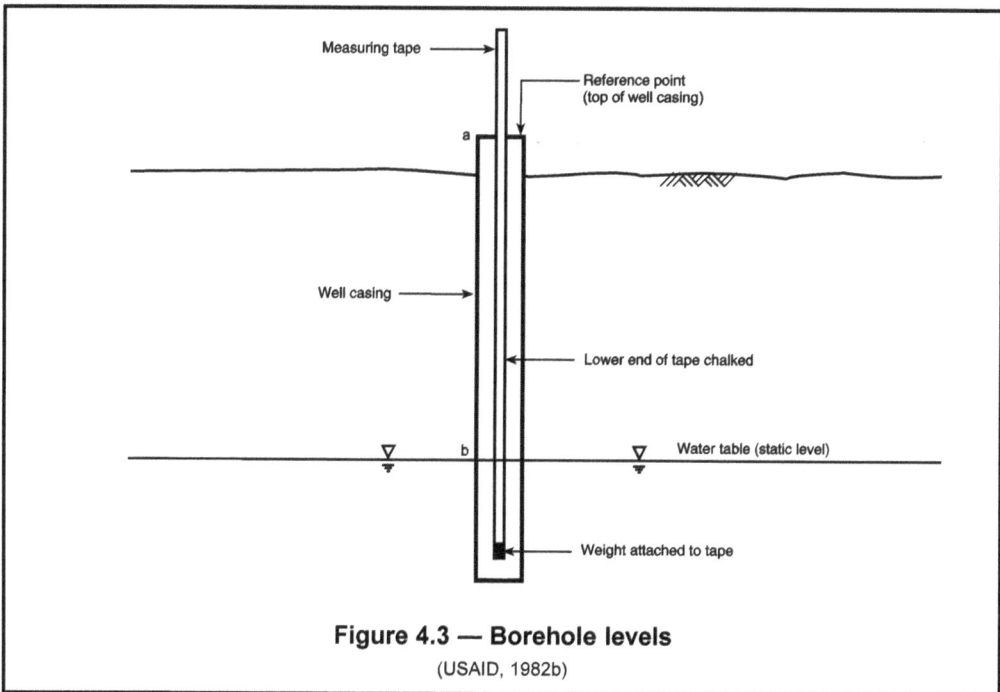

Figure 4.3 — Borehole levels
(USAID, 1982b)

2. **Measure the yield of the well**.
   - Operate the pump for about $1/3$ its capacity for a period of 1 to 4 hours. This will produce about $1/3$ of the full drawdown.
   - Whilst pumping measure the yield by filling a container of known size and measuring the time taken to do this. The container can be filled several times.

   $$\text{yield} \quad = \quad \frac{\text{volume of container}}{\text{time taken to fill the container}}$$

   - This is the yield at $1/3$ of the pump's capacity.

3. **Measure the new water level in the well**.
   - Measure the depth to the water level as described earlier (water level 2).

   Drawdown = water level 1 (static water level) – water level 2

4. **Calculate the specific capacity** at this one-third drawdown point.

   Specific capacity = $\dfrac{\text{yield}}{\text{drawdown}}$

5. **Repeat steps 2 to 4 but using $^2/_3$ the pump's capacity**.

6. **Repeat steps 2 to 4 but using the full pump capacity**. This will produce the maximum drawdown for the well using this particular pump.

7. Stop pumping and measure the recovery time for the water to reach its original static level. The shorter the time the better the aquifer. If it does not return within 24 hours then the aquifer may not be suitable.

8. A step-drawdown curve can be drawn through the three points plotting pumping rate versus drawdown. The maximum pumping rate can be determined from the curve.

The following figure and sections on hand dug wells and the constant rate pumping test has been modified from, and reproduced by kind permission of R. Brassington from *Field Hydrogeology*, pp134–5, published by John Wiley and Sons Ltd.

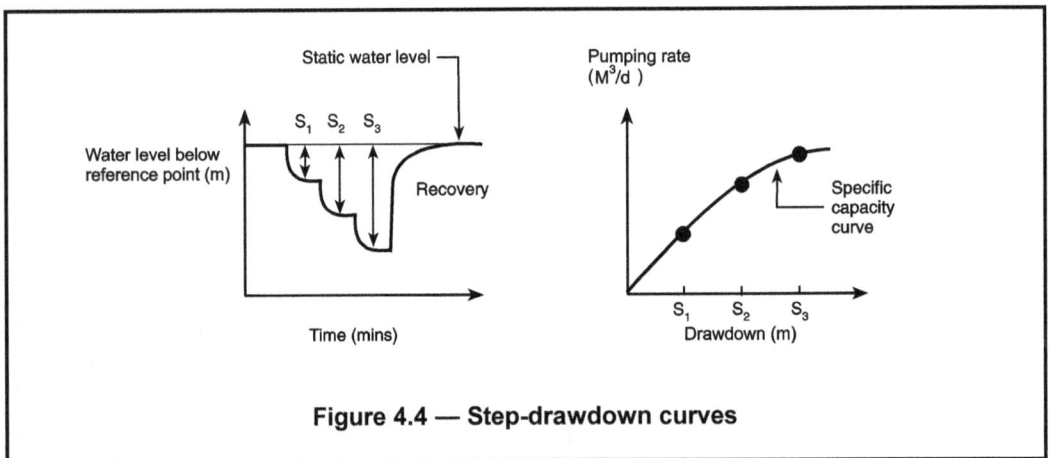

Figure 4.4 — Step-drawdown curves

In hand dug wells, the maximum yield can be assessed by a simpler method:

1. Pump out water from the well until the water level has dropped to just above the pump inlet.

2. Adjust the pumping rate until the level stabilizes. This pumping rate is the maximum yield of the well for the pump. It may vary throughout the year as maximum drawdown levels will be different.

Take care that the pump inlet always remains under water while pumping.

Constant-rate pumping test

To establish if stable pumping levels have been achieved it is useful to pump at a constant rate over several days. It will also help to ensure that the water levels will not drop too low and damage the pump. If it is possible to pump much harder than will actually be required, and the aquifer can cope, then this is a good sign for the long-term reliability of the aquifer. It will also help to assess whether abstraction from the well will affect surrounding sources.

Pumping rates of :
- $< 50 \text{ m}^3/\text{d}$ need about 3–4 days to test
- $50 \text{ m}^3/\text{d}$ need about 5–7 days to test
- $> 5000 \text{ m}^3/\text{day}$ need about 14–21 days or longer

Measurements should start a few weeks before the test start and continue for a similar period once pumping has finished to allow natural fluctuations to be identified.

Groundwater — springs ■

This section, including the figure, has been reproduced by kind permission of S. Cairncross from *Small Water Supplies* by S. Cairncross and R. Feachem, published by the Ross Institute.

Remember when measuring the yield of springs, that the yield can fluctuate during the seasons. 'Some of the springs which flow most powerfully after rain are the first to dry up in the dry weather' (Cairncross and Feachem, 1976 p71).

To measure the yield of the spring:
1. Gather the flowing water together, perhaps with a small earth dam.
2. If the flow is very small, it may be possible to bail a measured volume out of the pool with a bucket, and measure how long the pool takes to fill up again.
3. Otherwise, it should be arranged so that all of the water flows from the dam via a small pipe, or several pipes. The flow can be measured from each pipe and then totalled.
4. The simplest method of measuring flow is to fill up a bucket whose size is known. If it takes less than 5 seconds, a larger bucket should be used.
5. If you do not know the size of the bucket then this can be determined by weighing the full and empty bucket (one litre of water measures 1 kg).

$$\text{Flow (litres/ second)} = \frac{\text{volume of the bucket (litres)}}{\text{time (seconds)}}$$

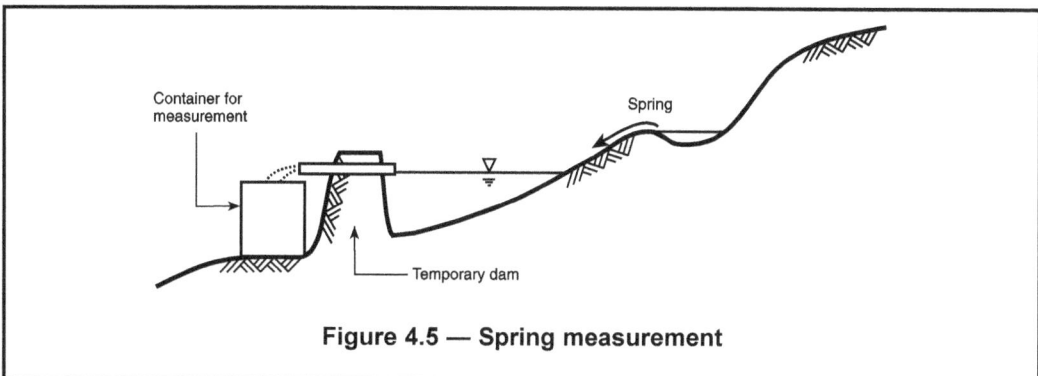

Figure 4.5 — Spring measurement

Surface water — streams and rivers ∎

This section has been modified and reproduced by kind permission of S. Cairncross from *Small Water Supplies* by S. Cairncross and R. Feachem, published by the Ross Institute.

To measure flow in a large stream or river:
1. Find a stretch of the stream which is straight, of fairly constant width, and clear of obstructions for a distance of at least 6 times the average water depth. The stream should be at least 300mm deep if possible.
2. Measure out a length along the bank and throw a floating object into the centre of the stream at the top end of this length. A plastic bottle with sand inside it, or an object such as an orange can be used for this.
3. Time how long it takes to reach the bottom end.
4. Repeat this three times and determine the average time.

$$\text{Approximate flow (litres/ second)} = \frac{850 \times \text{measured length (m)} \times \text{width of stream (m)} \times \text{average depth (m)}}{\text{average time (s)}}$$

For smaller streams an earth dam can be built across the stream and then the flow can be measured as noted above for springs or using a v-notch weir. **Note** that as a quick assessment is required and flows tend to vary throughout the year, measurements do not need to be exact. Hence the simpler assessments, such as using a float, are acceptable over the v-notch method and also have the advantage of being less time consuming.

Surface waters — lakes and ponds ∎

The yield of lakes and ponds can be estimated using the following method:
1. Measure the surface dimensions of the lake.
2. Measure the depth of the lake using a stick or weighted line. Take measurements at regular intervals across the diameter or width of the lake. Repeat this across several different widths.
3. Estimate the volume of water in the lake using the area and volume equations noted in *Catchment mapping: surveying techniques*, pp161–8.

Assuming that there will be no new inflow of water into the lake:

$$\text{Total predicted duration of pumping (hours)} = \frac{\text{Volume of lake (m}^3)}{\text{Flow (litres per second)} \times 3.6}$$

In reality, however:
*   there are likely to be inflows to the lake or pond, either from runoff during the rainy season or from streams or rivers feeding into the lake; and
*   the pond may lose a lot of water during the dry season by evaporation and may even dry up on its own, without the proposed new abstraction.

These factors are difficult to quantify. Information should be collated from local knowledge on the:
*   maximum and minimum water levels both during the seasons and the worst cases in the past; and
*   where the inflows such as streams or rivers are, and whether they dry up, or vary in flow during the seasons.

From this information, and observations on site which aim to identify physical signs of maximum and minimum water levels, an estimation will have to be made on the reliability of the source. If the source is to be utilised, then monitoring systems should be put in place as soon as possible to identify rates of lowering of the water level versus pumping rates. These should be continually scrutinised.

Key references:

- Brassington, 1988
- Cairncross and Feachem, 1978
- USAID, 1982b

Water quality assessment routines

Introduction ∎

Methods which can be used to assess water quality are:

- **Catchment mapping** can indicate potential sources of pollution (e.g. from populations upstream or from industries) and hence potential sources of present or future pollution.

- **Local knowledge, including medical information,** can provide information on the past and present pollution situations and hence potential recurrences in the future.

- **Sanitary survey / observation** investigates the local vicinity of the source and risks of faecal pollution. These risks relate to the present and future scenarios.

- **Water quality analysis** will give single results for that moment in time. They will not tell you for all parameters what happened in the past or what could happen in the future, even later in the same day. Some parameters, such as fluoride, will not fluctuate over short periods of time, but others can, such as turbidity or faecal contamination (indicated by the presence of *E.coli*) can.

- A **biological survey** indicates present and past pollution, although it is not suitable for indicating low levels of faecal pollution. It is especially useful where a quick assessment of potentially industrially polluted waters is required.

It is preferable to use as many of the methods of assessment as possible. If the results from all assessment methods are in agreement (e.g. high level of pollution) then there can be a greater degree of confidence in the prediction. However if they do not agree then thought must be given to why.

For example, if the water quality analysis notes that the *E.coli* level is very low but the sanitary investigation shows a high risk, or the local users report recurring problems with diarrhoea, then it is possible that the source is not presently polluted but that it may have been in the past and may be in the future, or that the water quality analysis results are wrong. Similarly, what if there appears to be no problem with the water quality analysis results but there is a lack of biological life, and hence an indication of high pollution level? Perhaps there is an additional pollutant which has not been tested for. In this case catchment mapping may identify the potential point of pollution and polluter. Therefore by using more than one assessment method, predictions can be cross checked. Care must be taken to consider which pollutants are being indicated when cross-checking methods.

Catchment mapping ∎

Catchment mapping involves the sketching of all features in a catchment area or in a region which includes several catchment areas. Visual assessment can then be made on sources of, and potential routes for pollution. See *Catchment mapping: maps and symbols,* pp154–60 and *Catchment mapping: surveying,* pp161–8 for further information.

Local knowledge including medical information ■

Answers to the following questions may be obtained from local governments, local populations, affected populations and other organizations working in the area. Ask as many different people as possible in the time frame to confirm answers.

Local knowledge including medical information

Question	Possible inference	Further investigation if positive response
Is there substantial animal rearing in the catchment area?	High levels of nitrates, nitrites, and / or faecal contamination	Test for nitrates, nitrites, and / or *E.coli*
Is there intensive agricultural farming in the catchment area?	High levels of nitrates, nitrites, and / or faecal contamination	Test for nitrates, nitrites, and /or *E.coli* and assess for industrial pollution
Are there industries in the catchment area?		Assess for industrial pollution
Are there reports that new users experience diarrhoea but not usual users?	High sulphates	Test for sulphates
Are there reports of tastes in the water?:		
· salty	High chlorides	Test for chlorides
· bitter	High manganese, iron and / or sulphates	Test for manganese, iron and / or sulphates and assess for industrial pollution
· metallic	High manganese, and / or iron	High manganese, and / or iron and assess for industrial pollution
· sweet	High levels of organic matter and possibly faecal contamination	Observe and test for *E.coli*
· flat / insipid	Low in oxygen	
What is the general health level of local users and what are the common diseases?	Common illnesses could indicate water quality, sanitation or hygiene problems	
What does the source look like in the rainy and dry seasons — does the water look muddy or clear?	The turbidity of the source is stable or varies with the season	
Are there any other problems with the water?		

Sanitary investigation / observation ■

(i) Sanitary investigation

The sanitary investigation looks at the environment in the local vicinity (within ½ km) of the source and hence predicts the risk of **faecal** pollution to the source. Use section A if the source does not have existing engineered facilities (spring box, borehole, etc.) and sections A & B if the source does have existing engineered facilities.

- Any yes answers in the high risk section implies that the source is of **high risk**.
- Any yes answers in the medium risk section (but none in the high risk section) implies the source is of **medium risk**.
- Any yes answers in the low risk section (but none in the high or medium risk sections) implies the source is of **low risk**.
- If there are no yes answers in the high, medium or low risk categories then there is only a **very low risk** of pollution (negligible).

All surface water sources will fall into the high risk category. However, the questions should still be answered to identify which of the risk factors are present and which can be improved. If two similar water sources are being compared it is unlikely that there will be a difference in the risk level indicated by the table. Independent judgement will be required to determine if one is slightly higher risk than another and if this should be taken into account during selection. An example of similar sources would be abstraction points up- and downstream of a bathing and animal-watering point in a river.

Repeat the questions allowing for improvements that can reasonably be made to protect the source. The risk indicated will then give the **'improved sanitary risk'**.

Sanitary investigation

Question (Answer the questions which are applicable to the source under consideration)	Yes	No	Not applic-able
A. Use for a source with or without existing engineered facilities			
High risk of faecal or other pollution			
· animals drink near to or from the source			
· water is being collected directly from the source in individual containers			
· human defecation occurs in or near the source			
· the source is used for bathing or laundry			
· the source is used upstream by other communities			
· surface run-off from the camp is likely to enter the source upstream of the abstraction point			
Medium risk of faecal or other pollution			
· industries or agriculture operate near to the source			
· refuse can be found around or in the source			
· there is standing water within 2m of the source (i.e. drainage is inadequate)			
· there are latrines <10m from source or on higher ground than the source and <30m away			
· the source has a wide boundary (such as a lake, river or stream) and hence is difficult to protect			
B Use for source with existing engineered facilities			
Medium risk of faecal or other pollution			
· protection structures are inadequate in design (borehole capping; drainage curtains or channels well lining; spring box)			
· if the source is a borehole it is <100m from uncapped wells or other sources of pollution such as sewers, septic tanks or refuse dumps			
· if the source is a borehole it is less than 800m from a graveyard			
· if the source is a spring the cut-off drain above the spring is inadequate			
When the source is from an existing piped supply:			
· the supply is intermittent			
· there is less than 0.4mg/l of residual chlorine entering the distribution system or 0.2mg/l of free residual chlorine at the collection point			
· the treatment systems are unreliable with possible interruptions			
· there are leaks from the pipework or valves			
· the pipes are closer than 10m to latrines, sewers or drains			
Low (but still possible) risk of faecal or other pollution			
· there is inadequate fencing around the source (if it is not enclosed in a building)			
· there is damage or cracks to the abstraction or protection structures (borehole capping; drainage curtains or channels; well lining; spring box)			
· if the source is a spring then the spring box contains silt or animals			
· if the source is a spring box the overflow pipe or air vents are damaged or blocked			
· the pump sumps are dirty			
· the pumps are not in good working order			
· the lifting or pumping devices are not secure and well fixed			
· storage tanks are uncovered or cracked.			

(Lloyd and Helmer, 1991; MSF Holland, undated; Smith, 1995; Siru, 1992)

(ii) Observations of the water source

The observations in the following table can be made of the water and surrounding area.

Observations of the water source

Question	Possible inferences	Possible actions if a positive response
Is there foaming which is >10cm high?		Assess for industrial pollution
Is there a lot of algae or plant life?	High nitrates or phosphates	Test for nitrates
Is there refuse or faecal matter in the water?	Faecal contamination and /or other contaminants may be present	Test for *E.coli*
Are there white deposits along the banks?	High chlorides	Test for chlorides
Are there oily deposits along the banks?		Assess for industrial pollution

Water quality analysis routine ■

See *Water quality analysis*, pp169–203 for details of individual parameters and tests and *Water quality analysis and surveying equipment*, pp261–82 for details of appropriate equipment.

Water quality analysis routine

Core tests	Question	Possible inference	Further investigation if the answer is positive
Turbidity	Is the turbidity >20 NTU (Survival level) >10 NTU (Minimum recommended level) or >5 NTU (Longer term level)		Undertake treatability test for sedimentation and / or undertake treatability test for assisted sedimentation
Odour	**Is there an odour? Does it smell of:**		
	rotten egg	High sulphates and / or low oxygen	Test for sulphates
	septic	High nitrites, nitrates and / or faecal contamination	Test for nitrates, nitrites, *E.coli*
	earthy / musty	High level of organic matter which could be algae or other	Observe
	disinfectant	High chlorine levels	Test for chlorine
	detergent		Assess for industrial pollution
	petrochemical		Assess for industrial pollution
	acrid/sharp		Assess for industrial pollution
Colour	**Is the settled colour of the water or staining of the rocks or sediments:**		
	orange / red	High level of iron	Test for iron
	black	High level of manganese	Test for manganese
	green	High level of nitrates and nitrites and algae	Test for nitrates and nitrites
	multi-coloured		Assess for industrial pollution
	earthy (yellow / brown)	High level of organic matter	
	other		Assess for industrial pollution
Conductivity	**Is the conductivity >1400 μS/cm?**	High levels of chlorides, sulphates and / or nitrates	Test for chlorides, sulphates and / or nitrates
pH	**What is the pH?**		Measure the pH and undertake treatability tests if there is likely to be a problem with treatment efficiency
E.coli	**Are there >10 *E.coli* (thermotolerant coliform) per 100 ml?**		Take extra care to ensure effective disinfection and monitoring of residuals

(i) Core tests

Undertake all of the tests in the first column of this table. Whether microbiological analysis *(E. coli)*, is needed in the assessment of a water source in an emergency situation is the subject of much debate. One opinion is that the test is essential to understand the degree of pollution, and the other is that the test results do not give useful information as it is always assumed that the water is polluted faecally. The recommendations is that testing for *E.coli* is **beneficial** and should be undertaken wherever possible. However it is not 'essential' if the water is going to be adequately treated. When used alongside other techniques such as the sanitary investigation it can provide complementary information which can highlight oversights and indicate the degree of faecal pollution. If microbiological testing is not undertaken at the initial assessment stage then judgements on pollution levels can be made using other techniques; but **extra care** must be taken to ensure that chlorination processes are effective when implemented. Testing should be undertaken as soon as possible for monitoring purposes.

(ii) Secondary tests

To be tested only if there is an indication from the core tests, visual observation, or local knowledge that there might be a problem with a specific parameter:

chloride; fluoride; iron; manganese; nitrates; nitrites; sulphates; taste; arsenic[1]; permanganate value[2]; chlorine demand (of the raw water)[3].

Notes:
1. Appropriate field equipment may not be available for this item to measure to WHO guideline levels.
2. Permanganate value can be used as an overall measure of pollution.
3. An increase in **chlorine demand** can be a useful indicator of changing pollution levels. However, as a stand-alone indicator it is limited. It is difficult to be sure of the exact strength of the chlorine as it becomes weaker over time.

(iii) Treatability tests

Treatability tests are used to check if the proposed treatment process is suitable for the particular water to be treated. See *Treatability tests*, pp176–83 for further details.

Treatability and treatment monitoring tests

Treatability tests	Treatment monitoring tests
Sedimentation	Chlorine residual
Assisted sedimentation (jar test)	Aluminium
pH adjustment	Temperature
Chlorination (chlorine demand of the pre-treated water)	

(iv) Industrial pollution

Note: The term 'industrial' has been used to represent 'industrial or agrochemical' pollution.

For the water source under consideration, are there:
- a smell of detergents, disinfectants or petrochemicals;
- colours unexplained by iron or manganese tests;
- reports of bitter tastes not explained by tests for manganese, iron or sulphates;
- reports of metallic tastes;

- foaming >10cm high;
- a multi-coloured surface to the water;
- reports of industries in the water source catchment area which are discharging or could possibly discharge to the source; or
- farming schemes in the source catchment area which could be using chemicals, pesticides, insecticides or fertilizers?

Steps to be followed if industrial/ agrochemical pollution is expected:

- Find out from the **industries** themselves or the **local government** the actual compositions of discharges.
- If the first step is not possible then find out what the industries are making from **local knowledge** and look at the **industry pollutants table** for possible pollutants.
- Undertake a **biological survey** if it is a surface water source.
- Undertake the **Permanganate Value** test.

The following scenarios could result:

Industrial pollution assessment scenarios

	Scenario	Action
1	*There is no indication from any of the above steps that industrial pollution may be a problem.*	The water can be used in the initial stages of the emergency with basic treatment without further investigation.
2	*One or two of the steps imply that there could potentially be a problem but not heavy industrial pollution.*	The source water can be used for survival level with basic treatment. Samples should be sent to a laboratory for analysis and the results sent to a capable institution for interpretation as soon as possible.
3	*One of the steps implies that there is a serious problem, or more than two of the steps imply that there could be a problem.*	The source water should not be used unless the water is treated using a mobile unit which incorporates activated carbon and / or reverse osmosis and whose performance is proven. Samples should be sent to a laboratory for analysis and the results sent to a capable institution for interpretation as soon as possible.
4	*Several steps imply that there is a serious problem.*	The source should not be used prior to testing.

If the samples are to be sent to a laboratory for testing then the **laboratory request form** may be used and the results should be **sent to a capable institution for interpretation** (see pp195–7).

Biological surveys

See *Biological survey*, pp204–13 for background information and assessment routines.

Catchment mapping: maps and symbols

Catchment mapping involves the mapping of all of the features in a catchment area or in a region which may include several catchment areas. Features to be highlighted by mapping include:

- Physical features (high and low areas, vegetation, water sources)
- Human features (settlements, industry, agriculture, roads)
- Distances between users and water sources
- Distances and approximate heights between features
- Rock and soil types (if known)

The maps are used for orientation in the area, the location of salient features, and the prediction of potential pollution pathways.

Security is an important issue when mapping. Land can be mined, and mapping activities can be seen as subversive, especially in conflict situations. Advice and permission should be sought before undertaking extensive mapping.

Catchment mapping: regional ■

If existing maps are available then this makes life much easier, especially for regional mapping. In this case potential polluters can be marked onto a copy of the existing map. If such maps are not available then key items can be recorded using tools such as a global positioning system receiver (in UTM Mode), altimeter, compass, or by observation if there is a high point giving a good view over the region.

The map on the next page is a regional map produced by ICRC of the area north of Uvira in eastern Zaire, where a number of camps are located.

The map shows the:

- main access roads;
- boundary between Burundi and Zaire;
- lines of the mountain ranges on both sides of the border;
- key tributaries leading into the Ruzizi plane and then feeding into Lake Tangyanika; and
- local settlements.

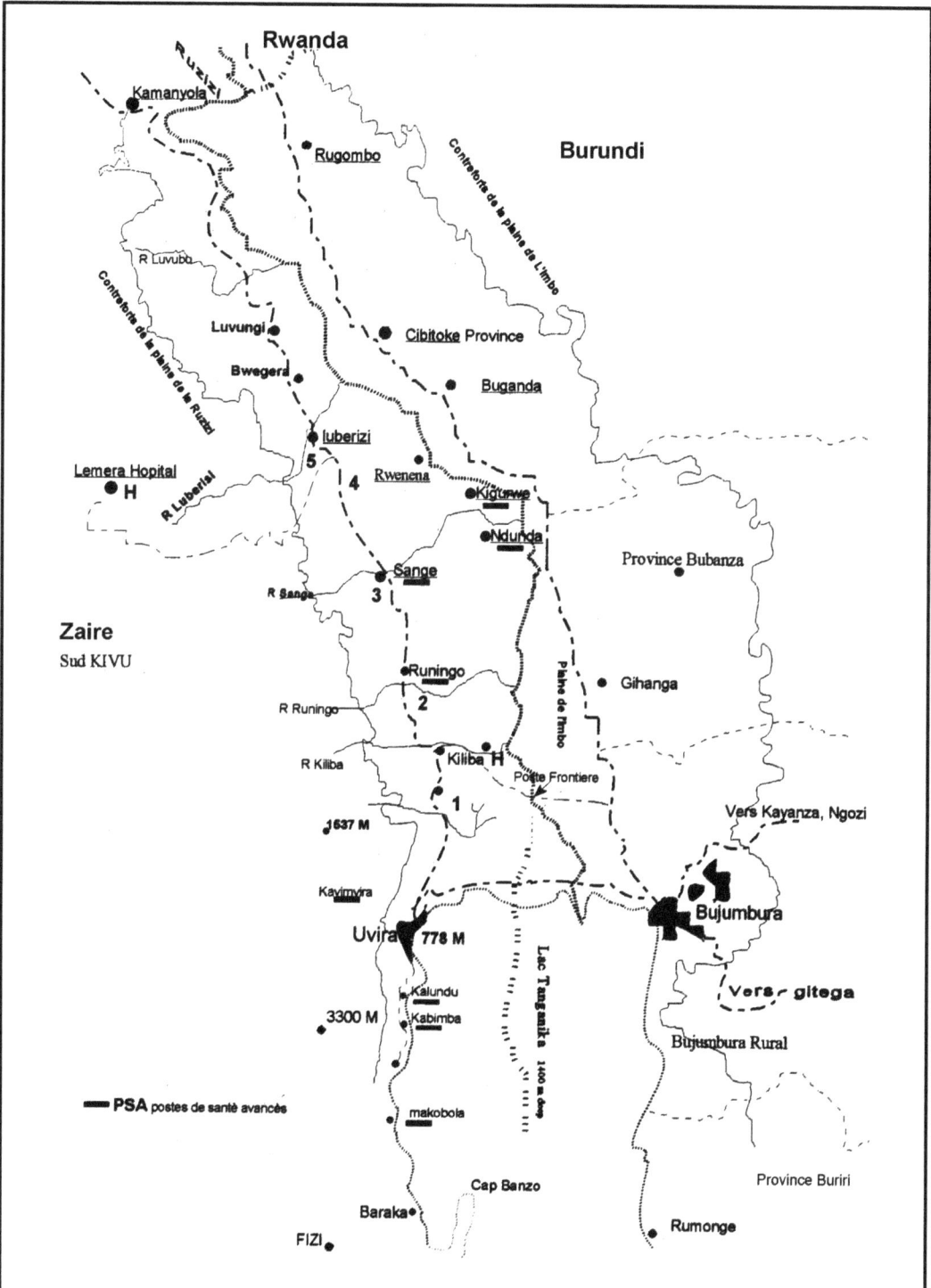

Figure 4.6 — Catchment map: regional

Reproduced by the kind permission of ICRC, from the document *Uvira Water Supply Project*, by J. Foerster

Catchment mapping: local ∎

If detailed maps are available of the local area around the source and camp then these should be used; if not alternative maps should be drawn.

It is difficult to judge heights and distances from the ground. Using a combination of a global positioning system receiver (using UTM Mode), a compass, an altimeter and possibly a clinometer an attempt can be made to sketch an area for the purpose of locating water sources and potential pollution pathways.

Panorama

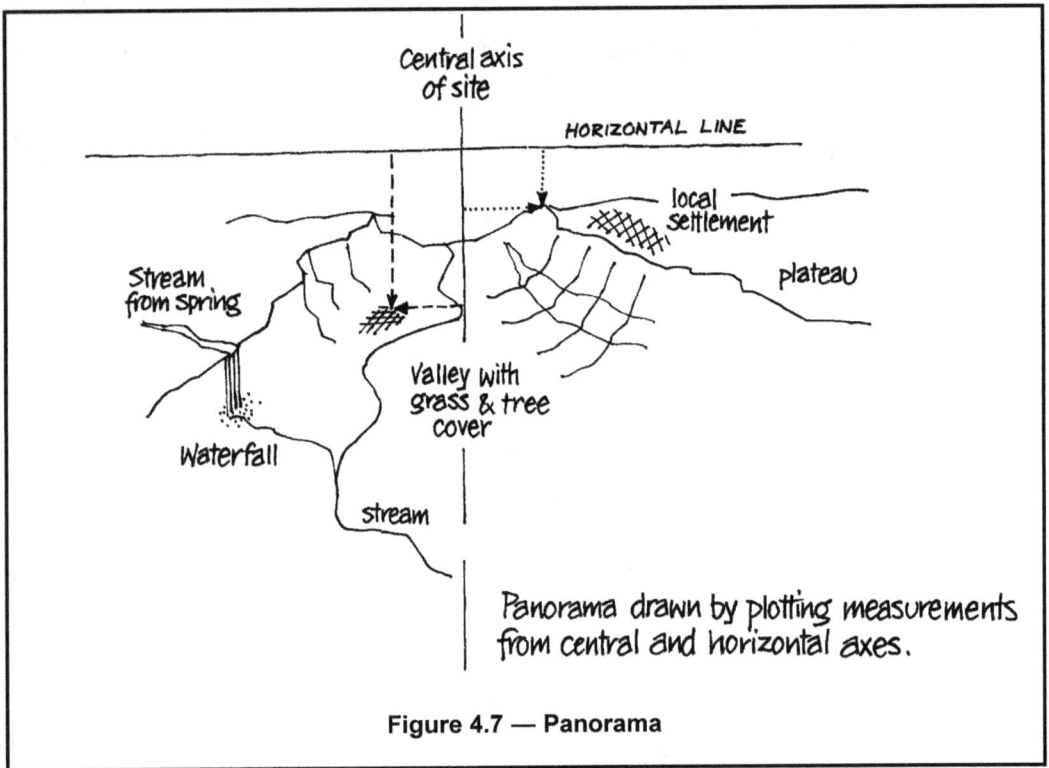

Central axis of site

HORIZONTAL LINE

local settlement

plateau

Stream from spring

Valley with grass & tree cover

Waterfall

stream

Panorama drawn by plotting measurements from central and horizontal axes.

Figure 4.7 — Panorama

Cross sections

These can be used to identify relative heights and longitudinal distances between certain features.

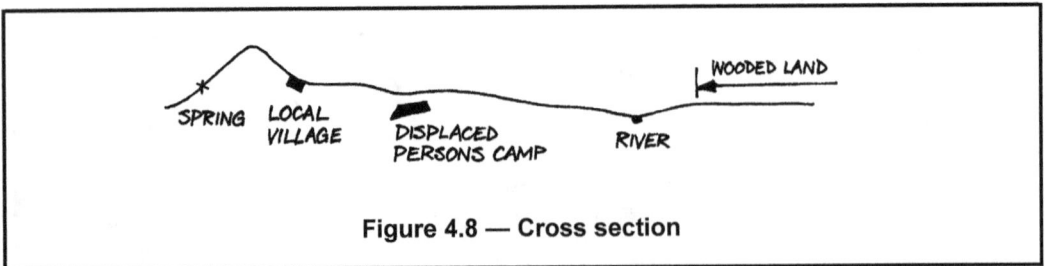

WOODED LAND

SPRING   LOCAL VILLAGE   DISPLACED PERSONS CAMP   RIVER

Figure 4.8 — Cross section

Simplified map

This map locates in plan the major features in relation to the populations, and identifies run-off patterns and water sources.

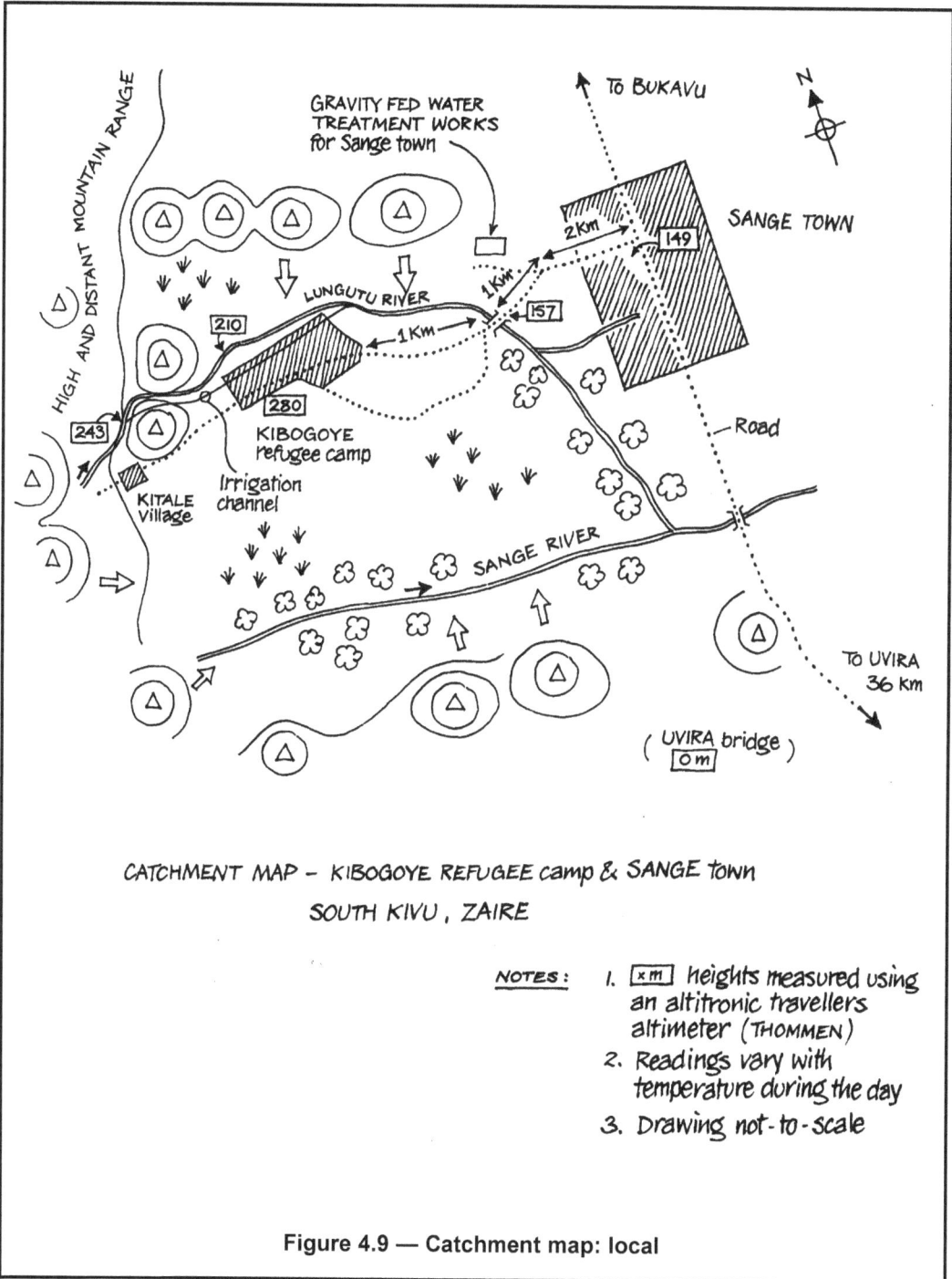

CATCHMENT MAP – KIBOGOYE REFUGEE camp & SANGE town

SOUTH KIVU, ZAIRE

NOTES:
1. ⬚ₓₘ heights measured using an altitronic travellers altimeter (THOMMEN)
2. Readings vary with temperature during the day
3. Drawing not-to-scale

Figure 4.9 — Catchment map: local

Camp mapping

If populations have already arrived at a site and a camp is already formed or forming then a camp map can be useful especially, where the source is near to the site. It can also be useful for locating tapstands and other features such as drainage points. The map may often be in greater detail and scale than they are shown here.

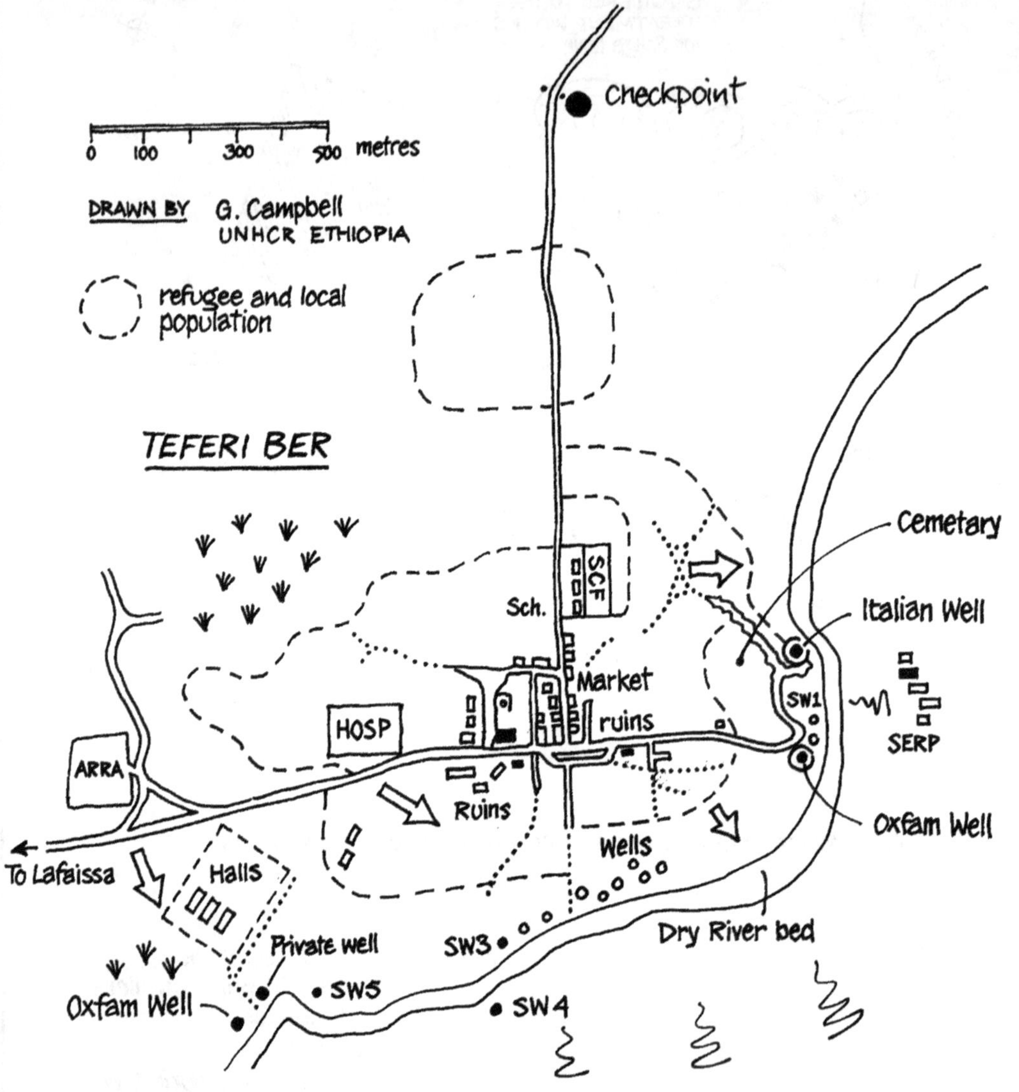

Figure 4.10 — Camp map

Modified and reproduced by kind permission of G.R. Campbell and UNHCR, Ethiopia

Detailed sketch of source ■

Detailed sketches of sources are useful for identifying potential pollution routes, and locating protection and construction requirements. They are also useful for expanding existing systems.

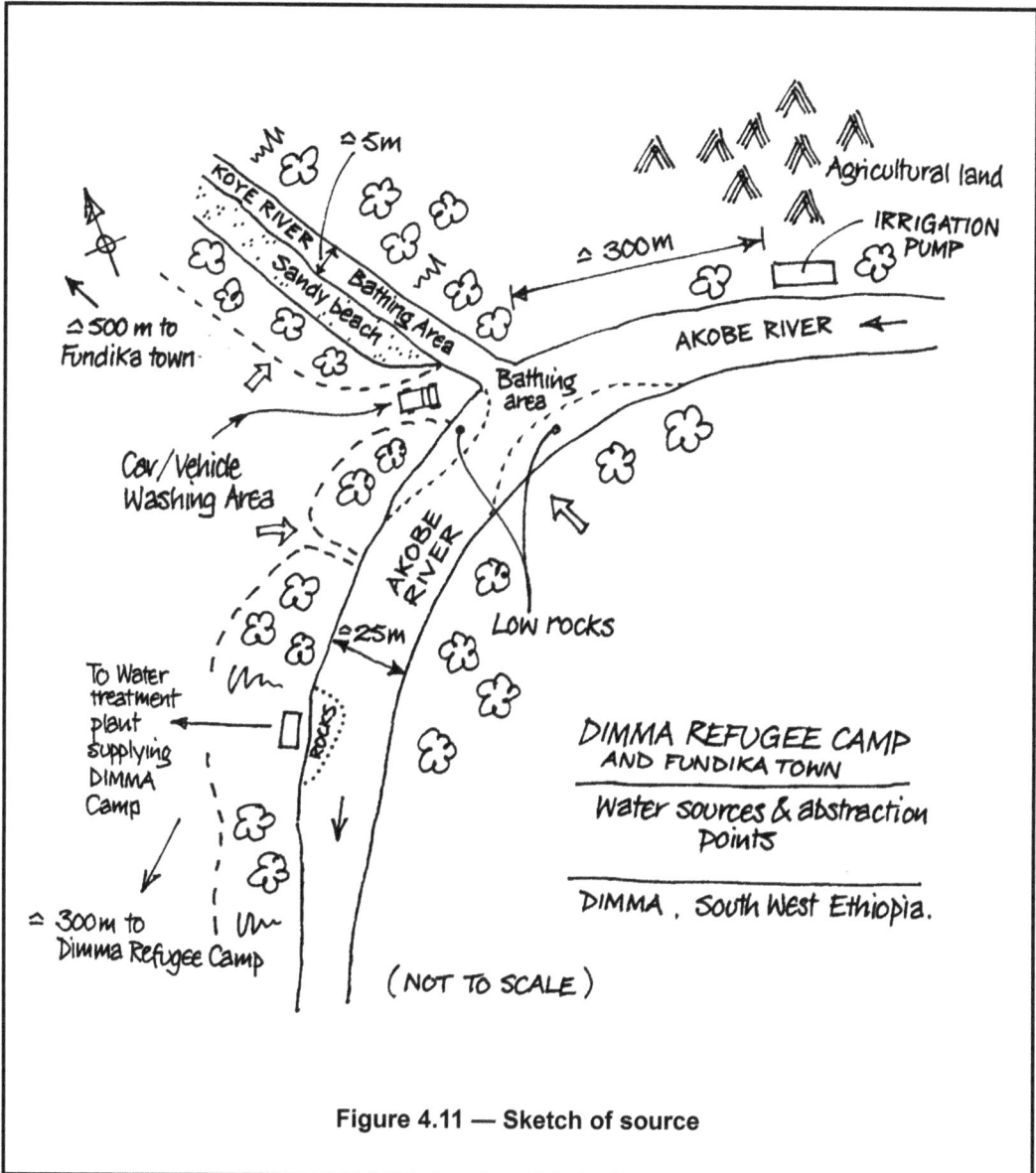

Figure 4.11 — Sketch of source

Key references:

- Ministry of Defence, 1970
- Silley, 1955
- Hodgkiss, 1970
- Sylvester, 1952
- Dickinson, 1969
- Greensmith, 1967
- Hilton, 1964
- Brink et al, 1984

Mapping symbols

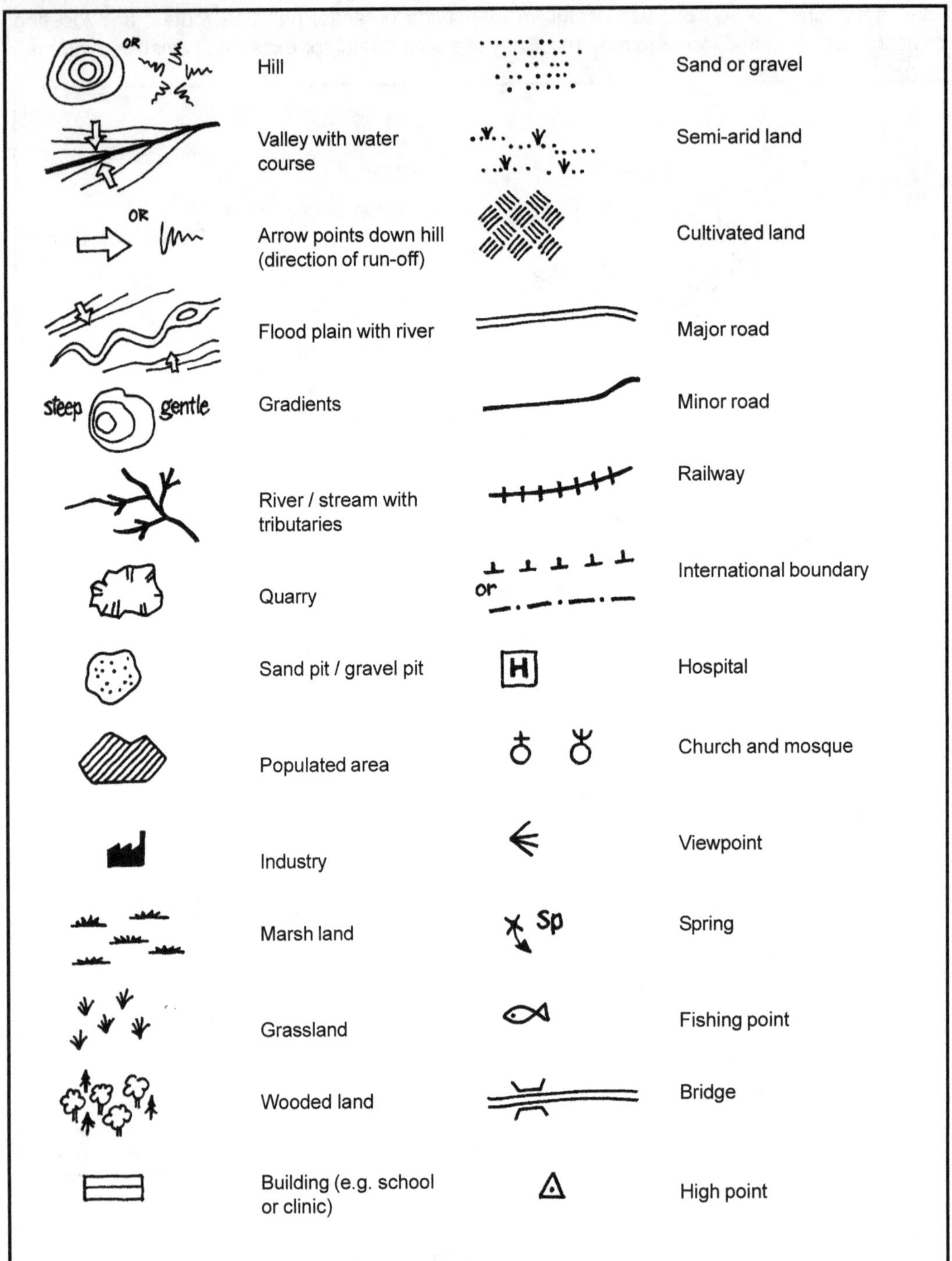

Symbol	Description	Symbol	Description
	Hill		Sand or gravel
	Valley with water course		Semi-arid land
	Arrow points down hill (direction of run-off)		Cultivated land
	Flood plain with river		Major road
steep gentle	Gradients		Minor road
	River / stream with tributaries		Railway
	Quarry	or	International boundary
	Sand pit / gravel pit	H	Hospital
	Populated area		Church and mosque
	Industry		Viewpoint
	Marsh land	Sp	Spring
	Grassland		Fishing point
	Wooded land		Bridge
	Building (e.g. school or clinic)		High point

Figure 4.12 — Mapping symbols

Catchment mapping: surveying

For details of equipment makes and suppliers see *Water quality analysis and surveying equipment*, pp261–2. Security is an important issue when surveying. Land can be mined and surveying activities can be seen as subversive, especially in conflict situations. Advice should be sought before undertaking extensive surveys.

Trigonometry ■

Areas, lengths and angles

Rectangle
• Area = length x width

Circle
• Area = π (radius)^2

Triangles
• sin ø = opposite / hypotenuse; cos ø = adjacent / hypotenuse;
• tan ø = sin ø / cos ø = opposite / adjacent

Right-angled triangles
• $a^2 + b^2 = c^2$
• $\sin^2 ø + \cos^2 ø = 1$

Oblique-angled triangles
• a/sinA = b/sinB = c/sinC (sine rule)
• $c^2 = a^2 + b^2 - 2a.b.\cos C$ (cosine rule)
• s = ½ (a+b+c);
• Area = ½ base x height = $\sqrt{(s(s-a)(s-b)(s-c))}$ = ½ a.b.sinC

Polygons
• In any closed polygon of 'n' sides, the sum of all the internal angles is equal to (2n-4) right angles, or (180n-360°).

Irregular shapes
• Divide the shape up into simpler shapes and add together the areas of each of the smaller sections.

Cross-section of a stream
• Divide the stream width into smaller portions of equal width.
• Measure the depth at the centre of each portion.
• Area of cross section of the stream approximates to = W (D1 + D2 + D3.....)

Volumes

• cube   V = Length x width x height
• right pyramid   V = $^1/_3$ (base area x height)
• right circular cone V = $^1/_3$ (base area x height)
• sphere   V = $^4/_3 \pi$ (radius)^3

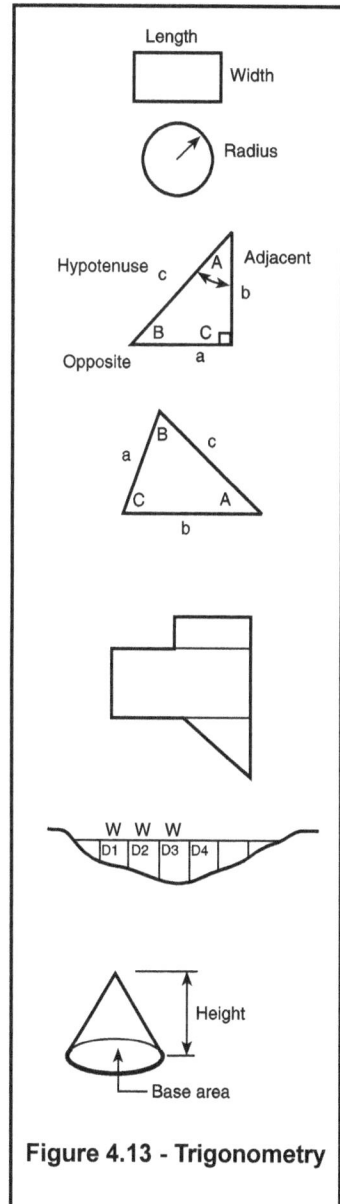

Figure 4.13 - Trigonometry

Pacing and using the vehicle mileage meter ■

Applicability to the assessment of water sources

Pacing is a simple method of measuring distances which can be used when mapping small areas. This method is particularly appropriate to camp mapping and for measuring distances between populations and sources where the distances are short.

Longer distances between populations and water sources can be measured using a vehicle mileage meter. This method is not as suitable as using a global positioning receiver if complicated networks of dirt tracks connect one point to another. The mileage meter does not indicate direction or location relative to a grid.

Compass traverse ■

Applicability to the assessment of water sources

A compass traverse may be useful for camp mapping where there is a need to record boundaries or locate existing facilities. It is difficult to undertake if there are obstructions in the line of site, for example when passing through a wooded area.

The following example has been reproduced by kind permission of P. Stern from *Field Engineering: An Introduction to Development Work and Construction in Rural Areas*, published by Intermediate Technology Publications, by P. Stern (Ed).

* Locate and mark stations (A,B,C etc.) which are to be used in the survey as location points.
* Standing over point A, the magnetic bearing of B is taken with the compass (a foresight).
* Distance AB is then measured and from B, stations A (backsight) and C (foresight) are observed on the compass.
* Distance BC is then measured.
* The process is repeated at C and then D, etc. until all points have been visited. Returning to A, a backsite is taken to the final point in the survey (in this case E).
* Distances measured up a slope need to be changed to horizontal distances by trigonometry, so the angle of slope is required.
* While working around the traverse double checks can be made to intermediate points (i.e. from D to B) if it can be sighted.

Compass traverse record sheet (Stern, 1983)

from station	to station	distance (m)	observed bearings (magnetic) foresight	observed bearings (magnetic) backsite	difference (should be 180 °)	accepted bearings (magnetic) foresight	accepted bearings (magnetic) backsite
A	B	325	33	212	179	32.5	212.5
B	C	615	327	140	187	327	147
C	D	490	45	231	186	51	231
D	E	1080	136.5	315.5	179	136	316
E	A	1070	248	67	181	247.5	67.5

The results should be logged as in the table on p162.
- A check should be made between the foresights and backsights which should differ by 180°.
- Using the formula for the closed polygon, the internal angle at A is the difference between bearing AE and AB.
- Plot the survey on paper using a compass. Squared paper is useful for this task.
- Closing error should be adjusted around the survey points. See Figure 4.14.

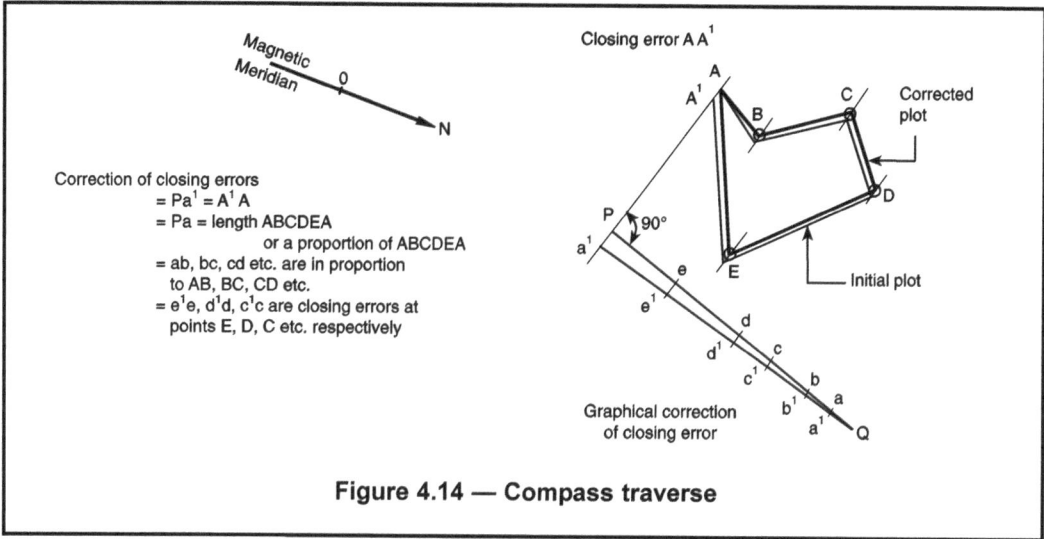

Magnetic Meridian

Closing error A A¹

Correction of closing errors
= Pa¹ = A¹ A
= Pa = length ABCDEA
    or a proportion of ABCDEA
= ab, bc, cd etc. are in proportion
  to AB, BC, CD etc.
= e¹e, d¹d, c¹c are closing errors at
  points E, D, C etc. respectively

Corrected plot

Initial plot

Graphical correction of closing error

Figure 4.14 — Compass traverse

Measuring inaccessible distances ∎

See the diagrams below for examples of using trigonometry to measure inaccessible horizontal distances. To measure inaccessible heights the clinometer can be used, but only when a second height and the distance to the object to be measured is known.

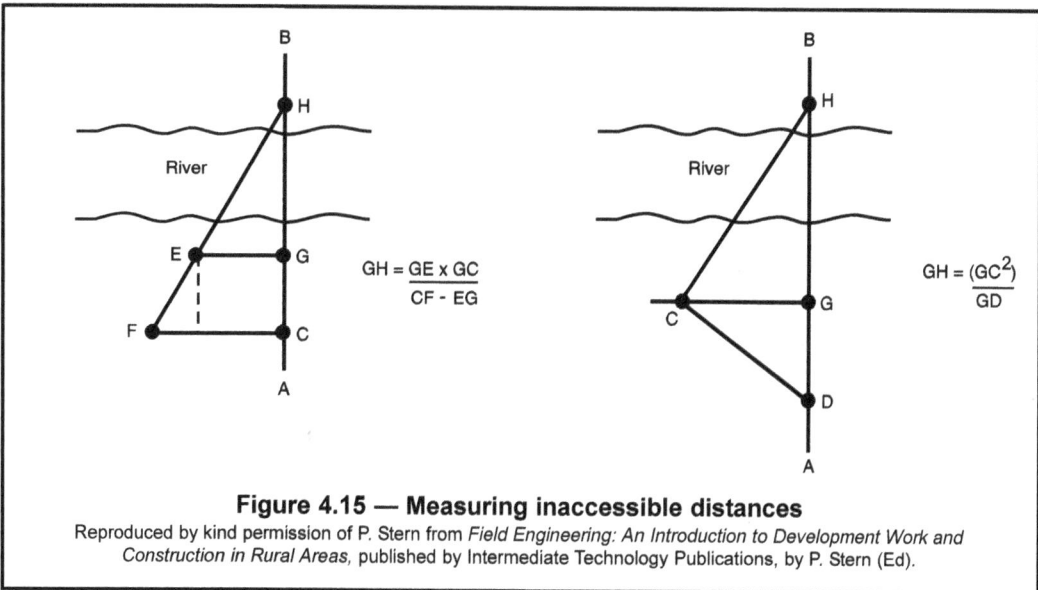

$$GH = \frac{GE \times GC}{CF - EG}$$

$$GH = \frac{(GC^2)}{GD}$$

Figure 4.15 — Measuring inaccessible distances

Reproduced by kind permission of P. Stern from *Field Engineering: An Introduction to Development Work and Construction in Rural Areas,* published by Intermediate Technology Publications, by P. Stern (Ed).

Using an aneroid barometer or an altimeter ■

The altimeter or the aneroid barometer measures height using the variation of atmospheric pressure with height. Temperature must also be noted as this affects the reading. If the reading of the barometer is taken over a whole day in one location the readings will vary considerably (mainly due to temperature). These daily variations follow a characteristic pattern. An observer should make his/ her own daily variation curve (see Figure 4.16). The Thommen Altitronic Traveller has an error limit of +/- 10 m not taking into account the variation due to changes in atmospheric pressure.

Applicability to the assessment of water sources

The altimeter (or aneroid barometer) can be a useful tool for the assessment of water sources, even with variations during the day. If measurements are taken close together in time, and the assessor returns and takes a reading at the starting point at the end of the survey, then errors can be approximated. Taking measurements with an altimeter is easier than using a clinometer or abney level, especially if the survey is over a large area (such as for catchment mapping) or there are obstructions en route such as may be found for camp mapping. A survey undertaken in this manner would not however be suitable for detailed scheme design.

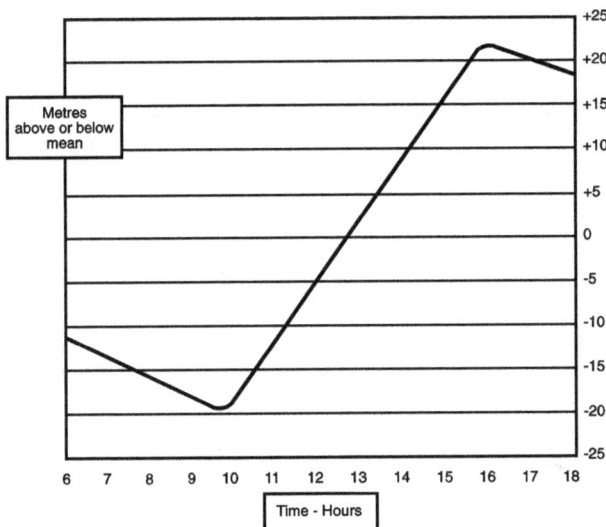

Figure 4.16 — Daily variation in atmospheric pressure

Reproduced by kind permission of P. Stern from *Field Engineering: An Introduction to Development Work and Construction in Rural Areas*, published by Intermediate Technology Publications, by P. Stern (Ed).

Using a clinometer or Abney level ■

A clinometer is the name given to any instrument which measures vertical angles to determine the shape of the land. The clinometer and Abney level are both simple items of equipment which do not need a power source. They are reliable tools but they are not appropriate for determining height differences over long distances, especially if the distance is unknown or there are obstructions blocking the view. To determine a height difference, measurements have to be made covering the whole route between the first point and the next.

Applicability to the assessment of water sources

The clinometer or abney level would be most useful for camp mapping or plotting detailed topography along a pipeline route for detailed design, but less useful for catchment mapping.

The following example and figures have been reproduced by kind permission by Viking Optical Ltd. from the *Manufacturers Instructions for the SUUNTO PM–5 Clinometer.*

- With both eyes open look through the viewpiece with the right eye.
- The instrument is aimed at the object by raising or lowering it until the hairline (see Figure 4.17) is sighted against the point to be measured. At the same time the position of the hairline against the scale gives the reading.
- The left-hand scale gives the slope angle in degrees from the horizontal plane at eye level. The right-hand scale gives the height of the point of site from the same horizontal level expressed in percent of the horizontal distance.
- Horizontal distances should be corrected using: H = h x cos ø ; H = corrected height; h = observed height using sloping ground distance; ø =ground slope angle.

Example:

- Measure the ground distance. This is found to be 82m. Then measure the slope angle = 9°. Read percentages of top and ground points. These are 29 and 23%.
- Calculate: 23/100 + 29/100 = 52/100.
- Take 52% of 82m. This is 42.6m. Multiply this by the cosine of 9°.
- 0.987 x 42.6m = 42m = H.

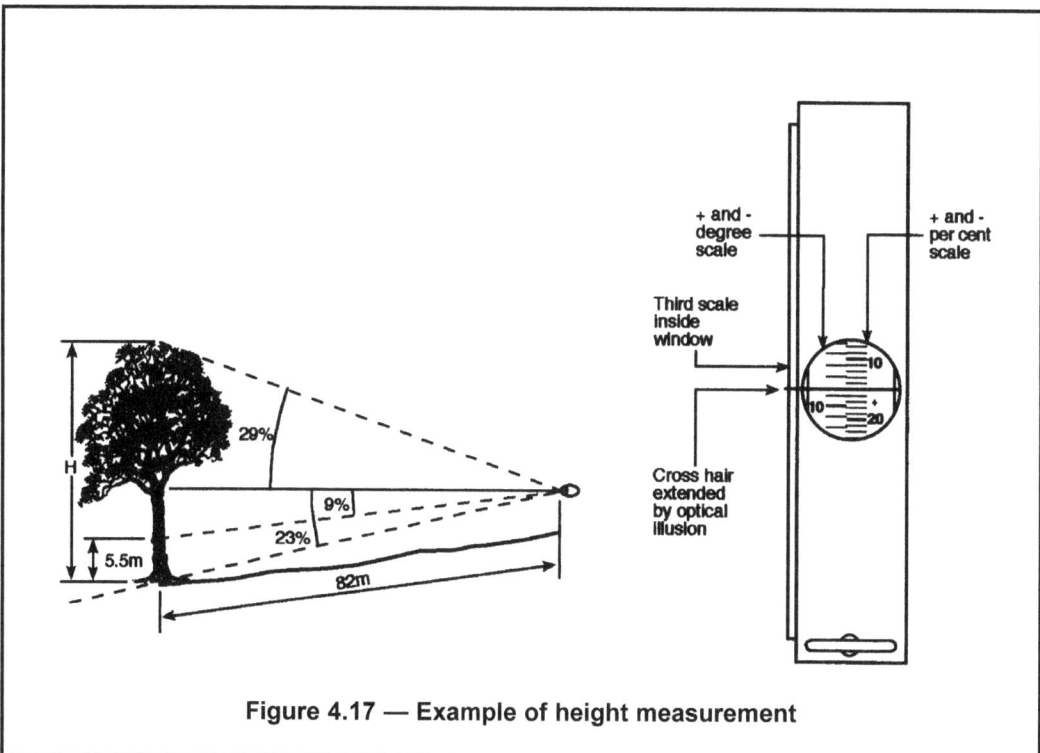

Figure 4.17 — Example of height measurement

The Abney level is another type of clinometer. The following example has been reproduced by kind permission of the publishers, Intermediate Technology Publications from a *Handbook of Gravity-Flow Water Systems* by Thomas D. Jordan, Jnr.

- To use the Abney level the instrument is held to the eye and sighted on a target, centring the cross hair on the target. The index arm is then adjusted until the bubble (visible in the right half of the field-of-view) is centred against the target and the cross hair (See Figure 4.18).

- The angle of view (vertical angle) is then read on the arc in degrees.

- Vertical distance = ground distance x sin ø (See Figure 4.18).

- The abney level should be checked before use and adjusted if necessary. Using the two post method (see Figure 4.18), a surveyor marks station A at the height of the abney level and the surveyor sights station B with the Abney level set at 0°. An assistant marks station B at this point. The surveyor and the assistant then swap places. The surveyor places the abney level at the mark at station B and sights station A with the Abney level set at 0°. If the original mark and the new mark at station A coincide then the Abney level is truly level and does not require adjustment. If they do not coincide, the assistant marks half way in-between the two A marks. The surveyor sights from the mark at B to the central mark on A. The surveyor should then adjust the bubble until it comes into alignment with the cross hair and target mark.

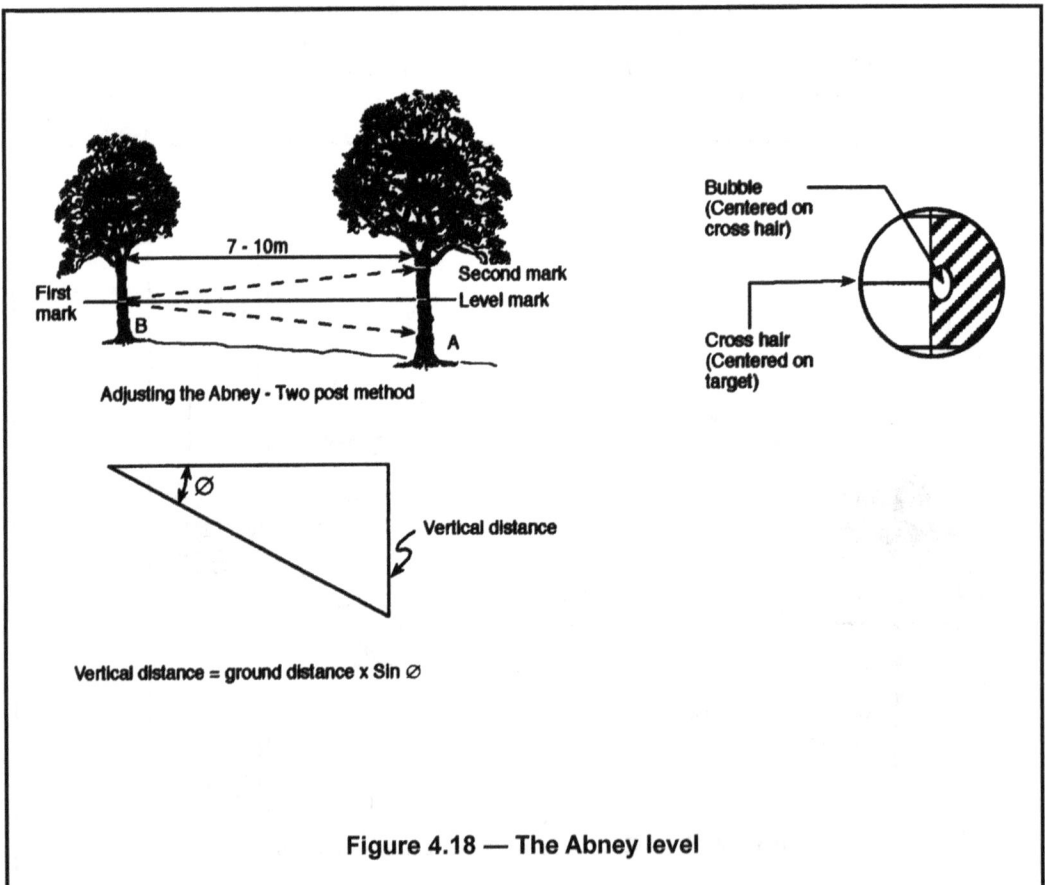

Figure 4.18 — The Abney level

Using the Global Positioning System (GPS) ∎

The following information has been modified and reproduced from Davies and Barclay 1996.

The Global Positioning System was designed to meet a US military need for precise positioning in hostile environments. The system is operated by the United States Government. It consists of twenty-four satellites orbiting the globe continually transmitting microwave signals. Using the GPS signals transmitted by at least four satellites simultaneously, a receiver can calculate precisely the time and a three-dimensional position and velocity. Since 1991 the GPS has been made available to the civilian community with no direct user-charges.

GPS receivers have largely replaced radio navigation services for the aviation and maritime industries and are increasingly being used for land-based transportation. A controversial aspect of the military control of the system has been the decision to limit the accuracy of the signals freely available. Selective Availability (SA) was introduced immediately prior to the Gulf War, and allows the US Military access to the Precise Positioning Service (PPS), whilst restricting other users to the Standard Positioning Service (SPS). Ninety-five percent of the time, SPS is accurate to 100 metres horizontally, 157 metres vertically, and 167 nanoseconds. The PPS, on the other hand, is capable of 17.8 metre horizontal accuracy, 22.7 metre vertical accuracy, and 100 nanoseconds. It is possible that in the near future the SA system will be switched off.

The requirement of many users for greater accuracy than provided by the SPS can be met by various augmentations to the GPS signals. Differential GPS signals can be broadcast which improve the accuracy of the GPS signals by correcting the errors at the receiver location with measured errors at a known location. If the errors at the two sites are correlated, positional accuracy as good as one metre can be achieved, even using SPS. Averaging over several hours will also remove the bias introduced by SA.

Applicability to the assessment of water sources

A single GPS hand-held receiver as it presently stands has significant uses but also limitations. Because of SA, the accuracy of the single hand-held receiver is limited to +/- 100m accuracy. This limitation restricts the GPS' usefulness for mapping over small distances, i.e. camp mapping for small or concentrated camps, but it does not restrict its usefulness for catchment mapping or for location identification. The GPS system can be a useful tool for locating water sources and other features such as high points, industries and communities within a catchment area, especially where standard maps are lacking or not available. Even ignoring the other features of the GPS system (altitude, time, recording data, compass readings), the single feature of horizontal location identification can be very useful in assessing water sources for emergencies and otherwise. Altitude readings can be obtained with greater accuracy using an altimeter.

Using two receivers to identify errors or spending long periods of time at one position to improve the accuracy of the SPS signals is not really necessary or feasible for the assessment of emergency water sources. The GPS system, although it has it's limitations at present will surely be the surveying tool of the future and assessors should keep abreast of the developments within this area.

Using a GPS receiver

- Specific instructions to use a receiver should be taken from the operating instructions provided by the supplier.

- The user should only focus on obtaining horizontal distances or grid references. The GPS handheld receivers often have several different grid references stored in their memory. The UTM mode gives readings in metres on a horizontal grid system and is recommended when mapping an area. Other modes give readings in northings and eastings and can be used to locate the users position in the world.

- UTM readings can be plotted against a grid to produce a rough map of an area.

Key references:

- SUUNTO, undated
- Jordon, 1984
- Stern, 1983

Water quality analysis

Introduction to physical, chemical and microbiological analyses ◼

There are three types of water quality features:

Water quality features

Feature types	Examples
Physical	colour, pH, taste, odour, temperature, turbidity
Chemical	arsenic, chloride, conductivity, dissolved oxygen, fluoride, iron, manganese, nitrate, nitrite, sulphate, pesticides, heavy metals
Microbiological and biological	bacteria, protozoa, viruses, helminths, higher organisms

Water quality features can affect health in the following ways:
- Some can be **directly harmful to health,** such as microbiological and biological contaminants, fluoride, pesticides and heavy metals.
- Colour, taste, turbidity and odour can make the **water objectionable to consumers** and cause them to use another less objectionable, but not necessarily safer source.
- Others features, such as pH and turbidity can **reduce the effectiveness of treatment processes** such as disinfection.

The water quality analysis tests for assessing water sources in emergencies have been split into several sections as follows:
- core tests;
- secondary tests;
- treatability tests; and
- industrial pollution assessment.

The **core tests** have been chosen as they provide:
- key information to determine treatment requirements (turbidity, pH, (*E.coli*)); and
- simple tests to indicate acceptability which can also highlight other potential pollution problems, and hence the need for further tests (odour, colour and conductivity).

The **secondary tests** mainly determine chemical quality and the features are less common than those measured in the core tests. They:
- can indicate acceptability of the water (chloride; iron; manganese; sulphates; taste);
- are linked to health (fluoride, nitrates, nitrites, arsenic);
- can provide another indicator of faecal or urinary pollution (nitrates, nitrites, chloride); and
- can provide an overall indicator of pollution (chlorine demand; permanganate value).

Treatability tests are an aid to the selection of a suitable water treatment process.

The **industrial pollution (including agrochemical pollutants) assessment** has been formulated to take into account that the pollutants are numerous and that they are much more difficult to analyse in the field than those in the core or secondary tests. Industrial pollution can be a serious risk to health as the pollutants may be toxic, carcinogenic or have other serious health effects, especially when consumed over a long period.

The need or otherwise for microbiological analysis (*E.coli*) in the assessment of a water source in an emergency situation is the subject of much debate. One opinion is that the test is essential to help the assessor understand the degree of pollution, and the other that the test results do not give any useful information as it is always assumed that the water is polluted faecally. The recommendation is that testing for *E.coli* is **beneficial** and should be undertaken wherever possible, but it is not 'essential' if the water is going to be adequately treated. When used alongside other techniques such as the sanitary survey it can provide complementary information which can highlight oversights and indicate the degree of faecal pollution. If microbiological testing is not undertaken at the early assessment stage then judgements on pollution levels can be made using other techniques on their own, but **extra care** must be taken to ensure that chlorination processes are effective when implemented.

Water quality parameter summary tables ∎

The World Health Organization (WHO) produce guidelines for acceptable parameter levels. Many countries also have their own national guidelines or standards. Some of the guideline values given by WHO are based on health criteria and some on aesthetic concerns (which could lead to the user using an alternative, but potentially less safe source). Most of the health criteria, especially for the chemical contaminants, are based on long-term use. In an emergency situation the immediate concern is to keep people alive, often by preventing deaths through dehydration. When considering chemical contaminants the immediate concern is short-term toxicity and the United States Environmental Protection Agency provides a range of figures for short-term consumption. See p184 for further details. The following tables note a range of guideline levels for core and secondary parameters relating to the various stages in an emergency and supply level:

* survival; and
* longer term: several months (minimum recommended) and several years (WHO guideline).

In some cases the value is the same for all stages (e.g. nitrates) but in others it becomes progressively more stringent (e.g. turbidity). It is generally accepted by international relief organisations that in the initial stages of an emergency a turbidity of 5NTU or 1NTU (for disinfection) is often not obtainable. To reject water on this basis, potentially limiting quantity and risking subsequent dehydration, could be more dangerous than supplying the water. On this basis turbidity guidelines which are slightly more lenient than WHO guidelines have been given for the earlier stages of an emergency.

The figures for survival level or longer term (minimum recommended) level have been modified from the WHO guideline levels **only** when the WHO criteria have been based on aesthetic concerns. The values selected have been taken from past WHO recommendations (e.g. iron or manganese) or generally accepted figures in the emergency field (e.g. *E.coli*, turbidity). WHO states in its guidelines that 'it is recongnized that, in the great majority of rural water supplies in developing countries, faecal contamination is widespread. Under these conditions, the national surveillance agency should set medium-term targets for the progressive improvement of water supplies, as recommended in Volume 3 of *Guidelines for drinking-water quality'*. Many of the figures could probably be less stringent but without further documentation they remain as noted.

Core tests

Test	Why the feature is of concern	Origins of the feature	When is testing required?	Suggested guideline levels (maximum) — Survival	Longer term: minimum recommended	Longer term: WHO guidelines, 1993 (criteria on which value is based are noted in brackets)	Ideal equipment range and accuracy
Turbidity	acceptability to the consumer and determines treatment requirements (reduces effectiveness of disinfection)	suspended matter e.g. clays, silts, organic matter, microscopic organisms	core test (when water is not totally clear)	20 NTU	10 NTU	5 NTU 1 NTU for disinfection (aesthetic and treatment)	1, 5, 10, 20, 50, 100, 200 NTU
Odour	acceptability to the consumer and can indicate the presence of other pollutants	hydrogen sulphide from septic conditions, organic matter, algae, fungi, industrial wastes	core test	no restriction	acceptable to the consumers	should be acceptable to consumers (aesthetic)	-
Colour	acceptability to the consumer and can indicate the presence of other pollutants	organic matter, metals, industrial wastes	core test	no restriction	acceptable to the consumers	15 TCU (aesthetic)	-
Conductivity	acceptability to the consumer (taste), corrosion and encrustation	dissolved solids	core test	no restriction	1400μS/cm	1400μS/cm (from 1000mg/l TDS (aesthetic))	500 - 1700 +/- 100μS/cm
pH	effects treatment requirements, corrosion and acceptability to the consumer (taste)	coloured peaty substances, acids or alkalis, acid rain	core test	no restriction	6 to 8 for coagulation with aluminium sulphate < 8 for disinfection	preferably < 8.0 for effective disinfection with chlorine (treatment)	4-10 +/- 0.5
E.coli	indication of the possible presence of pathogens	faecal contamination	(core test)	Always aim to disinfect supplies If this is not possible then: < 1000 thermotolerant coliform (E.coli) / 100ml	Always aim to disinfect supplies If this is not possible then: < 10 thermotolerant coliform (E.coli) / 100ml	0 thermotolerant coliform / 100ml (health)	<10, 10, 100, 1000, >1000

Secondary tests

Test	Why the feature is of concern	Origins of the feature	When is testing required?	Suggested guideline levels (maximum) — Survival	Suggested guideline levels (maximum) — Longer term: minimum recommended	Suggested guideline levels (maximum) — Longer term: WHO guidelines, 1993 (criteria on which value is based are noted in brackets)	Ideal equipment range and accuracy
Chloride	acceptability to the consumer (taste) corrosion; high levels can indicate contamination by urine	salt deposits, industrial pollution, sewage discharges, landfill leachate, sea water intrusion	complaints of salty taste or high conductivity	600mg/l	250mg/l	250mg/l (aesthetic)	100 - 800 +/- 50mg/l
Fluoride	health (fluorosis)	runoff from volcanic or igneous rock	local population have mottled teeth or skeletal fluorosis	3mg/l	1.5mg/l	1.5mg/l (health)	0.5 - 3.0 +/- 0.5mg/l
Iron	deposits, acceptability to the consumer (taste and colour)	rocks and minerals, acid mine drainage, landfill leachates, sewage, industrial effluents	reports of metallic or bitter tastes, red/orange staining or deposits, test if using iron as a coagulant for assisted sedimentation	no restriction	1.0mg/l (health long term)	0.3mg/l (aesthetic)	0.1 - 1.5 +/- 0.2mg/l
Manganese	deposits, acceptability to the consumer (taste and colour)	rocks and minerals, anaerobic groundwaters	metallic or bitter tastes, black staining or deposits	no restriction	0.5mg/l (health long term)	0.5mg/l (health) 0.1mg/l (aesthetic)	0.1 - 0.8 +/- 0.1mg/l
Nitrates	health (blue baby syndrome), can also indicate faecal contamination	breakdown of vegetation, fertilizers, sewage	agriculture is practised in the catchment area, reports of blue baby syndrome, high levels of algae; can be use for monitoring purposes	$50mg/l$ as NO_3^- (dangerous for babies under 6 months above this level)	$50mg/l$ as NO_3	50 as NO_3^- or 11 as N (health)	30 - 100 +/- 20mg/l as NO_3^-
Nitrites	as nitrates	as nitrates (plus indicates recent pollution)	as nitrates	$3mg/l$ as NO_2^-	$3mg/l$ as NO_2^-	$3mg/l$ as NO_2^- 0.91 as N (health)	1 to 5 +/- 1mg/l as NO_2^-
Sulphates	health (diarrhoea), acceptability to the consumer (taste), corrosion	rocks such as gypsum, acid mine water, industrial wastes	new users of the source usually experience diarrhoea, bitter tastes	400mg/l (can cause diarrhoea which in turn could lead to epidemics)	400mg/l	400mg/l (aesthetic)	100 - 600 +/- 100mg/l
Taste	acceptability to the consumer, can indicate other pollutants	organic matter, industrial pollution, rocks, anaerobic conditions, salt deposits, sea water intrusion	complaints from locals	must be drinkable	acceptable to the consumer	should be acceptable to the consumer (aesthetic)	-
Arsenic	suspected carcinogen on accumulation	refuse tips, weed killers, insecticides, industrial pollution. Some naturally occurring (usually < 0.1 mg/l but can be up to 12mg/l)	indication that industry may be discharging the parameter, or where the parameter is known as a problem regionally (especially for groundwater)	WHO guideline value is recommended for long-term consumption. However, as suitable alternative figures are not available for short-term consumption this figure should still be used as the guideline.	0.01mg/l (health)	0.01mg/l (health)	0.005 - 3mg/l (note: difficult to find suitable equipment)
Permanganate value	indicates organic pollution which could be faecal in origin, could affect the treatment processes, or could come from industrial pollution	Can be used when organic pollution is expected (either natural or industrial) Rough conversions can be made from PV to 'probable BOD'. These conversions have been formulated for sewage effluent: 'Probable BOD' = PV x 1.5 — BOD: < 2mg/l = low pollution level; 4mg/l = polluted, but rivers can usually accept this level without detriment to flora and fauna. Effluents from a sewage treatment works must have a BOD < 20mg/l entering a watercourse with an 8:1 dilution with freshwater. (Twort, 1994, p185)					Standard equipment measurers 0-10; 10-20; 20-30; and > 30 PV
Chlorine demand (of the raw water)	high demand an indication of pollution (organic matter, oxidizable compounds, micro-organisms)	Can be used as another test for overall pollution level 0 - 2mg/l = quite clean water (Cairncross and Feachem, 1988, p92); 1mg/l of chlorine is required to satisfy approximately 2 mg/l BOD_5 — Note: It is difficult to be sure of the original concentration of the chlorine used as it loses strength with time. However chlorine demand can be a useful tool to monitor changes in raw water quality over time.	Surface waters can have a chlorine demand up to 6 - 8mg/l (Twort, 1994, p332)				See treatability tests table, p173

Treatability tests

Treatment monitoring tests

Test	Why the feature is of concern	Origins of the feature	When is testing required?	Suggested guideline levels (max.)			Ideal equipment range and accuracy
				Survival	Longer term		
					minimum recommended	WHO guidelines, 1993 (criteria on which value is based are noted in brackets)	
Chlorine (residual)	acceptability to the consumer (when high) and treatment requirements	water treatment with chlorine or industrial effluents	always test when disinfecting	0.2mg/l minimum on disinfection 3.0 - 5.0mg/l max. (WHO, 1996)	0.2 - 1.0mg/l	0.2mg/l (aesthetic)	0-2.0 +/- 0.2mg/l & (2.0 to 8.0mg/l advantageous)
Aluminium	acceptability to the consumer, deposits and possible health effects on accumulation	water treatment with aluminium salts, industrial pollution, erosion, leaching of minerals and soils	test if treatment process involves assisted sedimentation with aluminium sulphate	If >0.3mg/l is present after treatment then there is a fault in the coagulation or sedimentation stages. Higher values are not dangerous to humans in the short term	0.2mg/l	0.2mg/l (aesthetic)	0 - 0.5 +/- 0.1mg/l
Temperature	acceptability to the consumer (taste) and treatment requirements	heating from sun or thermal pollution from industrial processes	physical assessment by touch, test if abnormally high				-10 to 110°C
Alkalinity	may be needed to improve treatment efficiency or to modify pH to prevent corrosion or for acceptability to the consumer	rock formations such as limestone	if there is a requirement to modify the pH or to improve the process efficiency of the assisted sedimentation process				5 - 100mg/l as $CaCO_3$ +/- 5mg/l

Treatability tests

Test	Why undertake the test?	What does the test tell you?	When is testing required?
Sedimentation	to reduce the turbidity to improve the acceptability of the water and the efficiency of the disinfection process	whether sedimentation is an appropriate method to remove turbidity	when there is a turbidity >20 NTU (survival level); >10 or >5 NTU (minimum recommended and WHO values respectively for longer term level)
Assisted sedimentation (jar test)	to reduce the turbidity to improve the acceptability of the water and the efficiency of the disinfection process	a rough guide to the quantity of coagulant which will be required and the most appropriate dosage	when there is a high turbidity and the sedimentation test results are not acceptable (>1 hour to sediment to acceptable turbidity)
pH adjustment	to modify the pH of the water for more effective chlorination, assisted sedimentation or to reduce corrosion	a rough guide to the quantity of chemical required to adjust the pH and the most appropriate dosage	if pH is high or low and chlorination or assisted sedimentation treatment process would be adversely affected
Chlorination (chlorine demand of the treated water)	to determine the chlorine volumes required for disinfection	a rough guide to the volume of chlorine which will be required for disinfection, the most appropriate dosage, and an indication of the chlorine demand (pollution level) of the water	always when disinfecting

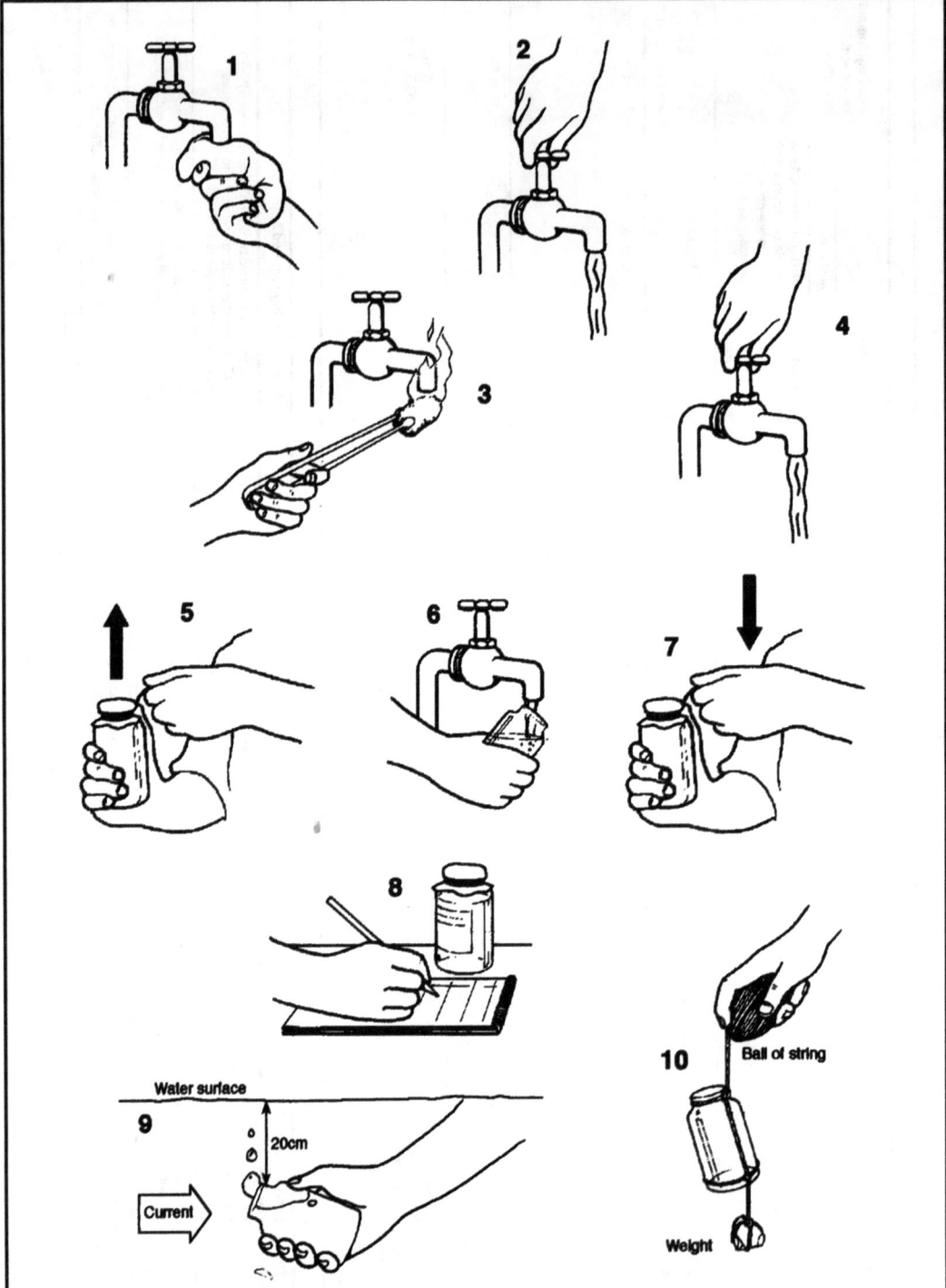

Figure 4.19 — Water sampling (WHO, 1985 and MSF, 1994)

Modified and reproduced by kind permission of Médecins sans Frontières from
Public Health Engineering in Emergency Situations

Water sampling ■

The following section has been slightly modified and reproduced by kind permission of Médecins sans Frontières from *Public Health Engineering in Emergency Situations*.

Method

Important : the sampling technique differs according to whether it is for bacteriological or chemical analysis.

Chemical analysis

- Collect at least 2 x 1l of water in plastic bottles (e.g. mineral water bottles), which must be clean and airtight.
- Rinse the bottles three times with the water to be analysed, fill them right to the top and label them.

Bacteriological analysis

- Collect at least 100ml in a sterile bottle.
- To sterilize the bottles, place the cap loosely on each one so that the steam can circulate inside.
- Wrap each bottle in tissue paper, newspaper or wrapping paper.
- Sterilize in an autoclave for **15 minutes at 121°C** (a small autoclave like the 'Prestoclav' is quite suitable).
- If there is no autoclave, the bottles may be sterilized by boiling: place each bottle and cap in the water and let it **boil for 20 minutes.**
- After 20 minutes of boiling, take out of the water, and let it cool, protecting the opening with the cap and flamed aluminium foil or a sterilized compress.
- Use as soon as possible.
- For the bacteriological analysis of water that has been chlorinated, add 0.15ml of 1% sodium thiosulphate solution per 100ml of sample to each bottle before sterilizing, in order to neutralize the chlorine which would otherwise affect the results.

Key to Figure 4.19

(1-8: water sampling from a tap for bacteriological analysis)

1. Clean the tap (alchohol or soap)
2. Let the tap run fully for about 30 seconds
3. Flame it with a pad soaked in alcohol
4. Let it run fully again for 30 seconds
5. Take off the cap and its protection from the bottle
6. Take the sample
7. Replace the cap and its protection
8. Label the sample and record it in a notebook
9. Sampling from a water course
10. Sampling from a well

Materials

Chemical

- Glass or plastic bottles, 1 litre: 2 per sample
- Marker pen for labelling
- Thermometer

Bacteriological

- 2 sterile 100ml bottles
- String and weighing stone (for sampling from a well or other inaccessible place).
- Cotton wool and forceps (e.g. hair tweezers)
- Thermometer
- Cool box

Important

- The 8 steps described above for sampling from a tap are not necessary for chemical analysis, but are absolutely necessary for bacteriological analysis. They are the only way to be sure that the results of the analysis reflect the quality of the water and are not affected by possible contamination on the tap or during handling.
- Always work with clean hands (washed with soap). Any contamination by dirty hands will distort the results.
- Never touch the inside of the sterilized bottle or its cap. When sampling, hold the cap by the outside, never put it down unless it is upside down. It is better, for security and reliability, to double each sample.
- **Mark the following on each sample** (and keep a copy)
  - an identification number, the place and the type of water sampled, as accurately as possible
  - the date and time of the sampling and dispatch
  - the substance(s) or organism(s) to be identified; techniques to be used
  - treatment, if any, of the water (product and dose)
  - water temperature at the time of sampling (if possible)
- Certain chemical tests require special sampling. Enquire about these.
- For bacteriological analysis, it is often simpler to use field testing kits (e.g. DelAgua or Millipore); as samples need to reach the analytical laboratory within an hour of sampling if they are kept at ambient temperature, or within 6 hours if they are kept between 4 and 6°C. They should not be frozen.

Treatability tests ■

The composition of water taken from sources will vary. Some generalities can be made about water from similar types of sources (e.g. groundwater will often have a lower turbidity than surface water) but there will always be differences. These differences can affect the efficiency of the water treatment process. The treatability tests are small-scale field trials which can indicate the potential effectiveness of a treatment process on the water and also approximate chemical quantities. In some cases (such as roughing or slow sand filtration) pilot-scale tests are really the only way to test for treatability. Pilot-scale tests are not suitable for the initial stages of an emergency, but may be suitable for the longer term when there is more time available.

The following treatability tests are discussed below:
- natural sedimentation
- assisted sedimentation
- filtration (roughing, slow sand and rapid sand)
- disinfection
- pH adjustment;
- other (includes specific treatments such as iron removal etc.)

Equipment necessary (varies with test):
- Beakers or containers preferably 1l x 5
- Spatula or spoon
- Chemicals: coagulant, chlorine, lime (or similar)
- Monitoring equipment: Chlorine residual test kit, turbidity tube, microbiological test kit, aluminium / iron test kit
- Pilot test equipment

Natural sedimentation

The smaller the particle the slower the sedimentation process will be. This test can be used to assess the effectiveness of natural sedimentation.

Method:
- Place a sample of the water in a container and watch it settle over time. Clear 1l beakers should be used.
- Time how long it takes the turbidity to sediment to the bottom 20% volume of the container, leaving a liquid which meets the turbidity guidelines for that stage of emergency.

Inference:

Natural sedimentation treatability test interpretation

Sedimentation time	Inference
< 1/2 hour	Sedimentation can be undertaken as the main treatment process prior to disinfection.
1/2 - 1 hour	Sedimentation could be undertaken as the main treatment process prior to disinfection. Availability of adequate treatment tank volumes to allow for sufficient retention time should be confirmed.
> 1 hour	Sedimentation on its own will not be enough to remove the turbidity. Chemical pre-treatment such as assisted sedimentation will probably be necessary.

Notes:
- A batch (rather than a continuous) process is most common for sedimentation in an emergency situation. Care must be taken when emptying treatment units that the sediment is not disturbed into the effluent.

Assisted sedimentation

See the table on p216 with details of coagulant pH ranges, dosage ranges and buffering capacity or alkalinity requirements. The following method can be used with one-litre beakers or adapted to be used with containers commonly found in the field such as buckets or oil drums.

Method:
To determine the optimum dosage of a coagulant (in this example aluminium sulphate) for the water treatment process the jar test method can be followed:
- Place a sample of the water in four or five 1l beakers (or larger) and mark each of the beakers with the concentration of aluminium sulphate which is to be added.
- Measure the pH of the water.
- Make up a 1% solution of aluminium sulphate.
  (A 100% solution of aluminium sulphate would be 1000g in 1 litre of water so a 1% solution is made up from 10g of aluminium sulphate in 1 litre of water. **The resulting 1% solution therefore has 10g/l = 10mg/ml**).
- From this 1% solution add a range of volumes to the separate water samples in 1l beakers or alternative containers as follows:
  - 1 ml of the 1% solution added to a 1l volume of water gives 10mg of aluminium sulphate per 1l or 10mg/l in the sample water.
  - 2ml would give 20mg/l
  - 4ml would give 40mg/l
  - 8ml would give 80mg/l etc.
- Stir the resulting solutions **very slowly** one after the other (e.g. stir each for five turns and then move on to the next) for a total time of 10 minutes and then leave them to sediment for half an hour.
- If none of the containers show any sign of flocculation (where the particles begin to clump together) then repeat the test using higher doses of alum. If all the containers show signs of flocculation and settlement then try lower doses. Note that a too high a dosage of alum leads to a reduction in the turbidity removal and a high concentration of the alum coagulant in the effluent.
- Measure the pH of the water of the clearest beaker.
- Measure the aluminium residual.

Inference:
- The beaker with the clearest solution on the top (and lowest concentration of coagulant if similar final turbidities are found), has the optimum solution of aluminium sulphate.

Notes:
- The pH of the water drops when a coagulant is added to the water as an acid is formed. The amount the pH drops will depend on the **buffering capacity of the water or in particular the amount of bicarbonate alkalinity**. Hence, to maintain the same pH, or to increase the pH after coagulation and prior to disinfection (optimum chlorination effectiveness occurs at or just below pH 8), pH adjustment may be required. More aluminium residual will remain in

solution at lower pHs. The pH should therefore be determined before, and after undertaking the coagulation test.

- Adjusting the pH before or after coagulation should be avoided wherever possible but may be more economical in some cases (see *pH adjustment*, p181).

Filtration (roughing, slow sand and rapid sand):

Some turbidity particles are more suited to filtration than others. Bentonite for example will tend to block a roughing filter very quickly and the filter will be difficult to clean. It is difficult to predict how well a water will be treated by filtration but there are no quick and simple tests. A pilot trial would be useful if time allows.

Method: Pilot-scale testing

A pilot-scale plant could be set up from a piece of pipe (of at least 150mm diameter) or an old drum with a system to feed the water through and to control the flow rate. The depth and specifications of the sand should be the same in the pilot filter and in the full-scale filter (Coad, 1995). The influent and effluent waters should then be tested over a few weeks to determine the resulting water quality and predicted run time.

Inference:

The water quality of the effluent and the run time should be identified. If both are acceptable and it is possible to produce the required quantity of water (see tables, p215 and 218 for hydraulic loading rates) the filters may be selected as part of the treatment process.

Disinfection

The most common method of disinfection in emergency situations is chlorination. This section on disinfection focuses on chlorination. It has been modified and reproduced with the kind permission of Médecins sans Frontières from *Public Health Engineering in Emergency Situations*.

Chlorine

Chlorine is a chemical whose strong oxidizing properties are used to disinfect and decontaminate. Other than its gaseous form (which is mentioned here just for information, because it is complicated to use), chlorine is supplied in the form of chlorine-generating products. Each product is described by its chlorine content.

The chlorine content should be labelled on the product's packaging and is expressed:
- in % of chlorine;
- in chlorometric degrees (°chl); or

Chlorine products:

Product	Chlorine content
Sodium hypochlorite solution, 12° chl	about 4% active chlorine
Sodium hypochlorite solution, 15° chl	about 5% active chlorine
Sodium hypochlorite concentrate, 48° chl	about 15% active chlorine
Calcium hypochlorite, high strength (HTH)	about 70% active chlorine
Calcium hypochlorite, chlorinated lime (bleaching powder)	about 30% active chlorine
Sodium Dichloro-iscyanurate or NaDCC [1]: • powder • tablets	 60-65% active chlorine 1.5g active chlorine / tab.

[1] The UK Department of the Environment authorizes the use of NaDCC for disinfecting drinking water in emergency or temporary situations as long as doses do not exceed 10mg of product per litre, and it is not used for more than 90 days per year.

- in parts per million (ppm) or mg of active chlorine/litre.
  (1°chl = about 0.3% active chlorine, 1ppm = 1mg/l = 0.0001% active chlorine)

Storage:
- Store chlorine products in airtight, non-metallic containers sheltered from heat, light and humidity.
- Chlorinated lime and all forms of sodium hypochlorite are unstable and do not store well.
- Calcium hypochlorite stores better (loss of active chlorine is about 2% per year), but NaDCC is by far the most stable chlorine-generating product.

Method:

Preparation of a 1% solution:
For chlorinating drinking-water a stock solution of 1% chlorine is used which is made from one of the chlorine-generating products at n% chlorine.

Starting with a product at n% active chlorine:
- A 1% solution of chlorine contains 10g of chlorine per litre, so it needs 10 x (100/n) grammes of product per litre of solution. Example: calcium hypochlorite at 70% active chlorine: 10 x (100/70) = 15g/l of solution.

Preparation of 1% chlorine solution

Starting with :	Dilution	Remarks
Calcium hypochlorite at 70% active chlorine	15g /l = 1 level soupspoon/litre	Let the deposit settle and use only the supernatant
Calcium hypochlorite at 30% active chlorine	33g /l = 2 level soupspoons/litre	
Sodium hypochlorite at suitable 5% active chlorine	200ml/litre	Only if manufactured very recently (< 3 months) and stored away from heat
Sodium hypochlorite concentrate at 15% active chlorine	75ml/litre	
Sodium dichloro-isocyanurate (NaDCC) at 1.5g active chlorine per tablet	7 tablets/litre	Ensure that the other chemicals in the tablets are non-toxic

The 1% stock solution should be kept in an airtight, opaque, non-metallic container, away from light and heat and should be replaced every 1 to 2 weeks. Calcium hypochlorite (HTH) and NaDCC are recommended for general disinfection (greater stability and high chlorine content).

Jar test:
The method to determine how much chlorine is required for a known volume of water in a reservoir is discussed below. The principle is to add enough chlorine-generating product to destroy all the organic matter contained in the water and to leave a small fraction of chlorine available for dealing with any possible reintroduction of organic matter.

- Prepare a 1% chlorine solution (see the table above).
- Take 3 or 4 non-metallic containers of known volume (e.g. 20 litre buckets).

- Fill the containers with some of the water to be treated.
- Add to each bucket a progressively greater dose of 1% solution with a syringe:
  - 1st container : 1ml
  - 2nd container : 1.5ml
  - 3rd container : 2ml
  - 4th container : 2.5ml
- Wait 30 minutes (essential: this is the minimum contact time for the chlorine to react).
- Measure the free chlorine residual in each bucket.
- Choose the sample which shows a free residual chlorine level between 0.2 and 0.5mg/l.
- Extrapolate the 1% dose to the volume of water to be treated.
- Pour the solution into the reservoir, mix well (during filling) and wait 30 minutes before distributing.

Example of extrapolation:
Chlorination of water in a 2000l reservoir

- Using the method noted above, the free residual chlorine levels of the water in the buckets, measured 30 minutes after adding 1, 1.5, 2 and 2.5ml of 1% chlorine solution respectively, are as follows:
  1: 0mg/l
  2: 0.1mg/l
  3: 0.4mg/l
  4: 1mg/l
- The dosing rate chosen should therefore be that for bucket number 3 (result between 0.2 and 0.5mg/l).
- If 2ml of 1% solution is needed to chlorinate 20 litres of water at the correct dosage, then it needs 100 times as much to chlorinate 2000 litres, e.g. 100 x 2ml = 200ml of 1% chlorine solution.

Inputs:
- 1% solution
- Several containers of the same known volume (buckets, jerrycans, etc.).
- 5ml syringe
- Measuring equipment (comparator and DPD1 tables)
- Stopwatch to measure the 30 minutes

Important
- Water to be chlorinated must contain as little visible suspended material as possible. If it is turbid, treatment such as sedimentation and / or filtration should be undertaken prior to chlorination. Turbidity particles can protect micro-organisms from the disinfectant.
- Chlorination is effective against most pathogenic micro-organisms in water except cysts and some viruses. It is important to measure the free residual chlorine frequently in order to be able to adjust the dosage rate to the varying water quality.
- Metal consumes chlorine, so never prepare strong solutions in metal containers (unless they are enamelled or painted).
- Concentrated chlorine products should be kept in a dry, shaded place, and guarded. (Chlorine is dangerous, particularly to children). When in contact with air, chlorine produces a corrosive and toxic gas heavier than air. Chlorine stores should therefore be ventilated by means of vents at the bottom of the walls.

- The taste of chlorine in water is no proof of the presence of free residual chlorine as the chlorine taste is due to the combination of chlorine with matter in the water.

Inference:
Required dosages can be calculated and chlorine demand estimated. It should be expected that the dosages will vary with time and that the dosages calculated are only approximations.

pH adjustment

pH adjustment may be required to:
- improve the assisted sedimentation process;
- increase the efficiency of disinfection; and
- prevent corrosion or bad tastes.

Usually if there is a requirement to modify the pH then it will be to raise it. Hydrated lime (calcium hydroxide) is often used for this purpose. It has a low solubility and so is normally fed as a slurry which needs constant agitation to prevent sedimentation. Where constant agitation is not provided sodium carbonate (washing soda) can be used, as it dissolves readily in water. Sulphuric acid is used in industrialized nations if the pH needs to be lowered but its use in emergencies is not advisable and **should be avoided wherever possible** due to the health and safety hazards and transportation restrictions.

Example calculation for pH adjustment (Semat Technical (UK) Ltd.):
- 1.0 mg/l of alkalinity as $CaCO_3$ is equivalent to:
  - 0.66 mg/l 85% quicklime (CaO)
  - 0.78 mg/l 95% hydrated lime ($Ca(OH)_2$) (also known as calcium hydroxide or slaked lime)
  - 1.08 mg/l soda ash (Na_2CO_3)
- 1 mg/l commercial aluminium sulphate reacts with 0.5mg/l alkalinity as $CaCO_3$.
- Raw water alkalinity should be 1/2 expected alum dose + 5 to 10 mg/l alkalinity.

e.g. for a water with no natural alkalinity:
- for 30mg/l alum dosage the alkalinity requirement is 20 to 25mg/l as $CaCO_3$ (19.5mg/l hydrated lime)
- for 50mg/l alum dosage the alkalinity requirement is 30 to 35mg/l as $CaCO_3$ (27.3mg/l hydrated lime)

If the assisted sedimentation process needs to be improved the lime should be mixed with the water prior to the addition of alum. If the assisted sedimentation process is operating satisfactorily without the prior addition of lime, however, it can be added afterwards to increase the pH to improve the chlorination process and to prevent corrosion.

Method:

When lime is to be added to improve the assisted sedimentation process:
- Measure the existing alkalinity of the water.
- Calculate the approximate volume of lime (or equivalent) which needs to be added and use this value to determine a range of dosages for the jar tests.
- Undertake a jar test (as explained in *Assisted sedimentation,* p177) but this time either:

- determine the optimum alum dose and then repeat the jar test using this alum dose but varying the lime dosage (to obtain the optimum combination at the coagulant dose chosen); or
- undertake a range of tests using different coagulant dosages and lime dosages.

Example:
- The natural alkalinity of the water is found to be 10mg/l as $CaCO_3$.
- The optimum alum dosage determined from a jar test is found to be 40mg/l.
- The approximate amount of alkalinity required (1/2 expected alum dose + 5 to 10mg/l alkalinity as $CaCO_3$) = (40 x 0.5) + 10 = 30mg/l as $CaCO_3$
- The volume of hydrated lime therefore required = (30 - 10) x 0.78 = 15.6mg/l
- For the purpose of this jar test use 5, 10, 15, 20, 25, and 30mg/l of lime with 40mg/l of alum.
- Make up a 1% solution of lime by adding 10g of lime to 1 litre of water.
- 1ml of the 1% solution added to a 1l volume of water means 10mg of lime will be used per 1l or 10 mg/l in the sample water.
- Measure the pH of the water.
- Add 0.5, 1, 1.5, 2, 2.5, and 3.0ml of the 1% lime solution to 1-litre beakers of the water under test. Stir them for a few minutes and allow to stand for 20 minutes.
- Make up a 1% solution of alum.
- Add 4ml of 1% alum solution to each beaker and stir the resulting solutions **very slowly** one after the other (e.g. stir each for five turns and then move on to the next) for a total time of 10 minutes and then leave them to sediment for half an hour.
- Measure the pH and alkalinity of the final solutions.
- Measure the turbidity and assess which provides the most effective turbidity removal. Check that the resulting pH is acceptable.

Note that the lime may not be as strong as the calculations assume, particularly if it has impurities. The volume of lime required may therefore be higher than expected from the calculations.

This example aims to improve the turbidity removal process and shows the lime being added before the alum. A fixed alum dosage has also been assumed. Alternatively, the lime could be added after the alum if the purpose was to raise the pH. A range of alum doses could also have been used with ranges of lime doses to see if the alum dose could have been reduced with the addition of lime.

When lime is to be added to raise the pH after assisted sedimentation (or an alternative treatment process):
- take a sample of the water produced after the assisted sedimentation treatment process (i.e. undertake the jar test and use the resulting liquid as the sample);
- add a range of dosages of lime to the water using jar test methodology (as noted in *Assisted sedimentation,* p177) but adding lime rather than alum; then
- test the resulting pH and select the lowest dosage producing the required pH.

Other

Iron or manganese removal

A simple pilot plant may be required to determine an appropriate treatment process for any specific treatment problem that has not been noted above (iron, manganese removal, etc.) In the initial stages of an emergency, however, it is unlikely that attempts will be made to remove specific pollutants other than as part of the standard treatment processes unless absolutely essential.

Temperature effects

The following should be noted:
- Coagulation is temperature-dependent and hence the jar test should be undertaken at the temperature of the natural water and not at room temperature;
- Colour and turbidity removal efficiency is also affected by temperature, with sedimentation and filtration being less efficient in the winter months than in the summer (WHO, 1984b, p301);
- The effectiveness of chlorination also increases with temperature especially when chlorinating outside of the pH range 7 to 8.5;
- Where there is a dramatic annual temperature change then the temperature should be taken into account when considering the possible efficiencies of treatment processes; and
- Viruses, cysts and ova of parasitic worms can survive longer at cold temperatures.

Industrial pollution ■

Potential industrial (including agrochemical) pollutants are numerous and may include:

arsenic, cadmium, chromium, copper, detergents, lead, mercury, pesticides, and petroleum products among others.

Keller et al, (1992) divided major potentially hazardous materials into the following groupings:
- heavy metals
- organic solvents
- inorganic toxins
- acids and alkalis
- organic toxins
- biodegradable materials
- infective agents

WHO divides its health-related guidelines in to the following sections:
- bacteriological quality
- inorganic chemicals
- organic constituents
- pesticides
- disinfectants and disinfectant by-products

WHO guideline values are mainly based on long-term consumption rather than short-term toxicity. In the immediate emergency rejecting a source because it does not meet the WHO guidelines based on long-term consumption could be dangerous if it means that the populations are therefore at an immediate risk from dehydration or from other health-related diseases due to ineffective hygiene practices. Where guidelines based on short-term toxicity are not available WHO guidelines should be met where possible, but used *with common sense*. Databases with up-to-date toxicological information are available and capable organizations should be sought for interpretations of laboratory data.

The United States Environmental Protection Agency has developed a series of 'Health Advisories (HA)' for drinking-water contaminants. They include tables of short-term guideline levels (one-day, ten-day and longer term use) for a wide range of contaminants. These would be suitable for use where there have been accidental spills or where drinking-water has been contaminated. They include a margin of safety to protect sensitive populations, e.g. children, the elderly and pregnant women (Davies, 1997). The figures are revised approximately every six months. Summary tables containing health advisory figures for varying periods of exposure can be found on the internet at the USEPA site http://www.epa.gov/OST (exact location: http://www.epa.gov/docs/ostwater/Tools/dwstds0.html). Copies may also be ordered free of charge from the Safe Drinking Water Hotline, (tel:1-800-426-4791) Monday to Friday 9 am to 5.30 pm US time. Supporting information containing information on the chemistry, health effects, analytical methods and treatment technologies for specific contaminants can also be purchased from the Educational Resource Information Centre (ERIC) tel: 1-614-292-6717.

Industrial pollution is difficult to assess in the field as there are:

- a large number of potential pollutants, with new ones being added all the time; and
- limitations in existing field-assessment procedures, methods and equipment.

Hence for a thorough assessment there really is no option other than to send the samples to a laboratory. *Water quality assessment: Introduction to methods and assessment routines, Industrial pollution,* p153 identifies indications that industrial or agrochemical pollution may be present and hence whether the sample should be sent to a laboratory for further analysis. **This section will have to be used with a great deal of common sense and personal judgement in the field. The assessment methods are not perfect and should only be undertaken where the potentially industrially polluted water source under consideration is the only option.**

Pages 185–92 identify potential industrial pollutants and associated industries. It can be used to highlight laboratory testing requirements. Laboratories require as much information on the potential pollutants as possible. Information which can be gleaned from the industries themselves or other local knowledge can be extremely valuable. Following also are: a list of recommended water sample preservation techniques, pp193–4; a draft letter to a laboratory requesting an assessment, pp195–6; and a draft letter to an interpreting organization, pp196–7.

The interpreting organization must have access to up-to-date toxicological data and have the experience and ability to translate this into acceptability for affected populations who may be physically weak and traumatized and may include a large number of infants and young babies.

Industries and activities and associated pollutants ■

The following table has been compiled from information in the following references with the assistance of P. Steadman of the University of Newcastle upon Tyne, UK:

Bahu et al, 1997;
Bridgewater and Mumford, 1979;
British Standards Institution, 1988;
Flemming, 1991;
HMSO, 1996;
Interdepartmental Committee on the Redevelopment of Contaminated Land (ICRCL), 1986;
Interdepartmental Committee on the Redevelopment of Contaminated Land (ICRCL), 1983;
National Rivers Authority, 1994;
Nemerow and Dasgupta, 1991;
Sawyer and McCarty, 1989;
Shen, 1995;
Tearle, 1973; and
Twort et al, 1994.

The table is a basic guide only and not fully comprehensive. Some pollutants may have been omitted. Specific information on the industries and their pollutants should be sought when the industries have been identified.

Industries and activities versus pollutants

Industry / activity	Pollutants (aqueous, solid or liquid)
Agriculture / horticulture	· Acids and alkalis · Ammonia · Arsenic (pesticides) · Cadmium (fungicides) · Copper (as pesticide) · Disinfectants · Faecal pollution · Herbicides · High BOD/COD · Insecticides · Mercury · Nutrients (nitrates and phosphates) · Pesticides (sharp / acrid odour) · Primary production waste · Turbidity from erosion
Animal (Food processing)	· Abattoir waste · BOD waste (high and low) · Disinfectants · Grease · Oil
Batteries	· Cadmium · Lead · Manganese · Mercury · Nickel · Zinc
Catalysts	· Cobalt · Iron · Manganese · Mercury · Nickel · Organometallics · Platinum · Silver · Vanadium
Beverage (Food processing)	· Acids · Alkali · BOD waste (low) · Detergent
Boiler house / power house	· Asbestos · Boiler dust · Chemical additives · Fly ash · Grease · Oil · Soot
Cannery and Bottling Plants	· Acids and alkalis · Detergents · Foodstuffs · Glass · High BOD/COD · Metals including tin · Paper waste / fibres (labelling) · Solvents
Cement, Bricks, Lime	· Chromium · Dust
Chemical Manufacture	· Activated carbon (from chlorine manufacture) · Asbestos (from electrolysis) · Metals (including heavy metals) · Solvents (including halogented solvents) · Acid solutions · Alkali solutions (calcium hydroxide, soda, ammonia) · Salts (including solutions containing cyanides)

Industry / activity	Pollutants (aqueous, solid or liquid)
Coal distillation, coal tar, coke ovens	· Ammonia · Aromatic hydrocarbons · Combustion products · Cyanate · Cyanide · Dust · Fluoride · Hydrocarbons · Phenols · Tar · Thiocyanate
Cooling towers / Cooling waters	· Chlorofluorocarbons · Fan tube oils · Heat · Solvents including chlorinated solvents · Process chemicals
Construction, building, demolition	· Asbestos · Dust · High pH (from cement) · Metals · Oil · Rubble · Timber · Turbidity due to erosion
Desalination	· Brines
Detergents	· Boric acid · Nickel · Phosphates · Sulphates
Domestic wastewater treatment works for sewered system	· Faecal pollution including pathogens · Metals in sludges · Nutrients (nitrites) · Oils · Sulphides
Domestic wastewater without sewered system	· As above for sewered system · Solids
Dry cleaning	· Chlorinated hydrocarbons · Hydrocarbon solvents
Dyestuffs	· Aniline · Chromium · Phenol · Selenium
Electrical, Electronics	· Copper · Other metals e.g. nickel, cadmium · Mercury
Electricity generation	· Clinker · Cooling water · Pulverized fuel ash
Electroplating	· Strong acids and alkalis · Boron · Cadmium · Chromium · Copper · Cyanide · Detergent · Fluoride · Iron · Nickel · Organic complexing agents · Phosphate · Precious metals · Silver · Sulphate · Tin · Zinc

Industry / activity	Pollutants (aqueous, solid or liquid)
Explosives, pyrotechnics	· Barium · Hydrocarbons · Lead · Manganese · Mercury · Nitric acid · Nitro-glycerine · Phenol · Phosphorus · Solvents · Strontium · TNT
Fibres and textiles	· Acids and alkalis · Bleach · Boron · Copper · Cyanide · Detergent · Dyestuffs · Grease · Halogenated wastes · Oil · Pesticides e.g. moth proofing - organophosphates · Resins · Silicones
Fish farming	· Nutrients · Pesticides (sharp / acrid odour)
Forestry	· Organic matter (musty odour) · Turbidity due to erosion
Foundries	· Dust · Heat · Heavy metals · Other metals · Sands
Garages	· Acids · Caustics · Degreasers containing chlorinated solvents · Grease · Oils · Petroleum · Solvents
Gas production / purification	· Ammonia · Asbestos · Cyanides · Catalysts containing zinc, nickel, chromium · Phenols · Sludges containing silver and other heavy metals · Sulphur compounds · Tarry residues
Glass and ceramic production	· Alkalis · Arsenic · Barium · Fluoride · Lead · Manganese · Nickel · Selenium
Hospitals	· Acids and alkalis · BOD waste (high / low) · Drug residues · Pathogens · Radioactivity · Sharp wastes · Solvents
Laundry	· Alkalinity · Bleach · Detergent · Organic solids · Phosphate · Sulphate · Turbidity

4

Industry / activity	Pollutants (aqueous, solid or liquid)
Machine shops	· Acids and alkalis · Cadmium · Caustics · Degreasing sludges containing chlorinated solvents · Nickel · Oils · Oil absorbents · Solvents
Metals: Anodizing	· Chromium · Other metals
Metals: Degreasing	· Detergents · Grease · Solvents
Metals: Extraction and refining	· Acid mine waters · Arsenic · Cadmium · Chloride · Chromium · Copper · Dust · Fluoride · Glass · Lead · Nickel · Selenium · Spoil · Sulphides · Tailings · Zinc
Mining	· Acids · Aluminium · Chlorides · Heavy Metals · Iron from acid mine drainage · Low / high pH · Metals · Phosphates · Radioactivity (uranium mining) · Salinity · Spoil · Sulphates · Sulphides · Tailings
Mortuary	· Blood salt · Formaldehyde · High BOD · Infectious diseases
Motor industry	· Asbestos (brake linings) · Chromate · Grease · Oil · Paint · Phosphates · Solvents
Nuclear fuel and power	· Cooling waters (heat) · Heavy metals · Radioactive substances · Radioisotopes
Oil extraction and processing	· Chlorinated oil emulsions · Chlorinated oils · Heavy metals · Hydraulic oils containing PCBs · Oily sludges · Phenols · Sulphide / sulphate · Tars

Industry / activity	Pollutants (aqueous, solid or liquid)
Paint and Coatings	· Acids and alkalis · Asbestos · Barium · Cadmium · Chromium · Copper · Emulsions · Lead · Manganese · Mercury · Organic Compounds (e.g. aliphatic / aromatic hydrocarbons) · Selenium · Solvents including halogenated solvents
Paper / pulp	· Alkalis · Bleach · Chlorine · Colour · Copper · Fibres · High BOD/COD · Hydrogen Sulphides · Lignin · Mercury · Methanol · Sulphides · Sulphite liquor · Titanium · Wax
Pesticide, herbicide production	· Zinc · Arsenic · Carbamates · Chlorinated hydrocarbons · Copper · Fluoride · Lead · Mercury · Organic solvents · Organic halogenated solvents · Organophosphorus compounds · Phenol · Polychlorinated biphenyl (PCB) · Selenium
Petrochemical (general)	· Alkalis · Asbestos · Benzene · Boric acid · Chlorocarbons · Fluorine · Fluorocarbons · Halogenoaliphatic compounds · Hydrocarbons · Hydrochloric acid · Hydrofluoric acid · Lead · Organic compounds · PCBs · Phenol · Solvents · Sludges · Sulphuric acid · Tar
Pharmaceuticals	· Drug intermediates and residues · Mercury · Phenols · Solvents including halogenated solvents
Photography	· Alkali · Cadmium · Cyanide · Mercury · Phenols · Selenium (photocopier manufacture) · Silver · Solvent-based developer and other solvents · Thiosulphate

Industry/ activity	Pollutants (aqueous, solid or liquid)
Pickling - Engineering	· Acid · Ferrous chloride · Ferrous sulphate · Hydrochloric acid · Hydrofluoric acid · Nitric acid · Phosphoric acid · Sulphuric acid
Pigment production	· Arsenic · Barium · Cadmium · Chromium · Cobalt · Cyanides · Iron · Lead · Manganese · Organic halogenated solvents · Organic solvents · Selenium · Silicone oils · Sulphates · Titanium
Polymers, Plastics, Resins, Rubber and Fibres	· Acid · Alkali · Asbestos · Cadmium · Cuprammonium compounds · Detergent · Dyestuffs · Fibres · Formaldehyde · Hydrocarbons · Methanol · Organic solvents · Organic halogenated solvents · Phenols · Phthalates · Pigments (carbon black) · Polychlorinated byphenyls (PCBs) · Solvents · Sulphide · Urea · Wood flour · Zinc
Printing	· Acids and alkalis · Inks · Paper products / fibres · Solvents including halogenated solvents · Metals e.g. cobalt, nickel, cadmium
Processing / engineering	· Acids and alkalis · Ammonia · Arsenic · Asbestos · Boron · Cyanide · Degreasers containing chlorinated solvents · Emulsions · Lubricating oils · Metalloids and compounds · Metals · PCBs (transformer / capacitor) · Phenols · Soluble oils · Solvents · Sulphates · Thiocyanates

Industry/ activity	Pollutants (aqueous, solid or liquid)
Refineries	· Acid alkyl sludges · Acid tars (other tars) · Alkali · BOD waste · Emulsions · Hydrocarbons · Mineral acids · Oily sludges and solid wastes · Phenol · Sulphides · Sulphur · Tar
Scrap yards and Reduction plants	· Acids and alkalis · Asbestos · Chlorides · Cyanides · Degreasers containing chlorinated solvents · Fluorides · Grease · Oils · Metals (especially iron, copper, nickel, chromium, zinc, cadmium, lead, magnesium, mercury, tin) · Polychlorinated biphenyls (PCBs) from transformer / capacitor breaking · Sulphides · Sulphates
Ship building	· Acids and alkalis · Asbestos · Degreasers containing chlorinated solvents · Emulsions · Halogenated solvents · Metals · Oils · Paint wastes · Solvents
Solid waste disposal	· Acids and alkalis · Battery acids · Garbage · Dust · Halogenated solvents · Heavy metals from leachates · High BOD/COD · Oils · Ammoniacal nitrogen · Pathogens · PCBs · Solvents · Sulphides · Sulphites · Sulphates
Tanneries	· Arsenic · Chromium · Degreasing wastes containing solvents · Fibres · Hair · Lime · Sulphides
Timber and wood processing	· Creosote (contains polycyclic aromatic hydocarbons) · Inorganic wood preservatives · Organochlorinted wood preservatives · Non-halogenated organic wood preservatives
Vegetable and fruit (food processing)	· Alkali · Bleach · BOD waste (high and low) · Foodstuffs · Oil · Solvent · Wax
Water treatment	· Chlorides · Coagulant residues · Filtered solids

Recommended water sample preservation techniques ■

The following section has been reproduced with kind permission of E. de Lange from *Manual for Simple Water Quality Analysis* published by the IWT Foundation.

Recommended water sample preservation techniques

Parameter	Container[1]	Sample vol (ml)	Preservative	Storage time
Total organic carbon	P, G	100	H_2SO_4 to pH<2 4°C	1-2 dy
Total inorganic carbon	P, G	100	Air seal 4°C	0
Chlorine demand	P, G	100-200*	None	0
Aluminium (Al)	P, G	100-200*	NHO_3 to pH<2	6 mo
Arsenic (As)	P, G	100-200*	NHO_3 to pH<2	6 mo
Cadmium (Cd)	P, G	100-200*	NHO_3 to pH<2	6 mo
Calcium (Ca)	P, G	100-200*	NHO_3 to pH<2	6 mo
Chromium (Cr)	P, G	100-200*	NHO_3 to pH<2	6 mo
Copper (Cu)	P, G	100-200*	NHO_3 to pH<2	6 mo
Iron (Fe)	P, G	100-200*	NHO_3 to pH<2	6 mo
Lead (Pb)	P, G	100-200*	NHO_3 to pH<2	6 mo
Magnesium (Mg)	P, G	100*	NHO_3 to pH<2	6 mo
Manganese (Mn)	P, G	100-200*	NHO_3 to pH<2	6 mo
Mercury (Hg)	G	500	NHO_3 to pH<2	2 wk
Nickel (Ni)	P, G	100-200*	NHO_3 to pH<2	6 mo
Selenium (Se)	P, G		NHO_3 to pH<2	90 dy
Zinc (Zn)	P, G	100-200*	NHO_3 to pH<2	6 mo
Ammonia-nitrogen	P, G		H_2SO_4 to pH<2 4°C	24 hr
Nitrate-nitrogen	P, G		H_2SO_4 to pH<2 4°C	24 hr
Nitrite-nitrogen	P, G		H_2SO_4 to pH<2 4°C	24 hr
Organic-nitrogen	P, G		H_2SO_4 to pH<2 4°C	24 hr
Total Kieldah nitrogen	P, G		H_2SO_4 to pH<2 4°C	24 hr
Oil and grease	G		H_2SO_4 or HCl to pH<2 4°C	24 hr
BOD	P,G	300	4°C	6 hr
COD	P,G	200	H_2SO_4 to pH<2 4°C	7 dy

[1] P = plastic; G = glass

* Sample can be used for other metal analyses.

** Sample can be used for total solids and volatile solids.

Parameter	Container[a]	Sample vol (ml)	Preservative	Storage time
PCBs	G	21	4°C	
Organochlorine pesticides	G	11	4°C	
Chlorinated phenoxy acid and herbicides	G	11	H_2SO_4 to pH<2 4°C	
Organophosphates and carbonates	G	11	H_2SO_4 to pH<3 10 g Na_2SO_4	
Phenolics	G	500	0.1-1.0 g $CuSO_4$ H_3PO_4 to pH<4 4°C	24 hr
				24 hr
Soluble reactive	P, G		Filter 4°C	7 dy
Total phosphorus	P, G		4°C	None
Redox potential	P, G	100	None	6 hr
pH	P, G	100	4°C	7 dy
Total solids	P, G	200**	4°C	7 dy
Volatile solids	P, G	200**	4°C	24 hr
Sulfides	P, G		2 ml ZnOAc	
Polyuncleated aromatic hydrocarbons	G			

* Sample can be used for other metal analyses.

** Sample can be used for total solids and volatile solids.

Source;   Plumb, Russell H. Jr.: 'Procedures for handling and chemical analysis of sediment and water samples'. U.S. Environment Protection Agency. Published by Environment Laboratory, U.S. Army Engineer Waterways Experiment Station, P.O. Box 631, Vicksburg, Mississippi 39180, U.S.A., in de Lange, 1994.

NHO_3 = Nitric Acid

H_2SO_4 = Sulphuric Acid

HCl = Hydrochloric Acid

H_3PO_4 = Phosphoric Acid

Na_2SO_4 = Sodium Sulphate

ZnOAc = Zinc Acetate

4

Draft letter to laboratory requesting assessment

The following letter format may be followed when requesting laboratory analyses for industrially polluted water. The letter will have to be modified to suit the situation and appropriate information included in place of the { } brackets.

Laboratory Manager / Chief Analyst
{Address}

Dear Sir/ Madam

Urgent request for water analyses

{Organization} are responding to the water needs of {scale} displaced persons recently arrived near {location}. I forward two one-litre samples of the water for analysis. The samples were taken at {time} on the {date} and {have or have not been preserved with ..}. Below I have provided as much information as I presently have available on the source and potential polluters. **I must emphasise that the results of the analyses are extremely urgent.**

Location of water source and possible polluters:
The only source of water near to the camp which can meet the demands of the displaced persons is potentially polluted. It is a small river of {flow} during the {dry or rainy season}. The variation during the year as identified from local knowledge is {variation}. Two kilometres upstream from the potential abstraction point it is believed that a battery factory may be discharging its effluents directly into the source. Alongside the river there is also agricultural land where pesticides may be used: see the sketch map attached. The surface strata is mainly volcanic rock and high levels of arsenic have been reported in some other sources in the region.

Field analyses
Some basic field analyses has been undertaken on the water in {location} on {date of assessment} at {time of assessment}. The results are attached with a list of equipment used to undertake these field analyses.

Pollution
From the information which I have available, I believe that a **battery factory** may discharge the following materials among others:
- cadmium
- lead
- manganese
- mercury
- nickel
- zinc

I am not aware of the exact type of **pesticide** which may be used in the vicinity of the source but local knowledge suggests that DDT is still commonly used in this region.

Local knowledge indicates that there may also be a problem with:
- arsenic

Minimum tests

Test for all of the pollutants noted above and any others which you feel are likely pollutants and will give useful information as to the potability of the water. Duplicates of all tests should be undertaken where possible.

Results

Results should be faxed to {.....} (or will be collected by {......}) **as soon as they are available**.

The results should be accompanied by the following information:
- date and time of test;
- equipment on which the parameters were measured with an indication of the degree of accuracy available;
- note as to whether the result is that of a single test or an average of more than one test; and
- name and qualification of analyst who undertook the tests.

If you have personnel qualified to interpret the laboratory results for the suitability of the water for short-term potability for traumatized and weakened communities with large numbers of small children and babies, then please also arrange for these interpretations to be forwarded with the data and details of the interpreters qualifications.

Payment for the analyses and interpretation
{details}

I would like to re-stress the urgency of this request. If you require further details please do not hesitate to contact me at {details}.

Yours faithfully,

Draft letter to interpreting organization ∎

The following letter format may be followed when requesting interpretation of laboratory analyses for industrially polluted water. The letter will have to be modified to suit the situation and appropriate information included in place of the { } brackets.

Dear Sir/ Madam,

{Organization} are responding to the water needs of {scale} displaced persons recently arrived near {location}. Two one-litre samples of the water were sent to a laboratory for analysis. The samples were taken at {time} on the {date} and {were or were not preserved with ..} before sending to the laboratory. Below I have provided as much information as I presently have available on the source, potential polluters, and the results of all analyses.

I require interpretation of these analyses for the **short-** and **long-term potability** of the water. The most **urgent interpretation of this data is for short-term potability** as the water needs of the displaced population are critical. If we do not increase water quantities quickly there may be serious health implications. The assessment for short-term potability should take into account that there are many young babies and children in the camp and that the people are weak from several days walking across a mountainous region and are traumatized from their experiences.

I must emphasise that the results of your interpretation are extremely urgent.

Location of water source and possible polluters:
The only source of water near to the camp which can meet the demands of the displaced persons is potentially polluted. It is a small river of {flow} during the {dry or rainy season}. The variation during the year as identified from local knowledge is {variation}. Two kilometres upstream from the potential abstraction point it is believed that a battery factory may be discharging its effluents directly into the source. Alongside the river there is also agricultural land where pesticides may be used: see the sketch map attached. The surface strata is mainly volcanic rock and high levels of arsenic have been reported in some other sources in the region.

Pollution
From the information which I have available, I believe that a **battery factory** may discharge the following materials among others:
- cadmium
- lead
- manganese
- mercury
- nickel
- zinc

I am not aware of the exact type of **pesticide** which may be used in the vicinity of the source but local knowledge suggests that DDT is still commonly used in this region.

Local knowledge indicates that there may also be a problem with:
- arsenic

Field analyses
Some basic field analyses has been undertaken on the water on location on {date of assessment} at {time of assessment}. The results are attached and also a list of equipment used to undertake these field analyses.

Laboratory analyses
The results from the {name} laboratory undertaken on the {date} are attached.

Please provide details of the interpretations, any references used and reasoning behind the interpretations and forward them along with details of the interpreters' qualifications.

Payment for the analyses and interpretation
{details}

I would like to re-stress the urgency of this request. If you require further details from us please do not hesitate to contact me at {details}.

Yours faithfully,

Organizations which may be able to interpret industrial pollution data ■

See *Useful addresses*, p285.

Key references:
- Davies, 1997
- de Lange, 1994
  and those noted on p185.
- Keller at al, 1992
- United States Environmental Protection Agency, 1996

WHO drinking-water guideline values ■

The following tables have been reproduced with kind permission of the World Health Organization from *Guidelines for Drinking Water Quality, Vol.1, Recommendations,* 2nd Edition, 1993, pp172–181.

Bacteriological quality of drinking-water (WHO, 1993)

Organisms	Guideline value
All water intended for drinking	
E.coli or thermotolerant coliform bacteria [b,c]	Must not be detectable in any 100ml sample
Treated water entering the distribution system	
E.coli or thermotolerant coliform bacteria [b]	Must not be detectable in any 100ml sample
Total coliform bacteria	Must not be detectable in any 100ml sample
Treated water in the distribution system	
E.coli or thermotolerant coliform bacteria [b]	Must not be detectable in any 100ml sample
Total coliform bacteria	Must not be detectable in any 100ml sample. In the case of large supplies, where sufficient samples are examined, must not be present in 95% of samples taken throughout any 12-month period.

[a] Immediate investigative action must be taken if either *E.coli* or total coliform bacteria are detected. The minimum action in the case of total coliform bacteria is repeat sample, the cause must be determined by immediate further investigation.

[b] Although *E.coli* is the more precise indicator of faecal pollution, the count of thermotolerant coliform bacteria is an acceptable alternative. If necessary, proper confirmatory tests must be carried out. Total coliform bacteria are not acceptable indicators of the sanitary quality of rural water supplies, particularly in tropical areas where many bacteria of no sanitary significance occur in almost all untreated supplies.

[c] It is recognized that, in the great majority of rural water supplies in developing countries, faecal contamination is widespread. Under these conditions, the national surveillance agency should set medium-term targets for the progressive improvement of water supplies, as recommended in Volume 3 of *Guidelines for drinking-water quality.*

Chemicals of health significance in drinking-water (WHO, 1993)

A. Inorganic constituents

	Guideline value (mg/litre)	Remarks
antimony	0.005 (P)[a]	
arsenic	0.01[b] (P)	For excess skin cancer risk of 6 x 10 [-4]
barium	0.7	NAD[c]
beryllium		
boron	0.3	
cadmium	0.003	
chromium	0.05 (P)	
copper	2 (P)	ATO[d]
cyanide	0.07	
fluoride	1.5	Climatic conditions, volume of water consumed, and intake from other sources should be considered when setting national standards. It is recognized that not all water will meet the guideline value immediately; meanwhile, all other recommended measures to reduce the total exposure to lead should be implemented
lead	0.01	
manganese	0.5 (P)	ATO
mercury (total)	0.001	
molybdenum	0.07	
nickel	0.02	
nitrate (as NO_3^-)	50	
nitrate (as NO_2^-)	3 (P)	The sum of the ratio of the concentration of each to its respective guideline value should not exceed 1
selenium	0.01	
uranium		NAD

B. Organic constituents

	Guideline value (μg/litre)	Remarks
Chlorinated alkanes		
carbon tetrachloride	2	
dichloromethane	20	
1,1-dichloroethane		NAD
1,2-dichloroethane	30[b]	for excess risk of 10^{-5}
1,1,1-trichloroethane	2000 (P)	
Chlorinated ethenes		
vinyl chloride	5[b]	for excess risk of 10^{-5}
1,1-dichloroethene	30	
1,2-dichloroethene	50	
trichloroethene	70 (P)	
tetrachloroethene	40	
Aromatic hydrocarbons		
benzene	10[b]	for excess risk of 10^{-5}
toluene	700	ATO
xylenes	500	ATO
ethylbenzene	300	ATO
styrene	20	ATO
benzo[a]pyrene	0.7[b]	for excess risk of 10^{-5}
Chlorinated benzenes		
monochlorobenzene	300	ATO
1,2-dichlorobenzene	1000	ATO
1,3-dichlorobenzene		NAD
1,4-dichlorobenzene	300	ATO
trichlorobenzenes (total)	20	ATO
Miscellaneous		
di(2 ethylhexyl)adipate	80	
di(2 ethylhexyl)phthalate	8	
acrylamide	0.5[b]	for excess risk of 10^{-5}
epichlorohydrin	0.4 (P)	
hexachlorobutadiene	0.6	
edetic acid (EDTA)	200 (P)	
nitrilotriacetic acid	200	
dialkyltins		NAD
tributyltin oxide	2	

C. Pesticides

	Guideline value (mg/litre)	Remarks
alachlor	20[b]	for excess risk of 10^{-5}
aldicarb	10	
aldrin / dieldrin	0.03	
atrazine	2	
bentazone	30	
carbofuran	5	
chlordane	0.2	
chlorotoluron	30	
DDT	2	
1,2-dibromo-3-chloropropane	1[b]	for excess risk of 10^{-5}
2,4-D	30	
1,2-dichloropropane	20 (P)	
1,3-dichloropropane		NAD
1,3-dichloropropane	20[b]	for excess risk of 10^{-5}
ethylene dibromide		NAD
heptachlor and heptachlor epoxide	0.03	
hexachlorobenzene	1[b]	for excess risk of 10^{-5}
isoproturon	9	
lindane	2	
MCPA	2	
methoxychlor	20	
metolachlor	10	
molinate	6	
pendimethalin	20	
pentachlorophenol	9 (P)	
permethrin	20	
propanil	20	
pyridate	100	
simazine	2	
trifluralin	20	
chlorophenoxy herbicides other than 2,4-D and MCPA		
2,4-DB	90	
dichlorprop	100	
fenoprop	9	
MCPB		NAD
mecoprop	10	
2,4,5-T	9	

D. Disinfectants and disinfectant by-products

Disinfectants	Guideline value (mg/litre)	Remarks
monochloramine	3	
di- and trichloramine		NAD
chlorine	5	ATO. For effective disinfection there should be a residual concentration of free chlorine of greater than or equal to 0.5 mg/litre after at least 30 minutes contact time at pH < 8.0
chlorine dioxide		A guideline value has not been established because of the rapid breakdown of chlorine dioxide and because the chlorite guideline value is adequately protective for potential toxicity from chlorine dioxide
iodine		NAD

Disinfectant by-products	Guideline value (μg/litre)	
bromate	25[b] (P)	for 7×10^{-5} excess risk
chlorate		NAD
chlorite	200 (P)	
chlorophenols		
2-chlorophenol		NAD
2,4-dichlorophenol		NAD
2,4,6-trichlorophenol	200[b]	for excess risk of 10^{-5}, ATO
formaldehyde	900	
MX		NAD
trihalomethanes		The sum of the ratio of the concentration of each to its respective guideline value should not exceed 1
bromoform	100	
dibromochloromethane	100	
bromodichloromethane	60[b]	for excess risk of 10^{-5}
chloroform	200[b]	for excess risk of 10^{-5}
chlorinated acetic acids		
monochloroacetic acid		NAD
dichloroacetic acid	50 (P)	
trichloroacetic acid	100 (P)	
chloral hydrate		
(trichloroacetaldehyde)	10 (P)	
chloroacetone		NAD
halogenated acetonitriles		
dichloroacetonitrile	90 (P)	
dibromoacetonitrile	100 (P)	
bromochloroacetonitrile		NAD
trichloroacetonitrile	1 (P)	
cyanogen chloride (as CN)	70	
chloropicrin		NAD

a   (P) — Provisional guideline value. This term is used for constituents for which there is some evidence of a potential hazard but where the available information on health effects is limited; or where an uncertainty factor greater than 1000 has been used in the derivation of the tolerable daily intake (TDI). Provisional guideline values are also recommended: (1) for substances for which the calculated guideline value would be below the practical quantification level, or below the level that can be achieved through practical treatment methods; or (2) where disinfection is likely to result in the guideline value being exceeded.

b   For substances that are considered to be carcinogenic, the guideline value is concentration in drinking-water associated with an excess lifetime cancer risk of 10^{-5} (one additional cancer per 100 000 of the population ingesting drinking-water containing the substance at the guideline value for 70 years). Concentrations associated with estimated excess lifetime cancer risks of 10^{-4} and 10^{-6} can be calculated by multiplying and dividing, respectively, the guideline value by 10.

In cases in which the concentration associated with excess lifetime cancer risk of 10^{-5} is not feasible as a result of inadequate analytical or treatment technology, a provisional guideline value is recommended at a practicable level and the estimated associated excess lifetime cancer risk presented.

It should be emphasized that the guideline values for carcinogenic substances have been computed from hypothetical mathematical models that cannot be verified experimentally and that the values should be interpreted differently then TDI-based values because of the lack of precision of the models. At best, these values must be regarded as rough estimates of cancer risk. However, the models used are conservative and probably err on the side of caution. Moderate short-term exposure to levels exceeding the guideline value for carcinogens does not significantly affect the risk.

c   NAD — No adequate data to permit recommendation of a health based guideline value.

d   ATO — Concentrations of the substance at or below the health based guideline value may affect the appearance, taste, or odour of the water.

Chemicals not of health significance at concentrations normally found in drinking water (WHO, 1993)

Chemical	Remarks
asbestos	U
silver	U
tin	U

U - It is unecessary to recommend a health-based guideline value for these compounds becasue they are not hazardous to human health at concentrations normally found in drinking water

Radioactive constituents of drinking water (WHO, 1993)

	Screening value (Bq/litre)	Remarks
gross alpha activity	0.1	If a screening value is exceeded, more detailed radionuclide analysis is necessary. Higher values do not necessarily imply that the water is unsuitable for human consumption
gross beta activity	1	

Substances and parameters in drinking-water that may give rise to complaints from consumers (WHO, 1993)

	Levels likely to give rise to consumer complaints[a]	Reasons for consumer complaints
Physical parameters		
colour	15 TCU[b]	appearance
taste and odour	-	should be acceptable
temperature	-	should be acceptable
turbidity	5 NTU[c]	appearance; for effective terminal disinfection, median turbidity less than or equal to 1NTU, single sample less than or equal to 5NTU
Inorganic constituents		
aluminium	0.2mg/l	depositions, discoloration
ammonia	1.5mg/l	odour and taste
chloride	250mg/l	taste, corrosion
copper	1mg/l	staining of laundry and sanitary ware (health-based provisional guideline value 2mg/litre)
hardness		high hardness: scale deposition, scum formation low hardness: possible corrosion
hydrogen sulfide	0.05mg/l	odour and taste
iron	0.3mg/l	staining of laundry and sanitary ware
manganese	0.1mg/l	staining of laundry and sanitary ware (health-based provisional guideline value 0.5mg/litre)
dissolved oxygen	-	indirect effects
pH	-	low pH: corrosion
		high pH: taste, soapy feel preferably < 8.0 for effective disinfection with chlorine
sodium	200mg/l	taste
sulphate	250mg/l	taste, corrosion
total dissolved solids	1000mg/l	taste
zinc	3mg/l	appearance, taste
Organic constituents		
toluene	24 - 170µg/l	odour, taste (health-based guideline value 700µg/l)
xylene	20 - 1800µg/l	odour, taste (health-based guideline value 500µg/l)
ethylbenzene	2 - 200µg/l	odour, taste (health-based guideline value 300µg/l)
styrene	4 - 2600µg/l	odour, taste (health-based guideline value 20µg/l)
monochlorobenzene	10 - 120µg/l	odour, taste (health-based guideline value 300µg/l)
1,2-dichlorobenzene	1 - 10µg/l	odour, taste (health-based guideline value 1000µg/l)
1,4-dichlorobenzene	0.3 - 30µg/l	odour, taste (health-based guideline value 300µg/l)
trichlorobenzenes (total)	5 - 50µg/l	odour, taste (health-based guideline value 20µg/l)
synthetic detergents	-	foaming, taste, odour
Disinfectants and disinfectant by-products		
chlorine	600 - 1000µg/l	taste and odour (health-based guideline value 5µg/l)
chlorophenols		
2-chlorophenol	0.1 - 10µg/l	taste, odour
2,4-dichlorophenol	0.3 - 40µg/l	taste, odour
2,4,6- trichlorophenol	2 - 300µg/l	taste, odour (health-based guideline value 200µg/l)

[a] The levels indicated are not precise numbers. Problems may occur at lower or higher values according to local circumstances. A range of taste and odour threshold concentrations is given for organic constituents.

[b] TCU, time colour unit

[c] NTU, nephelometric turbidity unit

Biological survey

Introduction ∎

Biological surveys can be undertaken to confirm or disprove the presence or absence of potential pollution problems. Small water animals, other water animals and plants respond to long-term changes in water quality and to the overall water quality. Hence their presence or absence can highlight intermittent pollution or pollution which may not be possible to test for in the field. Thorough biological surveys take time and are extensive. In an emergency time is not available so a simple version of a biological assessment can be undertaken, the results of which can be used to support results of other assessment methods.

There are different types of 'pollution' which can affect water life (both plant and animal) which may or may not be harmful to health. They include:

- temperature (different organisms have optimal temperature ranges in which to live);
- turbidity or silt loading (this reduces light penetration and can reduce diversity of the small water animals);
- pH (water life will vary with large pH variations);
- nutrients (high levels of nutrients can cause excessive plant or algae growth and hence eutrophication leading in turn to a variation in water life);
- organic load (high organic loads deplete oxygen levels in the water leading in turn to a variation in water life); and
- toxic pollution (can kill off or modify water life).

The nature of the stream bed and current also affects the populations. Small water animals may be washed away temporarily by flooding.

Use of biological surveys

The usefulness of simple assessments are limited by the range of factors noted above as it is difficult to determine which one has affected the water life. However, where the water is visibly clean (low turbidity) but is in fact polluted with a pollutant which is not visible, such as toxic pollutants from industrial discharges, this procedure could still be useful. It can also indicate high levels of organic pollution such as from fertilizers or sewage discharges. However, **the method is not suitable for detecting low levels of faecal pollution**. Pathogens and parasites may still be present even if 'clean water' is indicated. Microbiological testing will be required to identify their presence.

Small water animals ∎

Method

To collect samples undertake the following procedures:

- If the bed has small stones then stand upstream of the net and kick the stones while moving across a width of the stream for two to five minutes. The net should be placed in the water so that any small water animals which become dislodged will collect in it.

- If the bed has gravel then stir the gravel with the feet and sweep the net in the disturbed area for half a minute.
- If there are stones out of the current then kick and sample with the net and pick up stones by hand, collecting all small water animals within a square metre.
- If the bed is sand or mud then stir the bed with the feet and sweep the net over the area for half a minute.
- In lakes, ponds or large rivers search near the edges.

Identification:
- Pour water into a tray or collecting container and tip the contents of the net into the container.
- Remove the leaves, twigs and rubbish from the tray.
- Identify the types and numbers of small water animals in the tray using the identification pictures on the following pages and record what is found in the table below.
- Return all small water animals to the water.

Note that not all small water animals will be found in all types of waters so absence of one type does not necessarily indicate the water is polluted. Some observations on locations include:
- Optimum living areas for small water animals is a 'riffle' which is a rapid in a stream or river with a stony bottom.
- The deepest parts of very large rivers support few small water animals as the silty bottom is unstable and lacks oxygen.
- Silt or mud bottoms support small water animals such as tube-building worms, borrowing mayflies, blood worms, midges, mussels and clams.
- Sandy beds support very few small water animals.

This should be taken into account when interpreting the findings of the search. A simplified guide to level of pollution can be found in the following section.

Interpretation of results

Identify the numbers and types of small water animals in the table below. Use the right-hand side of the table to identify the rough pollution level. Other assessment methods and the statements below will have to be used to determine the type of pollution.

Small water animals interpretation chart (Modified from: Ellett, 1993, Shelembe, 1995 and Umgeni Valley Project)

Tolerance to pollution	Number found	Types	'✔' indicates that small water animals from this tolerance grouping are present				
			'X' indicates that small water animals from this tolerance grouping are not present				
intolerant			✔	X	X	X	X
slightly tolerant			✔	✔	X	X	X
moderately tolerant			✔	✔	✔	X	X
tolerant			✔	✔	✔	✔	X
		Interpretation ⟶	clean water	some minor pollution	moderate pollution	some major pollution	severe pollution

Other water animals, plants and algae ∎

The number and diversity of other water animals, plants and algae will also vary with the pollution level of the water:

- Invertebrates such as frogs and toads prefer cleaner water and there are few types which can survive in low oxygen conditions. Fish also prefer cleaner water but a few types can survive in polluted water.
- Massive fish death indicates severe depletion of oxygen caused by heavy organic or toxic pollution.
- Fish swimming near the surface, gasping for air at the surface, slowing down in movement or swimming in circles may indicate the presence of toxic substances.
- Birds are not likely to be found where there is no food in the form of freshwater animals.
- A large number of plants and algae (often indicated by a murky green colour) and low numbers of small water animals indicate a high nutrient level in the water. This could be from pollutants such as fertilizers, sewage or industrial wastes.
- Water which looks like pea soup (light green and murky) contains blue-green algae. They secrete foul-tasting substances and the water containing many blue-green algae is unfit for drinking.
- A huge number of dead plants in the water or total absence can indicate depletion of oxygen, heavy sedimentation or the presence of toxic substances.
- The presence of sewage fungus indicates heavy organic pollution (see Figure 4.24).

A selection of the following figures and descriptions have been modified and reproduced with kind permission by E. de Lange from the Manual for Simple Water Quality Analysis, published by the IWT Foundation. Several figures have also been modified from Hynes, 1974 and Choveaux, 1991.

Stonefly • Usually grey-brown but can also be brightly coloured • Most abundant in brooks with gravel or stone bottom but also in standing waters such as lake margins • Very sensitive to oxygen depletion • Crawls very slowly • Very sensitive to pollution • Up to 2.5 cm long	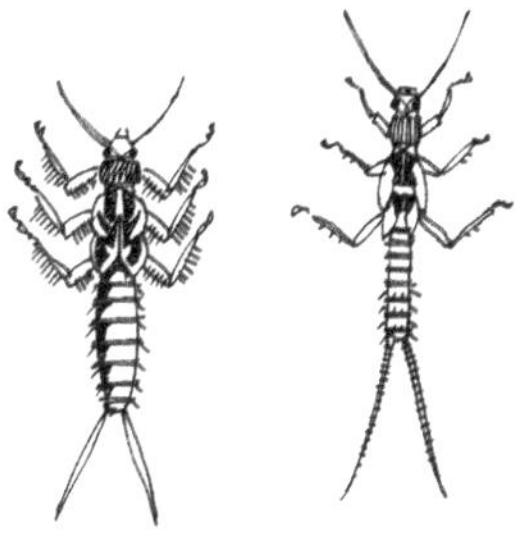	**Dobson-fly larvae** • Hairy tail • Often dull coloured yellow, brown and tan • Most often found in mud of lakes and wetlands but can be found in all kinds of waters • Up to 7.5 cm long	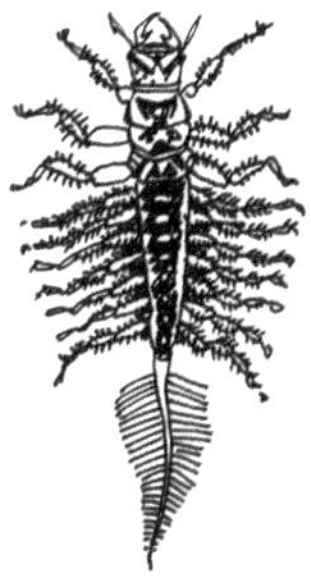
Snipe-fly larvae • Colour varies • Elongated slightly flattened bodies • Only live on the bottom of very clean flowing waters • Up to 1.2 cm long	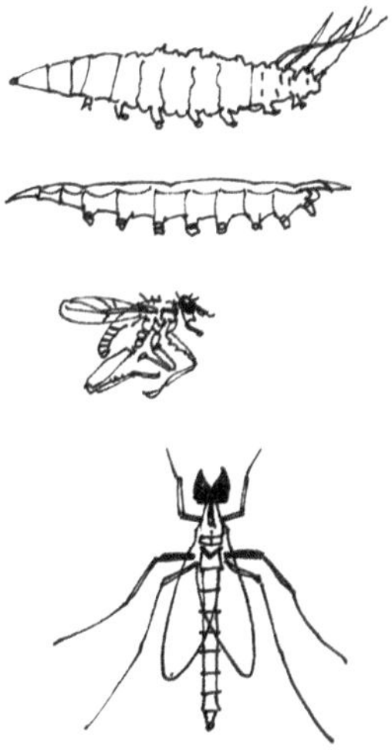	**Water spider** • Found in clear standing waters with lots of plants and oxygen	
Figure 4.20 — Small water animals intolerant to pollution			

Caddis-fly larvae		**Damsel-fly nymphs**	
• Three pairs of legs attached just behind head • Two small hooks from back section • Larvae construct hollow cases from grains of sand, leaves, grass, bark and twigs • Most types live in clear, flowing waters but some in standing waters • Larvae up to 2.5 cm long		• Long slender bodies with four wings • Ball shaped eyes • Three paddle like tails • They swim and run with a wriggling motion • Colour is green or brown to black • Live mainly among water plants • They prefer slow-moving or standing waters • They tolerate a little pollution • Up to 5 cm long	
May-fly nymphs		**Dragon-fly nymphs**	
• Similar to stone-fly but usually have three tails and a hook at the end of their legs • Colour varies from green to brown or grey but usually black • Swim by beating abdomen up and down • Occur in all types of freshwater but mostly in clear and flowing waters • Up to 2.5 cm long		• Ball shaped eyes • Vary in shape but have spider like bodies • Gills look like a small pyramid • Colour brown to black but often green • They are usually slow moving • Live in mud bottoms or among water plants. They prefer slow-moving or standing waters • Up to 5 cm long	
Beetle larva and adults		**Crane-fly larvae**	
• Adults are mostly found in shallow areas on plants or debris • Can be found in standing / flowing waters • Adult beetles are more tolerant of pollution than larvae • Whirly-gig beetles which swim on the surface in groups in a circular motion live in fairly nutrient rich water without further pollution		• Brownish-green to transparent or whitish • Pointed or rounded at the end and have disc like spiracles at the other • Bottom of shallow standing or flowing waters • Up to 7.5 cm long	

Figure 4.21 — Small water animals slightly tolerant to pollution (not to scale)

Gammarus / scuds • Fresh water shrimp • Grey, brown or creamy white colour • Flattened body • Moves on its side, flexing entire body • Hides in plants or under debris • Common in standing and flowing waters • Most are small but can reach 1.5 cm	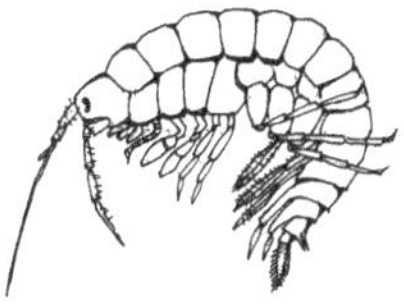	**Mussels** • Two halves of shells • Usually dark in colour • Found partially covered in sand, gravel or mud bottoms • Slight preference for flowing waters • Up to 20 cm in diameter	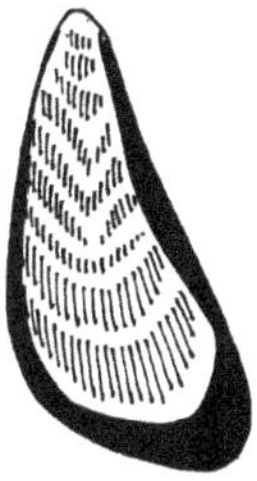
Flat worms • Standing and flowing waters • Found beneath rocks, logs or dead leaves • Sensitive to organic pollution but like moderate nutrient pollution • 0.5 to 4 cm when stretched	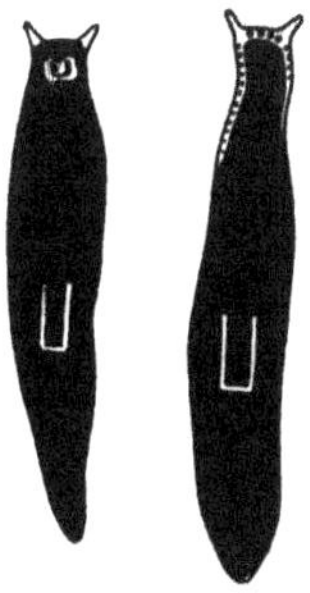	**Cray-fish** • Resemble tiny lobsters • Brown, green, reddish or black • Hide in stream banks or under rocks and logs • Found in standing or flowing waters • Rarely seen by day • Length up to 15 cm	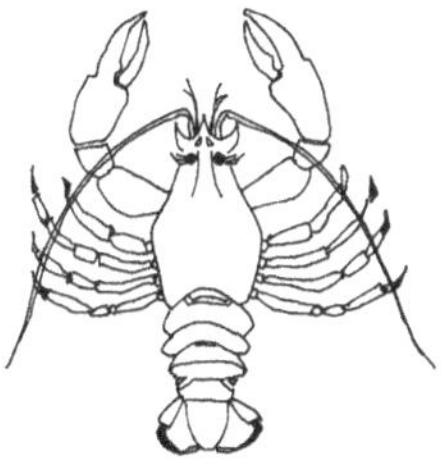
Water boatmen • Long flattened hind legs similar to paddles • Dark grey, brown and black • Shallow, slow moving sections of streams, rivers, ponds and lakes	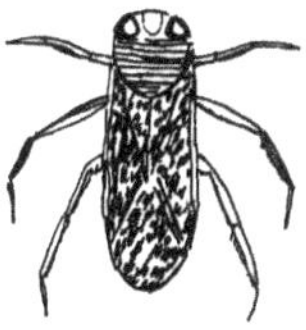		

Figure 4.21 (cont.) — Small water animals slightly tolerant to pollution (not to scale)

Blackfly larvae

- Small and worm like

- When out of water fold themselves in half

- Green and brown to grey but usually black

- They live on solid substrate often piled up in the current of brooks and rivers or in overflows of ponds

- Found attached to stones and plants at margins of streams

- Up to 0.8 cm long

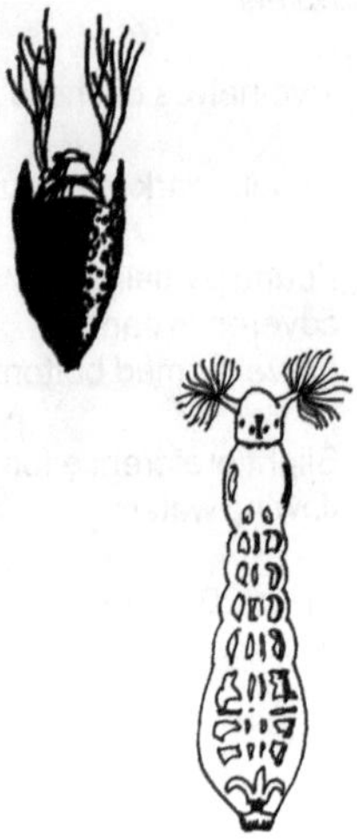

Asellus / water louse / snow bug

- Flattened body

- Grey or brown colour

- Crawls

- Seven pairs of legs

- Found hidden under rocks, plants and debris

- Prefer standing or slow moving waters

- Less than 2.5 cm long

Clams

- Two halves of shells

- Light coloured

- Found partially covered in sand, gravel or mud bottoms

- Slight preference for flowing waters

- Less than 1 cm diameter

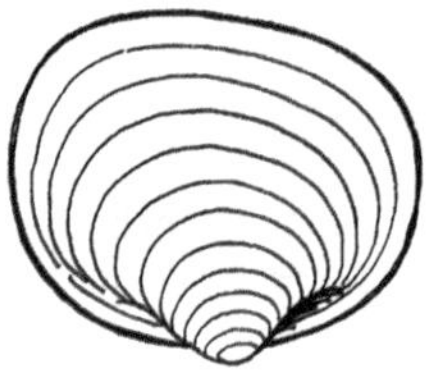

Midge larvae

- Gold or brown to green but tend to be black

- Blood worm (midge larvae) bright red in colour and swims by looping and un-looping

- Occur in almost all types of water

- Live in the silt bottom, on solid substrates or on water plants

- Wiggle intensely when out of the water

- Up to 1.5 cm long

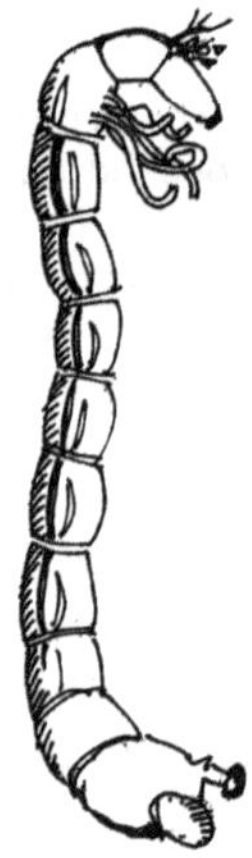

Snails

- Found in waters generally less than 2 m deep

- Can be found in standing or flowing waters

Figure 4.22 — Small water animals moderately tolerant to pollution

Aquatic worms

- Reddish, brown, grey or blood-red

- Usually skin of worms is transparent

- Many have two bunches of hair on their rings

- Live on and in the bottom both in standing and flowing waters

- Few mm to 30 cm

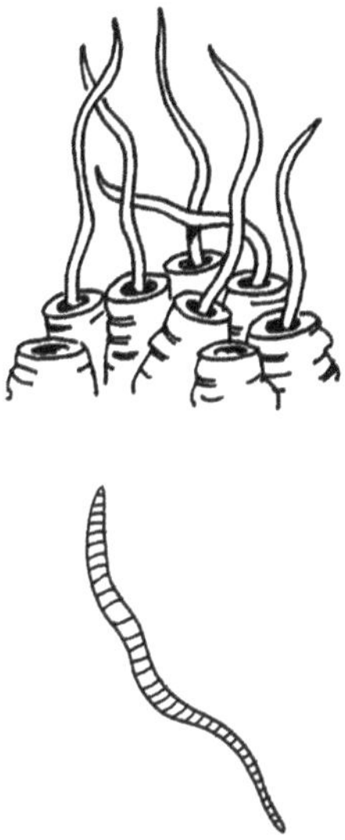

Leeches

- Colour can be green, black, brown or grey

- White, yellow, blue or red spots can occur

- Look like worms but do not have hair

- Two suction discs on belly side

- Prefer shallow waters rich in nutrients

- Usually found on underside of rocks and stones

- Up to 13cm long

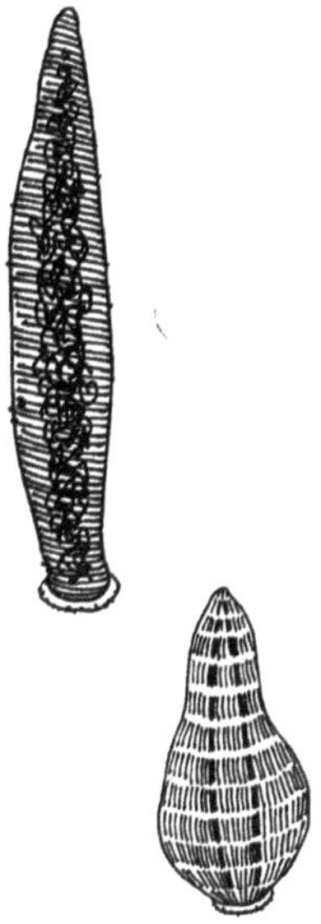

Mosquito larvae and pupae

- Usually found suspended just below the water surface

- Larvae are segmented and worm like with a tufted tail, round head and brush like jaws

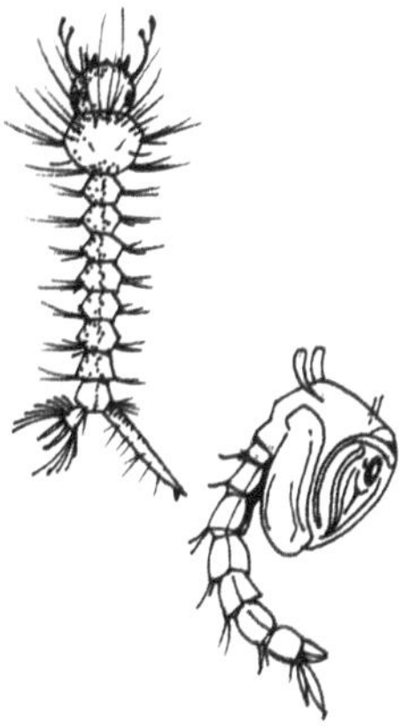

Rat-tailed maggot

- Grey with fat wrinkled body and long breathing tube

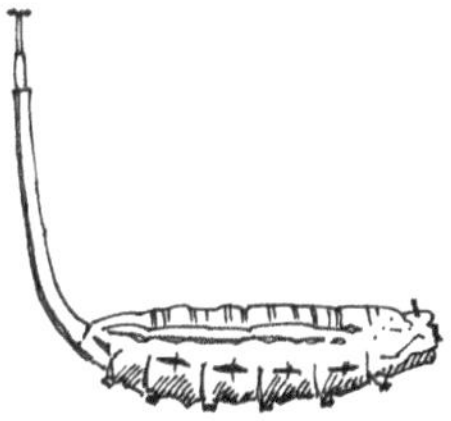

Figure 4.23 — Small water animals tolerant to pollution

Sewage fungus

- Slimy growth

- Ragged white, yellow, pink or brown masses formed on solid objects in the water and possibly also formed as a carpet over mud.

Other water animals

- Frogs, tadpoles

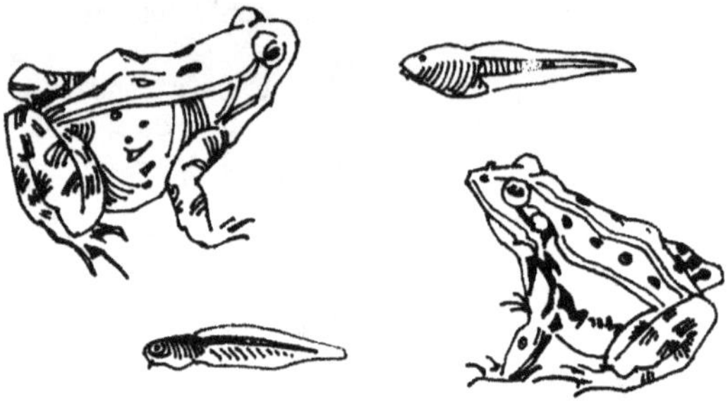

- Fish

- Birds

- Water terrapin

Figure 4.24 — Other biological indicators of pollution (not to scale)

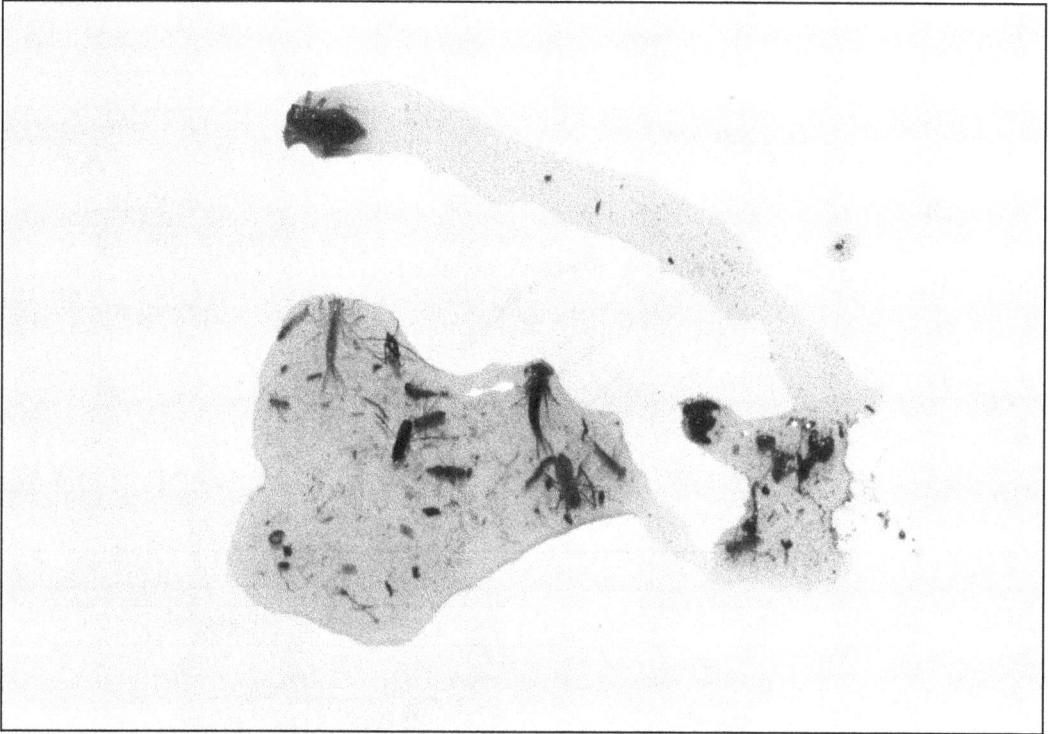

S. House

Small water animals from a spring supplying a refugee camp in Eastern Zaire

---

Key references:

- Choveaux, 1991
- Clegg, 1986
- de Lange, 1994
- Ellett, 1993
- Hynes, 1974
- Shelembe, 1995
- Umgeni Valley Project, undated
- United States Environmental Protection Agency, 1991

Water treatment: Treatment processes and health and safety

Features of treatment processes ∎

The tables, pp214–23 describe Pre-treatment, Main treatment and Advanced treatment processes. Note that equipment and structures for all of the processes will require structural and mechanical maintenance in addition to the items mentioned in the tables.

Pre-treatment

These processes are used mainly to reduce solids and turbidity, reduce of specific problems (e.g. iron or manganese) and to enhance the main processes.

Screening

Description and comments	Physical barrier to prevent inflow of large solids. Algae can be strained using a microstrainer.
Treatment restrictions and design criteria	· Coarse bar screens have 75-100mm centres · Fine screens holes are approximately 5 - 20mm · Flow-through screens should be < 0.7m/s to prevent soft material being forced through the holes (Hofkes, 1983, p146) · Micro-strainers 23 - 35 microns (Twort et al., 1994, pp229–30) · Screen slot sizes for borehole casings of 0.054-6.7mm (Davis and Lambert, 1995, p 274) · Gabion baskets filled with stones with inlet in the centre
Action on water	Removes large floating particles
Key O&M requirements	· Cleaning of screen

Infiltration (galleries or wells)

Description and comments	Water abstracted through natural material (such as a river bed or bank) or imported graded media. Infiltration gallery is a pipe surrounded by gravel leading to a bankside well Infiltration trench / well is a trench sometimes filled with gravel constructed into the bank and leading to a bankside well. Sometimes the natural bank material is used.
Treatment restrictions and design criteria	**Infiltration gallery** · Round 12-25mm stones should be used around the pipes and a graded filter built out from this first layer using sand and gravel · Filter should be 30-40cm from the pipe's outside diameter (WRC / WHO, 1989) **Infiltration trench and infiltration well** · Soils with a high clay content are not suitable for infiltration · Water with high silt loadings can reduce infiltration capacity dramatically
Action on water	· Removes a proportion of the turbidity · Protects inlet from gross solids · Uses screening, filtration and bacteriological processes
Key O&M requirements	· Occasional unblocking of large sediments from inlet of the filter section to improve filtration rates · Replacement of scoured materials · Difficult to maintain as filter is submerged

4

Roughing filtration

Description and comments	Usually horizontal flow or upflow in action. Can use one size of media or multiple sizes.
Treatment restrictions and design criteria	· Roughing filtration is most efficient at 20 to 150 NTU · Can be used for turbidities up to 100 NTU (example in Davis and Lambert, 1995, p 327) · Can remove between 40-80% of turbidity depending on depth and size of media and the characteristics of the water

<table>
<tr><td></td><td></td><td>flow rate</td><td></td></tr>
<tr><td></td><td>· Horizontal RF (> 150mg/l s.solids)</td><td>0.5 - 0.75m/h</td><td></td></tr>
<tr><td></td><td>· Horizontal RF (< 150mg/l s.solids)</td><td>0.75 - 1.0m/h</td><td></td></tr>
<tr><td></td><td>· Downflow RF</td><td>0.3 - 1.2m/h</td><td></td></tr>
<tr><td></td><td>· Upflow RF</td><td>0.5 - 1.0m/h</td><td>(Wegelin in Davis and Lambert, 1995)</td></tr>
</table>

	· Size ratio of media roughly 2:1 from each section ranging from 30mm at inlet (course) to 4mm at outlet (fine) (for more details see WRC/WHO, 1989 and Davis and Lambert, 1995) · Length of bed usually 9-12m (horizontal) · Depth of media 0.85-1.25m (upflow) (Galvis et al., 1993)
Action on water	· Reduces the turbidity by screening, filtration and sedimentation · Also removes some bacteria and other pathogens associated with turbidity
Key O&M requirements	· Backwashing once or twice a month in the wet season and two or three times a month in the dry season (upflow) · Physical cleaning of media once every several years (upflow) · Regulation of flow

Storage / sedimentation

Description and comments	· Particles fall by gravity to the bottom of the tank · The smaller the particles the longer the required retention time · Colloidal turbidity will not sediment out within acceptable time periods using this method · Sedimentation characteristics of different waters will vary. As a guide to particle sedimentation times, gravel (10mm); fine sand (0.1mm); bacteria (0.001mm) and colloidal particles (0.0001mm) will settle 30cm in approximately 0.3s, 38s, 55hr and 230 days respectively (Schulz and Okun, 1984, p32)
Treatment restrictions and design criteria	**Storage** · Raw storage is usually limited from a few hours to a maximum of one day in an emergency. · A minimum of one day's supply of treated water should be stored if possible **Sedimentation** · Sedimentation retention time will depend on the characteristics of the water. A field test can estimate the characteristics. If 1 hour retention time (maximum) is needed to reduce turbidity to acceptable level, then the water will not require additional pre-treatment · Rectangular sedimentation tanks need a retention time of 0.5-3 hours · Batch-operated sedimentation tanks need a retention time minimum of 1 hour · Care is required to prevent short-circuiting and disturbing the sediments at the bottom of the tank
Action on water	· Suspended particles sediment out · Also removes some bacteria, viruses, cysts and ova · Some reduction in bacteria can also occur from solar radiation if uncovered tanks are used · Algae growth and wind-blown contamination can occur if uncovered tanks are used · Natural bacterial die off can occur in storage tanks, especially with long retention times
Key O&M requirements	· Desludging and occasional cleaning of tank · Flow regulation

Assisted sedimentation (coagulation, flocculation and sedimentation

Description and comments	A chemical coagulant is added to the water and rapidly mixed. The water is then stirred slowly until flocs are formed. The flocs are then allowed to sediment.

Treatment restrictions and design criteria

Manufactured coagulants	pH boundaries (Twort, 1994)	Dosage ranges
· aluminum sulphate(s) $Al_2(SO_4)_3 \cdot xH_2O$ (x= 14 to 21)	5.5 - 7.5	10 - 100mg/l as commercial product
· ferric chloride (l) $FeCl_3$	4 - 9	5 - 25mg/l as iron
· ferric sulphate (l) $Fe_2(SO_4)_3$	4 - 9	5 - 25mg/l as iron
· PAC (polyaluminium chloride) (l)	6 - 9	

<u>Natural coagulants</u> (Jahn, 1981)
Natural / traditional coagulants include: plant seeds, vegetables, tree bark, burnt coconut shells and many others. The organic matter caused by natural coagulants must be carefully removed before disinfection.

One of the most effective of the natural coagulants is *Moringa Oleifera*. The white seed is crushed and mixed in the water in the same manner as a manufactured coagulant. It can be used as a primary coagulant on its own or as a coagulant aid at a lower dosage primary coagulant. The dosage range is 50-250mg/l and it works best at a pH <7.

A 50mg/l dose of *Moringa Oleifera* requires approximately 1 crushed seed per 4l.
Hence, a 150 mg/l dose would require 3 crushed seeds per 4l.
One tree has approximately 5000 seeds and an average pod has 13 to 14 seeds

Another example of a natural coagulant is broad beans. Here the required dosage range is 400-500mg/l: 2.5 beans for every 4l.

For further and more detailed information on natural coagulants refer to Jahn (1981)

Alkalinity neutralization:
· 1 mg/l alum. sulphate reacts with 0.5mg/l alkalinity as $CaCO_3$ (Semat Technical (UK) Ltd)

· Hydraulic flocculators, 0.1 - 0.3 m / sec with retention time of at least 30 min (Davis and Lambert, 1995, p274)

Action on water	· Removes turbidity including some bacteria, viruses, cysts and ova · The processes of coagulation and focculation include charge neutralization, colloid entrapment (sweep floc), double-layer compression and bridging · The process may also remove some chemical contaminants such as fluoride (see fluoride removal p223)
Key O&M requirements	· Flow regulation · Desludging and occasional cleaning of the tank · Disposal of sludges · Regular jar tests to determine the chemical requirements · Dosing of chemicals · Chemical storage · Health and safety precautions required · Water quality / process monitoring

pH adjustment

Description and comments	pH or acidity / alkalinity modified by adding chemicals

Treatment restrictions and design criteria

To raise the pH
1.0mg/l alkalinity as $CaCO_3$ is produced by:
· 0.66mg/l 85% quicklime (CaO)
· 0.78mg/l 95% hydrated lime (Ca(OH)$_3$)
· 1.08mg/l soda ash (Na$_2$CO$_3$)   (Semat Technical (UK) Ltd.)

· Soda ash is more expensive and can 'cake' in storage but does not clog dosing lines
· Lime is relatively insoluble in water and clogs dosing lines
· Quicklime needs to be hydrated (slaked) with water before use
· Hydrated lime does not need hydrating before use and has fewer impurities than quicklime and hence clogs less

To reduce the pH
Acids such as sulphuric can be used to reduce the pH but this is not advisable if it can be avoided because of the hazardous nature of the chemicals

Action on water	· Modifies the pH and acidity / alkalinity.
Key O&M requirements	· Flow regulation · Desludging and occasional cleaning of the tank · Disposal of sludges · Regular jar tests to determine the chemical requirements · Dosing of chemicals · Chemical storage · Health and safety precautions required · Water quality / process monitoring

Pre-chlorination

Description and comments	Water is chlorinated prior to assisted sedimentation or rapid filtration (but *not* prior to slow sand filtration).
Treatment restrictions and design criteria	· If algae is a problem or *E.coli* are > 1000 / 100ml, pre-chlorination can be considered · For algae removal it is usual to pre-chlorinate the supply to slightly above breakpoint (i.e. to leave a very small free residual) if this does not involve an exceptionally high dosage. Contact time is not as important for pre-chlorination as it is for post-chlorination for disinfection, as the chlorine reaction required occurs during the first few minutes. (Degremont, 1979, p 615) · Pre-chlorination has been reduced in some parts of the world due to an increased awareness of the carcinogenic properties of the chlorinated organic by products such as trihalomethanes (THMs). This risk is associated with long term use
Action on water	· Kills or stuns algae and bacteria which improves the effectiveness of the assisted sedimentation or filtration processes · Oxidizes iron and manganese, causing their precipitation · Combines with ammonia compounds
Key O&M requirements	· Flow regulation · Dosing of chemicals · Chemical storage · Health and safety precautions required · Water quality / process monitoring

Aeration

Description and comments	· Water is trickled over media or sprayed into the air to ensure contact with air / oxygen · Resulting solids then need to be sedimented or filtrated out of the solution
Treatment restrictions and design criteria	· For iron removal the pH should be > 7.0. Aeration does not remove complexed iron · When aerating to remove aggressivity in a water with 100mg/l alkalinity, the pH needs to be about 8.6 · Spray systems remove 60-70% excess CO_2 · A cascade 3m high at 10-30m³/m²/h can remove up to 70% CO_2 · A percolating filter at 100-400m³/m²/h can remove up to 80% CO_2 (WRC / WHO, 1989)
Action on water	· Reduce bad tastes and smells · Precipitate (non-complexed) iron or manganese from solution · Reduce aggressivity of the water (CO_2) and raise the pH · Increases the dissolved oxygen of the water
Key O&M requirements	· Cleaning of media · Operation and & maintenance of pumps used to raise water to a suitable height · Sedimentation or filtration O&M as noted in the tables, pp215–8

Main treatment

To reduce bacteriological contaminants and / or further reduce turbidity

Slow sand filtration

Description and comments	Water is passed slowly through a sand bed in a downflow mode.
Treatment restrictions and design criteria	· Inlet turbidity should be limited to 20 NTU (50 absolute max.) wherever possible. Up to 200 NTU can be treated but only for a few days · Hydraulic loading 0.1-0.3m³/m²/h (usual operation is between 0.1 and 0.2) · Sand effective size 0.15-0.35 mm · Sand uniformity coefficient 1.5-3.0 · Depth of sand 0.6-0.9m on top of coarse gravel (total 1.0-1.3 m) · Needs to be covered where freezing can be severe, or in exposed sites. · The surface of the filter can also be covered with a fabric which simplifies the cleaning procedure

Action on water	· Turbidity is reduced by straining, sedimentation and adsorption
	· Microbiological pollution is reduced by bacterial and biochemical action in the *schmutzdecke*
	· Bacteria, protozoan cysts and viruses are removed
	· It also removes some iron, manganese, heavy metals, colour and organic matter
	· A filter working at 0.1-0.2m/h, with a sand depth of > 0.5m and at a temperature of > 5ºC can remove the following:
	  · entero-bacteria 90-99.9%
	  · protozoan cysts 99-99.99%
	  · turbidity to < 1 NTU if the influent is < 10 NTU
	  · colour 30-90% (Galvis et al., 1993, p16)
	· Iron in the influent should be less than 2 mg/l to prevent frequent blocking
	· Reduction of process efficiency occurs at low temperatures, at low nutrient levels (carbon, nitrogen and sulphates) and at low levels of dissolved oxygen
	· Galvis, 1993, p17 notes that 'Huisman reports that *E.Coli* removal will be reduced from a normally achieved 99% at 20ºC to 20% at 2ºC'. Removal efficiency can be improved by reducing the filtration rate

Key O&M requirements	· Removal of 1-3cm of the top sand layer (once every one or two months) · Cleaning and stockpiling of removed sand · When a minimum depth of 0.6m is remaining the cleaned and stockpiled sand removed earlier should be replaced on top of the bed · Maintenance of the water levels and flow rates · Head-loss monitoring and flow control

Rapid sand filtration

Description and comments	Water is passed through a sand bed at a faster rate than for slow sand filtration. Layers of activated carbon or calcareous material can replace some or all of the sand
Treatment restrictions and design criteria	· Inlet turbidity usually < 20 NTU · Hydraulic loading 3-12m³/m²/h (usually 6, Twort, 1994) · Sand effective size 0. 5-1.5mm · Sand uniformity coefficient 1.3 - 1.8 · Sand bed thickness: 0.45-0.9m · Backwash frequency controlled by head loss, filtrate quality or duration of run
Action on water	· Straining, sedimentation, adsorption, coagulation in the bed and limited biological action · Removes 50-90% of turbidity without assisted sedimentation and 90-99% of turbidity with assisted sedimentation
Key O&M requirements	· Backwashing of media with water and sometimes air scour · Head-loss monitoring and flow control

G.R. Campbell

Water treatment

Above: Sand cleaning for slow sand filter, Dumdumia Refugee Camp, Bangladesh

Below: Mobile water treatment units, Rwanda

P. A. Larcher

S. House

Water treatment

Above: Assisted sedimentation tank, Rwenena Camp,
Eastern Zaire

Right: Jar test for assisted sedimentation, Eastern Zaire

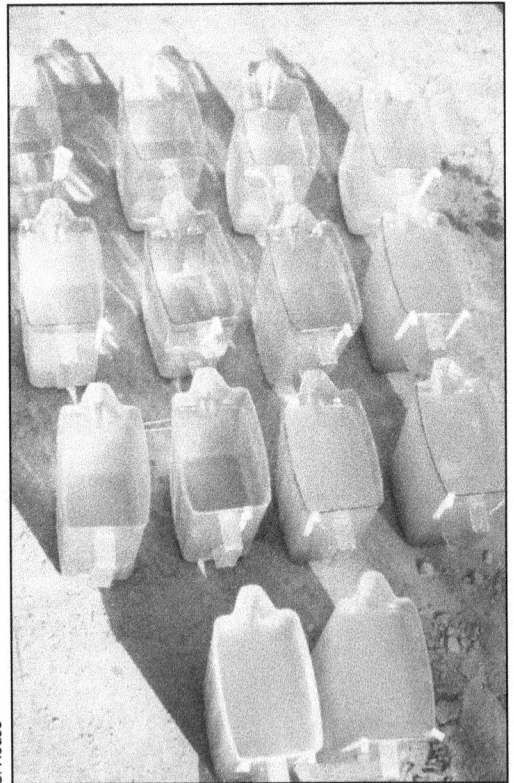

S. House

Disinfection

Description and comments	The most common disinfectant, chlorine, is added to the treated water at a known dosage. Other disinfectants include iodine and UV light

Treatment restrictions and design criteria	**Chlorination**
	· t = contact time (minutes); C = free chlorine residual concentration at the end of the contact time (mg/l)
	· Recommended dosage: 0.5 mg/l after 30 mins at pH 8.0 i.e. Ct = 15mg.min/l (at 20 °C) (WHO, 1993)
	· For potable water 't' should be between 20 and 60 mins (Twort et al., 1994)
	· References on the effects of temperature vary:
	  · 'Generally about 50% more free available chlorine would be required for effective disinfection at < 5°C compared with 10 °C' (Sterritt and Lester, 1988, p264)
	  · To achieve a 99.9% inactivation of *Giardia Lambila* the Ct values for chlorine need to be approximately doubled for each drop of 10°C (United States Environmental Protection Agency, 1990, p59), e.g. if the temperature drops by 10°C then either the free residual concentration should be doubled while keeping the same contact time or the contact time should be doubled to achieve the same free residual.
	· Effects of pH:
	  · At high pHs the rate of disinfection decreases so a longer contact time is required (WRC / WHO, 1989) or a higher dosage. 'Typically, concentrations of free available chlorine five to ten times higher than those at pH 7 would be required to achieve the same kill as at pH 8.5' (Sterritt and Lester, 1988, p264)
	· If < 1 NTU, pH < 8, t = 30min and a free residual of 0.5mg/l then the majority of viruses are killed
	· Typical doses of chlorine 0.5-2.0mg/l of free chlorine
	· Surface waters can require a high chlorine dose of 6-8mg/l
	· Quite large doses of chlorine (> 2.0mg/l) cannot be tasted (Twort et al., 1994)
	· Tastes are principally caused by chlorine reacting with other compounds in water

Action on water	· Kills bacteria and most viruses but not cysts at standard doses · Oxidizes iron and manganese causing them to precipitate. · Combines with ammonia compounds · Combines with organic matter
Key O&M requirements	· Flow regulation · Regular jar tests to determine the chemical requirements · Dosing of chemicals · Chemical storage · Health and safety precautions required · Water quality / process monitoring

Advanced treatment

Used to reduce chemical pollutants or further reduce pathogens.

Diatomaceous earth coated filters

Description and comments	Stainless steel wire-wound candles are enclosed in a cylindrical filter chamber Raw water is injected with diatomaceous earth or cellulose powder which forms a thin coating on each candle Water is then filtered through the candle
Treatment restrictions and design criteria	
Action on water	Filtration and adsorption
Key O&M requirements	Re-coating with diatomaceous earth or replacement of filter candles

Activated carbon

Description and comments	Filtration through a media of activated carbon In an emergency situation this would probably only be used with mobile units
Treatment restrictions and design criteria	· Filters 6-12m³/m²/h · Sand effective size 0.6-1.3mm (Twort et al., 1994, p106) · Activated carbon can be made from wood, coal, coconut shells or peat. It is first carbonized by heating and then 'activated' by heating to a high temperature while introducing oxygen in the form of a stream of air or steam. It is then ground into a granular form · Empty bed contact time (EBCT) 5 to 30 minutes · The breakthrough time depends on what is being adsorbed (pesticides 6-24 months, THMs 6-12 months, taste and odour 2-3 years with a EBCT of approximately 10 minutes). (Twort et al., 1994)
Action on water	· Filtration occurs as with any other media, but the activated carbon also removes other contaminants by adsorption · Removes organic compounds and other trace elements
Key O&M requirements	· As the rapid sand filter above · Regeneration when the activated carbon is spent

Reverse osmosis

Description and comments	· In an emergency a reverse osmosis unit will probably be included in a mobile unit · When osmosis occurs water molecules pass through a semi-permeable membrane from a weaker solution to a solution with a higher number of contaminants until equilibrium is achieved. With reverse osmosis, pressure is applied to the stronger solution so that the water passes from the stronger to the weaker solution, leaving a concentrated brine.
Treatment restrictions and design criteria	· Can treat a TDS of 1000-5000mg/l using standard membranes and > 5000 mg/l with high rejection membranes. · Membranes need cleaning due to fouling. Fouling is caused by suspended solids, organics, silica, iron, manganese, and some salts (e.g. carbonates and sulphates of calcium). Biological action and chemical attack (from pH and chlorine) can also affect the performance of the membrane. · Water requires pre-treatment · Concentrates produced are highly contaminated · To desalt sea water a flow of 0.5-2.5m³/m².d is needed · The membranes tend to be made out of cellulose acetate or a polyamide base · Removal levels: sea water (35%); brackish water (90%); fluoride (95-99%) · Also removes bacteria and viruses
Action on water	· Separation process
Key O&M requirements	· Disposal of high-concentration waste products · Defouling with chemicals or replacing the cartridge · Flow control

4

Fluoride removal

Description and comments	Three main methods: · Chemical precipitation · Adsorption · Membrane processes
Treatment restrictions and design criteria	**Chemical precipitation** (Twort et al., 1994, p293) · Hydrated lime precipitates fluoride as calcium fluoride at an optimum pH of 12 · Aluminium sulphate coagulation reduces fluoride by 10-60% but the pH needs to be in the optimum range for the coagulation process. Dosages quoted include 200-300mg/l (Kawamura, 1991, p532) and 150-1000 mg/l (Degremont, 1979, p639) · The 'Nalgoda' process uses lime and aluminium sulphate. It produces good removal rates but uses high doses. Dosages in Dahi, et al., 1996 were between 700-900mg/l of aluminium sulphate and 75-350mg/l of lime (CaO used in this example). These dosages reduced 12mg/l of fluoride to 3.0-1.5mg/l respectively. **Adsorption** · Activated alumina: optimum pH 5.5-6; contact bed depth 1.0-1.5m; grain size 0.3-0.6mm; EBCT = 5 mins; breakthrough = 3-5 days. To regenerate the media requires backwashing with water and two stage regeneration with caustic soda and sulphuric acid. The process can reduce the fluoride levels to < 1.0 mg/l. Kawamura (1991) also identifies a process where 3mg/l of fluoride is reduced to 0.5mg/l with a flow rate of 12.5-17.5m/h at a pH of 5.5. · Bone char can also be used as an adsorption media **Membrane process (reverse osmosis)** · See reverse osmosis table, p222 The main problem of the processes above is the disposal of the fluoride concentrates.
Action on water	Varies with the process. See the relevant table.
Key O&M requirements	Varies with the process. See the relevant table.

Health and safety ∎

General health and safety points:

- All treatment units must be secured in position. Bladder tanks can roll down slopes so should be retained using a bund if this is a risk.
- All steps leading up to the treatment units should be provided with handrails.
- All treatment platforms should have handrailing on three sides.
- Chemicals should be handled with care at all times (see the tables below). Chemicals should be secured in a locked room and *on no account* should be stored in the same room as a guard uses to sleep.

Calcium Hypochlorite (synonyms: HTH, Bleaching powder, chlorinted lime)

Appearance	White powder
Hazard classes	· Harmful · Irritant · Oxidizing · Restricted for transportation: IMDG (hazard class): 5.1; Pkg group III; IATA: 2208
Other known hazards	· Produces toxic chlorine gas in contact with acids · Powerful oxidizing agent · Can cause fires if in contact with combustible material. In case of fire use water to extinguish · May evolve toxic fumes of hydrogen chloride in fire · Can react vigorously or explosively with ammonium chloride, carbon, amines, ammonia and sulphur
Health hazards	· Irritating to skin, eyes and respiratory system · Harmful if swallowed
Toxicological information	· LD50 oral, rat 850mg/kg
First aid measures	**Eyes:** Rinse thoroughly with water for at least 15 minutes **Lungs:** Move to fresh air **Skin:** Take off contaminated clothing immediately and cover affected area with plenty of water for at least 15 minutes. Wash contaminated clothing before re-use **Mouth:** If swallowed wash out mouth with water provided the person is conscious and give plenty of water to drink In all severe cases or if in doubt obtain medical advice.
Accidental release measures	· Evacuate area · Wear appropriate protective clothing including full-face chlorine respirator · Shut off all sources of ignition · Avoid raising dust · If local regulations permit mop up with plenty of water and run to waste, diluting greatly with running water. · Ventilate area · Wash site of spillage thoroughly with detergent and water · Dry off area · Large spillages liquids should be contained with moist sand or earth
Disposal	· Dispose of through disposal companies if available. · If not bury material away from water.
Storage, handling and personal protection	· Store in tightly closed containers · Care must be taken when opening containers as pressure may have developed · Store in a cool, dry place away from acids and strong reducing agents · Avoid inhalation of dust and eye, skin and clothing contact · Use rubber or plastic gloves for handling · Use a dust respirator and goggles especially when in an enclosed space · Use a plastic apron, sleeves and boots if handling large quantities · Wash thoroughly after handling

Hydrated lime (Ca(OH)$_3$, slaked lime)

Appearance	White powder
Hazard classes	· Corrosive · Not restricted for transportation: IMDG (hazard class): NR; IATA: NR
Other known hazards	· Emits toxic fumes under fire conditions · Use dry chemical powder to extinguish fires · Will burn skin · Incompatible with strong oxidizing agents and absorbs carbon dioxide from the air
Health hazards	· Harmful if swallowed, inhaled or absorbed through the skin · Corrosive and causes burns
Toxicological information	LD50 oral, rat 7340mg/kg
First aid measures	**Eyes:** Rinse immediately with plenty of water for at least 15 minutes **Lungs:** Move to fresh air **Skin:** Take off contaminated clothing immediately and cover affected area with plenty of water for at least 15 minutes. Wash contaminated clothing before re-use. **Mouth:** If swallowed wash out mouth with water provided person is conscious and give plenty of water to drink In all severe cases or if in doubt seek medical advice.
Accidental release measures	· Evacuate area · Wear appropriate clothing including self-contained breathing apparatus, rubber boots and heavy rubber gloves · Absorb with moist sand or inert absorbent · Sweep up and place in a container · Ventilate area · Wash the spill area with water and detergent after the material has been removed · Dry off area
Disposal	· Dispose of through disposal companies if available · If not bury material away from water sources
Storage, handling and personal protection	· Store in tightly closed containers · Store in a cool, dry place away from incompatibilities · Avoid inhalation of dust and eye, skin and clothing contact · Use rubber or plastic gloves for handling · Use a dust respirator and goggles especially when in an enclosed space · Use a plastic apron, sleeves and boots if handling large quantities · Wash thoroughly after handling

Soda ash (Na$_2$CO$_3$)

Appearance	White granular powder
Hazard classes	· Harmful · Irritant · Not restricted for transportation: IMDG hazard class: NR; IATA: NR
Other known hazards	· Non-combustible. Use extinguishing media appropriate to surrounding conditions if in a fire. · Emits toxic fumes of carbon monoxide and carbon dioxide under fire conditions. · Incompatible with strong acids and aluminium. Material is moisture-sensitive. · Reacts vigorously with fluorine.
Health hazards	· Harmful if inhaled, in contact with skin and if swallowed. · Causes severe irritation.
Toxicological information	LD50 oral, rat 4090mg/kg
First aid measures	**Eyes:** Rinse immediately with plenty of water for at least 15 minutes. **Lungs:** Move to fresh air. **Skin:** Take off contaminated clothing immediately and cover affected area with plenty of water for at least 15 minutes. Wash contaminated clothing before re-use. **Mouth:** If swallowed wash out mouth with water provided person is conscious and give plenty of water to drink. In all severe cases or if in doubt seek medical advice.
Accidental release measures	· Evacuate area. · Wear appropriate clothing including self-contained breathing apparatus, rubber boots and heavy rubber gloves. · Avoid raising dust. · Sweep up and place in a container or bag. · Ventilate area. · Wash the spill area with water and detergent after the material has been removed. · Dry off area.
Disposal	· Dispose of through disposal companies if available. · If not bury material away from water sources.
Storage, handling and personal protection	· Store in tightly closed containers. · Store in a cool, dry place away from incompatibilities. · Avoid inhalation of dust and eye, skin and clothing contact. · Use rubber or plastic gloves for handling. · Use a dust respirator and goggles especially when in an enclosed space. · Use a plastic apron, sleeves and boots if handling large quantities. · Wash thoroughly after handling.

Quicklime (CaO, Calcium Oxide)

Appearance	Off-white powder
Hazard classes	· Corrosive · Restricted for transportation: IMDG hazard class: NR (8); IATA: 1910; Packaging group III
Other known hazards	· Will burn skin · Non-combustible. Use extinguishing media appropriate to surrounding conditions if in a fire. · Reacts with fluorine to evolve heat and light. · Can react exothermically with limited amounts of water and the heat liberated may cause ignition of combustible materials. · Incompatible with acids and moisture and absorbs carbon dioxide from the air.
Health hazards	Harmful if swallowed, inhaled or absorbed through the skin. Corrosive and causes burns
Toxicological information	Not available
First aid measures	In cases of exposure *obtain medical attention immediately* **Eyes:** Rinse immediately with plenty of water for at least 15 minutes and seek medical advice. Apply cool packs to eyes while transporting patient to a medical facility. **Lungs:** Move to fresh air. **Skin:** Wipe off excess material with a dry cloth. Wash remaining material off with copious amounts of water for at least 15 minutes. Remove clothing and shoes prior to showering. Wash contaminated clothes before re-use. **Mouth:** If swallowed wash out mouth with water provided person is conscious and give plenty of water to drink. *Do not induce vomiting.*
Accidental release measures	· Evacuate area. · Shut off all sources of ignition. · Wear appropriate clothing including self-contained breathing apparatus, rubber boots and heavy rubber gloves. · Avoid raising dust. · Sweep up and place in a container or bag. · Ventilate area. · Wash the spill area with water and detergent after the material has been removed. · Dry off area.
Disposal	· Dispose of through disposal companies if available. · If not bury material away from water sources.
Storage, handling and personal protection	· Store in tightly closed containers. · Store in a cool dry place away from incompatibilities. · Wear a respirator, chemical-resistant gloves, safety goggles and other protective clothing. · Do not breathe in the dust or get it in the eyes, on the skin or on clothing. · Avoid prolonged or repeated exposure. · Wash thoroughly after handling.

Aluminium sulphate

Appearance	White crystals or a solid block which breaks down into a white powder
Hazard classes	· Harmful · Not restricted for transportation: IMDG hazard class: NR; IATA: NR
Other known hazards	· May evolve toxic fumes of aluminium oxide and oxides of sulphur in a fire. · Incompatible with strong oxidizing agents and sensitive to moisture. · Non-combustible. Use extinguishing media appropriate to surrounding conditions if in a fire.
Health hazards	· Irritating to eyes. · Ingestion of large amounts may lead to senile dementia (not proven).
Toxicological information	
First aid measures	**Eyes:** Rinse thoroughly with water for at least 15 minutes. **Lungs:** Move to fresh air. **Skin:** Wash off skin thoroughly with water. Remove contaminated clothing and wash before re-use. **Mouth:** If swallowed wash out mouth thoroughly with water provided person is conscious and give plenty of water to drink. In severe cases obtain medical attention.
Accidental release measures	· Evacuate area. · Wear appropriate clothing including self-contained breathing apparatus, rubber boots and heavy rubber gloves. · Avoid raising dust. · Sweep up and place in a container or bag. · Ventilate area. · Wash the spill area with water and detergent after the material has been removed. · Dry off area.
Disposal	· Dispose of through disposal companies if available. · If not bury material away from water sources.
Storage, handling and personal protection	· Store in tightly closed containers. · Store in a cool, dry place away from incompatibilities. · Avoid inhalation of dust and eye, skin and clothing contact. · Use rubber or plastic gloves for handling. · Use a dust respirator and goggles especially when in an enclosed space. · Use a plastic apron, sleeves and boots if handling large quantities. · Wash thoroughly after handling.

4

Ferric chloride (anhydrous and hexahydrate)

Appearance	anhydrous: solid; hexahydrate: yellow powder and lumps
Hazard classes	· Corrosive · Anhydrous: Restricted for transportation: IMDG hazard class: 8; Packaging group III; IATA: 1773
Other known hazards	· Will burn skin. · Emits toxic fumes of hydrogen chloride gas under fire conditions. · Non-combustible. Use extinguishing media appropriate to surrounding fore conditions if in a fire. · Anhydrous: very sensitive to moisture · Incompatible with strong oxidizing agents and forms explosive mixtures with sodium and potassium
Health hazards	· Harmful if inhaled, in contact with the skin and if swallowed. · Corrosive and causes burns.
Toxicological information	anhydrous: LD50 oral, rat 450 mg/kg
First aid measures	**Eyes:** Rinse immediately with plenty of water for at least 15 minutes. **Lungs:** Move to fresh air. **Skin:** Take off contaminated clothing immediately and cover affected area with plenty of water for at least 15 minutes. Wash contaminated clothing before re-use. **Mouth:** If swallowed wash out mouth with water provided person is conscious and give plenty of water to drink. In all severe cases or if in doubt seek medical advice.
Accidental release measures	· Evacuate area. · Wear appropriate clothing including self-contained breathing apparatus, rubber boots and heavy rubber gloves. · Avoid raising dust. · Sweep up and place in a container or bag. · Ventilate area. · Wash the spill area with water and detergent after the material has been removed. · Dry off area.
Disposal	· Dispose of through disposal companies if available. · If not bury material away from water sources.
Storage, handling and personal protection	· Store in tightly closed containers. · Store in a cool, dry place away from incompatibilities. · Avoid inhalation of dust and eye, skin and clothing contact. · Use rubber or plastic gloves for handling. · Use a dust respirator and goggles especially when in an enclosed space. · Use a plastic apron, sleeves and boots if handling large quantities. · Wash thoroughly after handling.

Key references:

- BDH, 1997
- Dahi, et al., 1996
- Davis and Lambert, 1995
- Degremont, 1979
- Galvis, 1993
- Hofkes, 1983
- Nothomb, 1995

- Schulz and Okun, 1984
- Semat Technical (UK) Ltd
- Sigma Chemicals, 1997
- Tebbutt, 1992
- Twort et al, 1994
- WHO / WRC, 1989

Background to groundwater and aquifers

Soils and rocks ■

The uppermost layer of the earth, the crust, consists of soils and rocks. The definitions of these two material groups vary depending on the definers background and training. For assessing groundwater resources the two main variations are between the geologist and the engineer. For the purposes of these supporting notes the geologist's definitions will be used.

Soil - A complex mixture of inorganic minerals (clay, silt, gravel and sand), decaying organic matter, water, air and living organisms.
a) *To the geologist*: accumulation of loose, weathered material which covers the earth's surface.
b) *To the engineer*: any soft, unconsolidated, deformable material.

Sub-soil -
a) *To the geologist*: a layer of shattered and / or partly weathered rock between the soil and bedrock layers.
b) *To the engineer*: soil as defined above but below the surface layer.

Rock (or bedrock) -
a) *To the geologist*: Any mass of mineral matter which makes up a large, natural, continuous part of the earth's crust. ('Soft' material that is found in the ground is 'rock' as well as hard material).
b) *To the engineer*: Material that is hard, consolidated and load-bearing.

Weathering - The process by which rocks are broken down and decomposed by the action of external agents such as wind, rain, temperature changes, plants and bacteria.

A **'mineral'** is of a single chemical composition.

The composition of a **'rock'** can vary. It is made up of minerals and other rock fragments.

Hydrological cycle ■

The movement of water through the hydrological cycle determines the presence and availability of groundwater. The quality of the groundwater will depend on the presence of polluting sources, the length of time the groundwater has been in the ground, and the type and permeability of the material in which the groundwater is held. See Figure 4.26 of the water cycle, pp232-3.

Precipitation - Water in the form of rain, sleet, hail and snow that falls from the atmosphere onto the land and bodies of water.

Evaporation - Physical change in which a liquid changes into a vapour or a gas.

Transpiration - Process by which water is absorbed by the root systems of plants, moves up through the plant, passes through pores in their leaves or other parts, and then evaporates into the atmosphere as water vapour.

Desalination - Purification of salt water or brackish (slightly salty) water by removing dissolved salts.

Water in soils and rocks ▪

The soil or rock in the upper part of the earth's crust has openings called pores, fractures or voids. Water which is below the ground is held in these spaces (which are often microscopic in size) and some of this water can be exploited for supply.

Pores or voids - The holes in soil or rock.

Fractures - Longitudinal breaks in the fabric of a rock.

Infiltration - The entry of water through the surface layers of the soil.

Percolation - The downward flow of water.

Saturated zone - Where the rock or soil pores are totally filled with water.

Unsaturated zone (or zone of aeration) - Some of the rock or soil pores are filled with water, some are partially filled and some are empty.

Water table - The upper surface of the saturated zone or the plane between the saturated and unsaturated zone.

Surface water - Water that is above the ground surface.

Sub-surface water - All of the water which is underground, whether in the saturated or unsaturated zone.

Groundwater - Water that is below the water table.

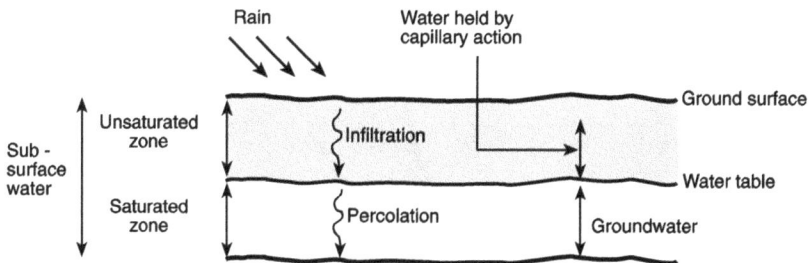

Figure 4.25 — Water in soils

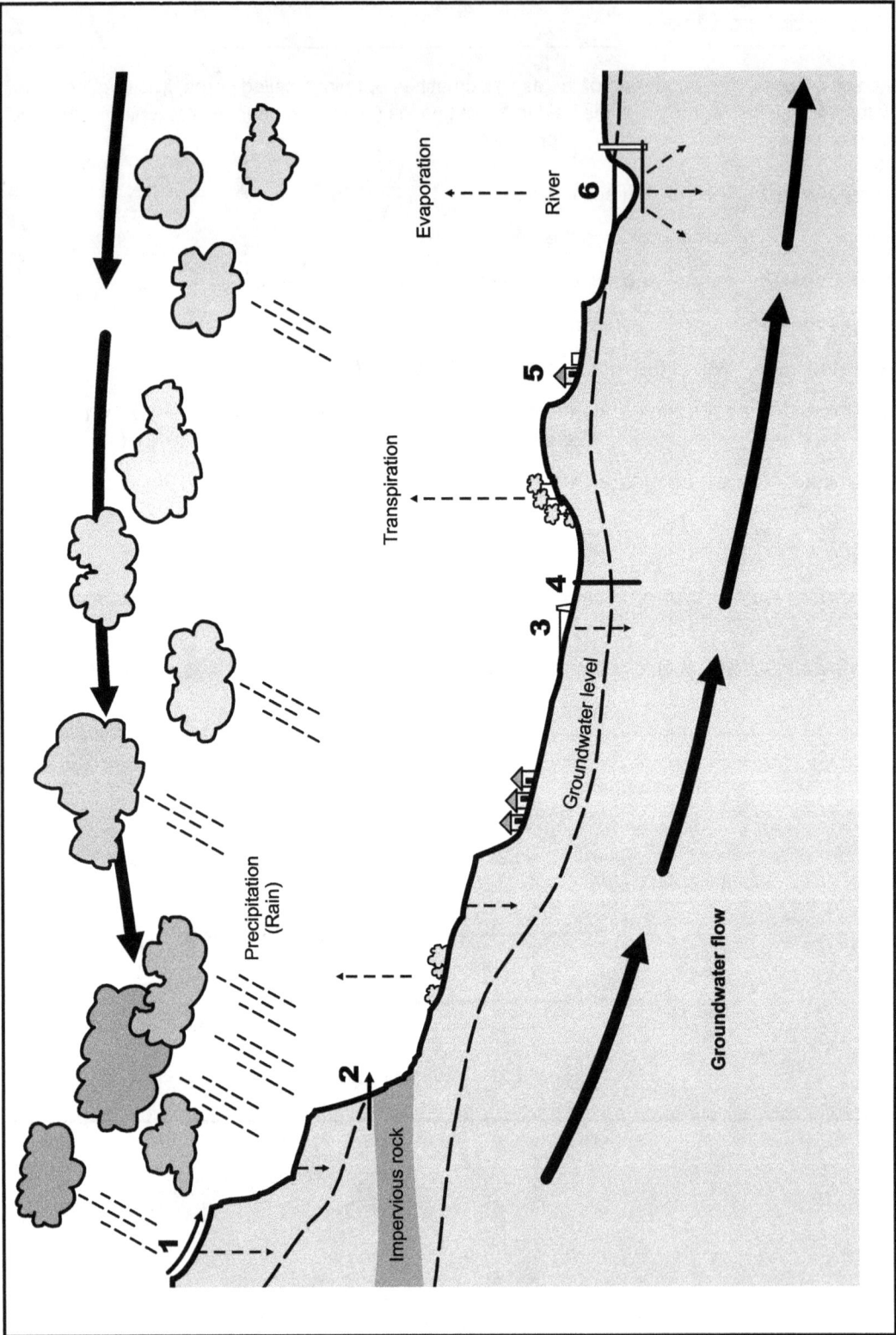

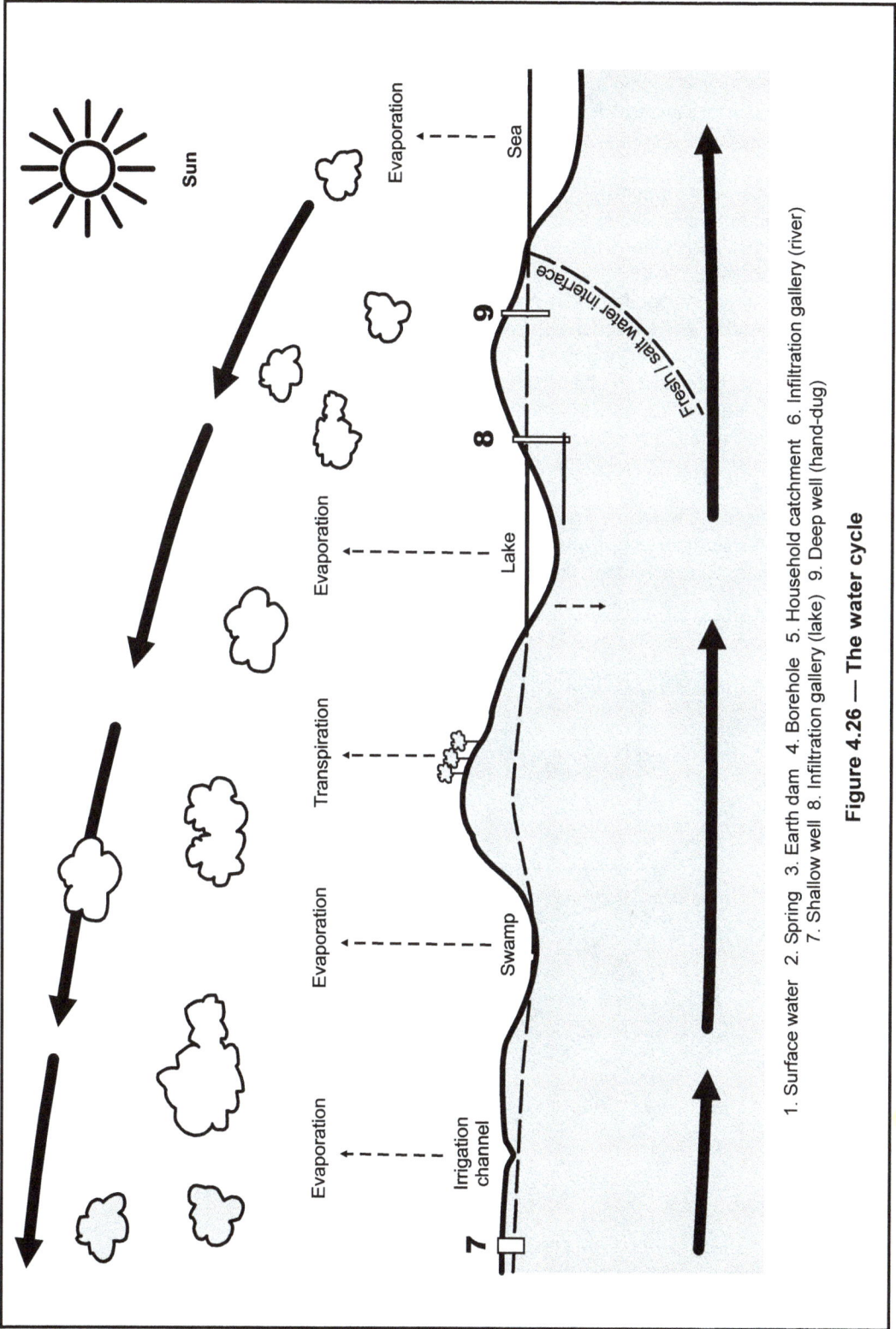

Figure 4.26 — The water cycle

1. Surface water 2. Spring 3. Earth dam 4. Borehole 5. Household catchment 6. Infiltration gallery (river)
7. Shallow well 8. Infiltration gallery (lake) 9. Deep well (hand-dug)

Groundwater ∎

Groundwater occurs in a variety of conditions and forms, but most is not discharged naturally and is contained in rock formations below the ground. Rock formations which hold water are known as aquifers.

Aquifer - Porous, water-saturated layers of sand, gravel or rock that can store water and are permeable enough to allow water to flow through them in useable quantities.

Confined aquifer - An aquifer which is between two layers of low permeability material and has no air spaces above it.

Unconfined aquifer - An aquifer that is above but not totally confined by low permeability material and has a water table and air spaces above it.

Perched aquifer - The underlying rock is located above the main body of groundwater and the groundwater is not extensive. It has a limited volume of water.

Aquiclude - Material which may contain water but has a low permeability and does not allow water to move through it, e.g. clay.

Aquitard - Material that permits water to move through it but at much slower rates than neighbouring aquifers, e.g. silt.

Artesian borehole - A borehole that penetrates a confined aquifer where the water table (and hence piezometric surface) level is above the unconfined aquifer water table level. If the piezometric surface is above ground level then the water will flow out under pressure.

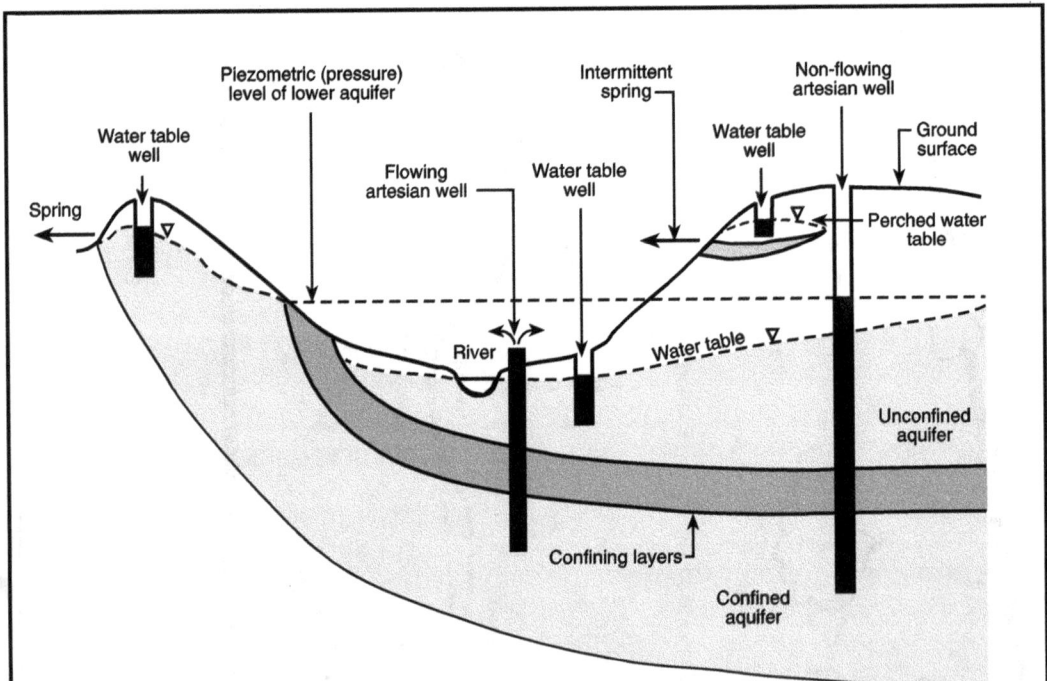

Figure 4.27 — Aquifers

Redrawn and reproduced by kind permission of R. Brassington from *Field Hydrogeology* published by John Wiley and Sons Ltd.

Aquifer characteristics ■

The water-yielding capacity of an aquifer is identified by the rock characteristics: porosity, permeability and specific yield.

Porosity - The ratio of volume of open space to the total volume of rock (%).
Permeability (hydraulic conductivity) - The 'interconnectivity' of the pore spaces in a rock, i.e. a measure of the ease with which water can flow through the rock (measured on a saturated sample).
Transmissivity - Permeability x thickness of the aquifer.
Specific yield - Ratio of the volume of water released per unit volume of rock (when fully saturated). It depends on the transmissivity and the adhesion between the water molecules and the host rock.
Fault - A fracture in a rock where relative movement has occurred.
Joint or **Fracture** - A fracture in a rock between the sides of which there is no observable relative movement.
Fissure - A joint which is open and the two sides are tens of millimetres apart.
Dyke - A sheet-like body of intrusive igneous rock which cuts across bedding or structural planes of the host rock.
Sill - A sheet-like body of intrusive igneous rock which conforms to bedding or other structural planes.

Aquifers also require confirming strata to ensure water is held at an accessible depth.

Rock and soil identification

Identification of rocks and aquifers ■

See table p236.

Aquifer properties ■

See table p237.

References used for figures for porosity, permiability and specific yield include: Brassington, 1988, pp52–60; Ayoade, 1988, pp115–7 and USAID, 1982d.

Identification of rocks and aquifers

Rock types		Examples	Description / material identification	Aquifer identification methods
				· Satellite imagery and aerial photography can be used in the location of potential aquifers in most situations
Sedimentary				
Unconsolidated sedimentary	Clay	-	Particle size < 0.002mm; no particles visible, no dilatancy, hard to crumble and sticks to hands when dry, feels smooth, has plasticity	· Visual field identification · Materials often soft, so can drill by hand · In arid areas lines of dense vegetation can indicate presence of water · Geophysics can be used to locate the presence of the water table · Commonly found in layers in river valleys
	Silt	-	Particle size 0.002-0.06mm; some particles just visible, exhibits dilatancy, easy to crumble and can be dusted off hands when dry, feels rough, some plasticity, mainly silica or quartz	
	Sand	-	Particle size 0.06 to 2mm; individual particles visible, exhibits dilatancy, easy to crumble and falls off hands when dry, feels gritty, no plasticity, will not form a ball when wet	
	Gravel	-	Particle size 2 to 60mm, when moist will not form a ball, coarse pieces of rock like quartzite or limestone, etc.	
Consolidated sedimentary	Sandstone and mudstone	Shale, grit	Angular or rounded grains commonly cemented by clay or other minerals	· Sandstone often leaves ridges · Jointing perpendicular to bedding planes may also be visible
	Limestones and dolomites	Chalk, oolite (spheres)	Crystalline, can be scratched with steel, reacts strongly with dilute hydrochloric acid, can find fossils or nodules of flint embedded in it	· Dry drainage channels can indicate possible underground channels and cave systems from dissolution of limestone rocks · Layering and sink holes in limestones are often visible from aerial photographs and on the ground · Can use geophysics to find the water table and joints
	Conglomerates (rounded) and breccia (angular)	-	Rounded or angular boulders, cobbles and gravel cemented together with sand and silt	
Igneous and metamorphic				
Igneous (formed by melting)	Extrusive (volcanics)	lava	Crystalline, fine-grained, sometimes glassy	· Water exists in cracks, fissures and joints · Need to reconstruct geomorphological history
		ash (unconsolidated layers)	Sorted to poorly sorted lava particles	
	Extrusive (fine-grained crystalline)	dolerite, basalt (dark) andesite (intermediate) rhyolite (light)	Cannot be scratched with steel, crystalline texture, not structured (homogeneous)	· Geophysics can be used to find major fissure systems
	Intrusive (coarse crystalline)	gabbro (dark), diorite (intermediate), granite (light)	Cannot be scratched with steel, crystalline texture, not structured (homogeneous)	
Metamorphic (formed by pressure and / or heat)	Crystalline	gneiss (crystals segregated into light and dark layers), schist (mica rich with undulating layers), slate, quartzite	Cannot be scratched with steel, often foliated (layered) with mica, structured (homogeneous)	
Basement complex (very old igneous and metamorphic rocks)		Complex mixtures of igneous and metamorphic rocks	Masses of strong crystalline rocks	· Basement rock does not often follow the surface topography · Geophysics can be used to find fissure systems

Aquifer properties

	Possible location	Water storage (porosity) %	Ease of water flow (permeability m/day)	Usefulness as aquifer (specific yield %)	Flow rate (l/min)	Water quality	Recharge
Sedimentary							
Unconsolidated sedimentary							
Clay	· Floodplains · Abandoned meanders of rivers	Very good (45–55)	Very low	Very poor (1–10%)		· If a river is in close proximity to the groundwater source and the permeability of the ground is good then the groundwater may be similar in quality to the river water.	· Often substantial due to permanent or intermittent flow of nearby streams or rivers · Tends to follow topography and accumulate in valleys · Direct recharge to buried river channels may be less significant due to overlying clays
Silt	· Floodplains · Abandoned meanders of rivers	Very good (35–50)	Low	Poor (5–10%)		· However unconsolidated materials have good purification capacity and can be used for initial purification of surface	· Deposits at foot hills of mountains can get substantial recharge and have springs at the base
Sand	· River channel beds	Very good (25–40)	Very good (10–10³)	Very good (10–30%)	Sand and clay - 1900	water if distances are sufficient and permeability not too high (e.g. no fissures or	
Gravel	· River channel beds · Where steep valley suddenly widens at foot of mountain	Good (25–40)	Very good (10–10³)	Very good (15–30%)	Sand, gravel and clay - 1900–3800 Sand and gravels - up to 11,400	gravels)	
Consolidated sedimentary							
Mudstones	· Anywhere	Low (0–5)	Low			· If highly fractured pollution can occur	· Infiltration through fractures and pores
Sandstones and mudstones	· Anywhere	Varied (5–30)	Good especially through fissures (1–10)	Good (5–15%)	Fractured sandstone 1900		
Limestones and dolomites	· Anywhere	(1–20)	Good through fissures (10³)	0–15% depending on fissures	40–200 or greater if heavily jointed	· High in calcium and magnesium carbonate · If highly fissured then pollution can travel long distances	· Infiltration through surface soils except in areas with sink holes or weathered fissures at the surface
Conglomerates	· Anywhere	As sandstone					
Igneous and metamorphic							
Igneous							
Extrusive (volcanics)	· Anywhere	Low Weathered, faulted or jointed zones (10–50)	Good through joints and fractures Clay layers in weathered zones can lead to confined conditions	Young basalt 8%	Very variable Depends on nature of jointing	· Can be high in minerals from dissolution of rocks; can have high fluorides, iron, sulphates, metals, and chlorides · Usually good microbiological quality as is deep groundwater · High pollution risk if wide fissures	· Good through joints and fractures · Recharge depends on surrounding topography - high features implies more recharge · Buried soils during lava flows can be routes for flows
Extrusive (fine grained crystalline)	· Anywhere	Low (in joints)	Low but variable	Poor			
Intrusive (coarse crystalline)	· Anywhere	Variable	Good through fissures	Granite 5%			
Metamorphic							
Crystalline	· Anywhere	Not weathered low, except in faults or joints (<1)	Very low	Variable Schist very poor	Limited		
Basement complex (igneous and metamorphic)							
Crystalline	· Basement complex remnants of old mountain ranges	Weathered upper zones can produce limited aquifers	Very low except joints	Poor	Limited		

Unconsolidated sediments (soil) identification and infiltration rates ∎

Loess - Accumulations of wind-borne dust of silt size derived originally from desert areas.

Laterite - Highly weathered soils which contain large, though extremely variable, proportions of iron and aluminium oxides, as well as quartz and other minerals. Their colour varies from ochre through to red, brown, violet and black, depending largely on the concentration of iron oxides.

Loam - A soil containing a mixture of clay, sand, silt and humus.

Identification of soils and infiltration rates

Characteristic	gravel	sand	sandy loam	silt	silty loam	clay loam	clay
particle size (mm)	> 2	0.06-2		0.002-0.06			< 0.002
visibility of particles	individual particles visible	individual particles visible		some particles visible			no particles visible
feels gritty, rough or smooth (touch test)		gritty / rough	gritty / rough	rough	almost smooth	smooth	smooth
will form a ball when wet	no	no	difficult	yes	yes	yes	yes
does the ball take a polish when smeared (lustre test)	no	no	no	no	no	no	yes
after washing wet soil it can easily be rinsed off the hands (washing test)							no, fine particles stick to hands
dry lump of soil can be easily crumbled (dry strength test)		yes		yes			no
dilatency (dilatency test)		yes with very fine sands		yes			no
plasticity (the soil can be deformed without rupture i.e. without losing cohesion)	no	no		some			yes

Note that the soil may be a combination of materials. Soils that have a mixture of sizes of materials are named according to the proportion of different materials e.g. 'clayey sand' indicates that more than 50% of the coarse material is sand and more than 50% of the fine materials is clay.

Agricultural soils are different to engineering soils. Agricultural soils tend to be disturbed by cultivation, mixed with humus and are unlikely to be homogeneous. Engineering soils are often undisturbed, consolidated and often homogenous (Stern, 1997). When investigating infiltration, percolation or permeability, care must be taken to determine which type of soil is being referred to and what conditions the water will be under when moving through the soil (relative water table levels, homogeneity of the soil, etc.).

Rock types

Unconsolidated, sedimentary

Left to right: gravel, river gravel, coarse sand, fine sand, silt and clay

Consolidated, sedimentary

Sandstones and mudstone

Limestones and dolomites

Rock types

Consolidated, sedimentary (cont.)

Breccia and conglomerates

Igneous intrusive (volcanics)

Lava

Igneous extrusive (fine grained crystalline)

Left to right: dolerite, basalt, andesite and rhyolite

Rock types

**Igneous intrusive
(coarse crystalline)**

Granite

Diorite

Gabbro

Rock types

Metamorphic (crystalline)

Schist

Gneiss

Slate

Quartzite

Infiltration / percolation of water through soils for the purpose of water abstraction

If infiltration is being considered for the abstraction or treatment of water it can occur either through the *in situ* material or imported gravels and sands. If the *in situ* material is to be used then an assessment will be required of the suitability of the soil for this purpose.

It is very difficult to predict how a soil will perform as the yield will depend on many factors, including the:
- permeability of the soil;
- structure and homogeneity of the soil;
- depth of the pumping well below the water surface;
- quality of the water being infiltrated (especially with respect to the turbidity); and
- rate of deposition of solids and clogging of the infiltrative surface.

Soil permeability tests under laboratory conditions identify that soils with a high percentage of silt or clays are not suitable for infiltration. In these cases the soil should be replaced with gravels or sands.

Permeability of soils

	Permeability of soil (Smith, 1990, p 47) mm/day
Clay	< 0.0864
Silt	0.0864-8.64
Fine sands, coarse silts	8.64-864
Sands	864-8,640,000

If an infiltration well using *in situ* materials is being suggested as a means of abstraction or treatment then a trial well or a hand-augered borehole should be constructed and pumping trials undertaken. Note that yield from an full-sized well will be much higher than that from a small-diameter survey bore. See the Oxfam Water Supply Scheme Well Digging Pack Survey Auger Kit for further details (Oxfam, 1991).

For an infiltration gallery with slotted pipes under a river bed the pipes should be surrounded with sand and gravel rather than using the *in situ* material unless the *in situ* material is sand or gravel. Sedimentation of silt or erosion are the most common problems with this technique.

Simple infiltration and percolation tests such as those on the next page from Davis and Lambert, 1995 or Carroll, 1991 will give a general feel for the infiltrative capacity of a soil under test (related to, but not the same as permeability). However they provide more appropriate information for infiltration from soak pits, latrines or reservoirs than infiltration through soils to infiltration wells. This is due to variations between the test conditions and the field conditions for infiltration galleries or wells e.g. the relative heads of water between the river and well chamber, the effects of pumping, variation in soil along the line of flow, and the direction of travel of the water.

Seepage from water collection reservoirs or ponds

The seepage from an engineered reservoir where the soil is relatively homogeneous and undisturbed is best approximated from laboratory tests or estimated from the soil type and its theoretical permeability. Typical values for permeability range from <0.0864mm/day in clays to 8,500,000mm/day in sands (Smith, 1990). Seepage or infiltration into the ground in areas where the soil is agricultural or where it has been disturbed by cultivation, mixed with humus and likely to be unhomogeneous, is more empirical and best measured in the field (Stern, 1997). Typical values for infiltration into agricultural-type soils range from 24mm/day in clays to 2400mm/day in sands (Stern, 1979).

Simple methods to estimate infiltration in the field are highlighted below. They should be undertaken at the bottom of the proposed reservoir or pond to ensure that the test is not distorted by a variation in material with depth. Note that infiltration rates for turbid water will be less than those for clean water as the fines from the turbidity will block the pores. Infiltrative capacity is likely to decrease with time, especially for turbid waters.

Field tests for infiltration

Simple field test
Reproduced by kind permission of the publishers Intermediate Technology Publications, from *Engineering in Emergencies: A practical guide for relief workers* by J. Davis and R. Lambert, p685.

Method: Force a steel cylinder (without ends) of about 300mm diameter into the soil so that it stands upright. Place an upright ruler or gauge stick marked in millimetres into the cylinder. Fill the cylinder with water and measure the fall in water level at convenient intervals (5, 10, 20, 30 minutes) as water infiltrates into the soil.
Interpretation: Determine the infiltration rate during each time period and average the results for a very rough guide to infiltration rate.

Falling head percolation test (approximate but less so than the simple field test above)
Reproduced by kind permission of the International Division of the Building Research Establishment from, *Disposal of domestic effluents to the ground, Overseas Building Note 195* by R.F. Carroll, pp6–7.

Method:
- Dig or bore a 150mm diameter test hole to the depth of the bottom of the proposed soakage system. The hole can be opened out to a wider diameter at the top if the pit is deep. Scratch the wall of the test hole with a sharp pointed instrument and remove any loose material from the bottom of the hole. Place a 50mm depth of gravel in the hole to protect the bottom from scouring action when water is added.
- Carefully fill the test hole with at least 300mm depth of clean water. This depth of water should be maintained by topping-up for at least 4 hours and preferably overnight if in a clay soil. It is important that the soil is soaked for a sufficient time to allow the soil to swell so as to give accurate results. In sandy soil or soil with no clay soaking is unnecessary.
- Except for sandy soils, water level measurements should be made at least 15 hours but no more than 30 hours after soaking began. Remove any soil that has collected in the hole

during the soaking period and adjust the water level to 150mm above the gravel. Do not allow the water level to rise more than 150mm above the gravel during the test. Immediately after adjusting the depth, measure the water-level from a fixed reference point and repeat at 30-minute intervals. The test is continued until two successive water level drops do not vary by more than 2mm. At least three measurements are made and **after each** the water level is adjusted to maintain the 150mm depth over the gravel. The last water level drop is used to calculate the percolation rate. If the water soaks away in less than 30-minute intervals then use 10 minute intervals instead.

e.g. if the water level dropped 20mm in 30 min

The percolation value (or infiltration rate) in mm /day = $\dfrac{20 \times 60 \times 24}{30}$ = 96 mm/day

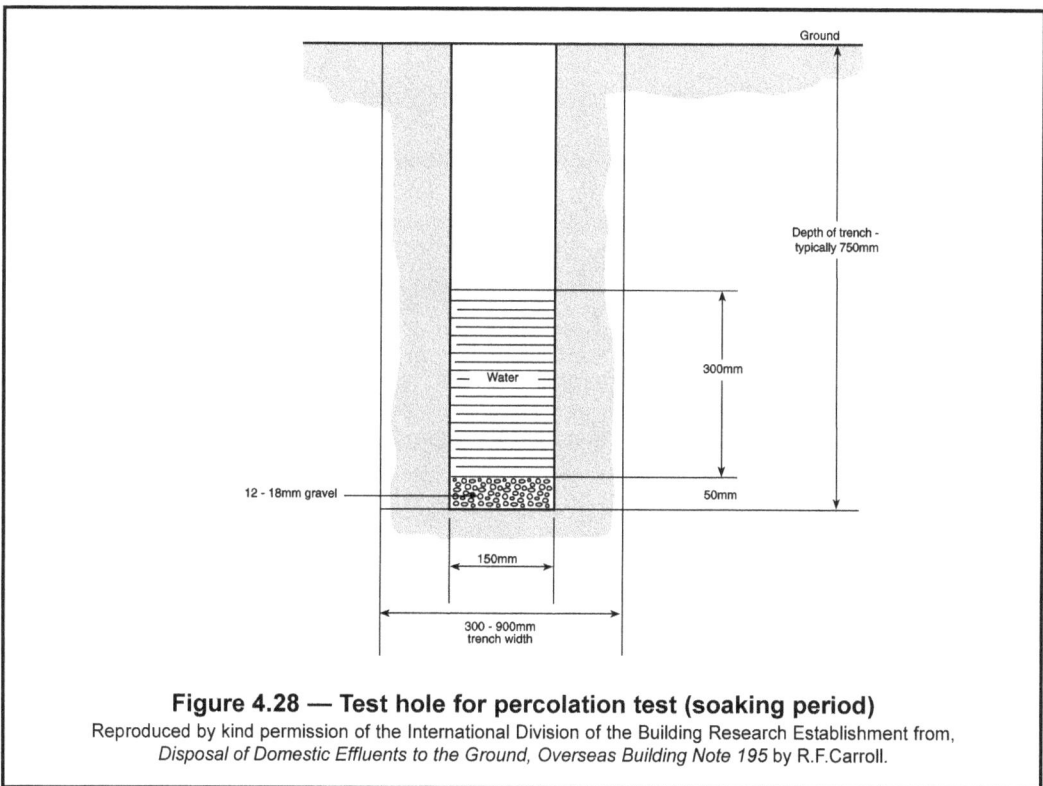

Figure 4.28 — Test hole for percolation test (soaking period)
Reproduced by kind permission of the International Division of the Building Research Establishment from, *Disposal of Domestic Effluents to the Ground, Overseas Building Note 195* by R.F.Carroll.

Soil identification field tests

The majority of the tests and figures noted below have been reproduced by kind permission of the publishers SKAT from *Appropriate Building Materials: A Catalogue of Potential Solutions* by Roland Stulz and Kiran Mukerji, 1993.

(i) Odour test:

Method: Immediately after removal, smell the soil.
Interpretation: Organic material smells musty, and this smell becomes stronger on moistening or heating.

(ii) Touch test

Method: After removing the largest particles (gravel), a sample of soil is rubbed between the fingers and palm of the hand.
Interpretation:
- a sandy soil feels rough and gritty and has no cohesion
- a silty soil still feels slightly rough, but has moderate cohesion when moist
- hard lumps that resist crushing when dry, but become plastic and sticky when moistened indicate a high proportion of clay

(iii) Lustre test

Method: Cut a slightly moist ball of the soil.
Interpretation:
- a fresh cut revealing a dull surface indicates a predominance of silt
- a fresh cut with a shiny surface indicates a higher proportion of clay

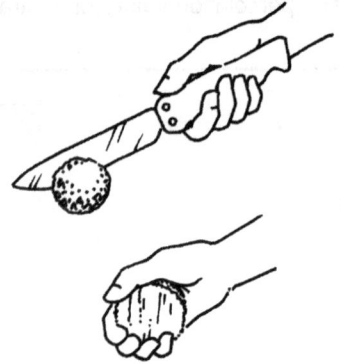

(iv) Adhesion test

Method: Push a knife into a moist ball of soil.
Interpretation:
- if it easily penetrates the ball then the proportion of clay is usually low
- if the knife does not easily penetrate and the knife sticks when pulling it out then the proportion of clay is probably high

(v) Washing tests

Method: Wash hands after handling soil for some time
Interpretation:
- silt and sand are easy to wash off
- clay needs to be rubbed off

(vi) Vibration test (grading test)

Method: Place a handful of dry soil on a board. Slightly lift one end leaving the other on the ground or on a horizontal surface and then tap the board gently
Interpretation: The particles will drift down the board at speeds relating to their sizes (small at the top and large at the bottom)

(vii) Sieving test (grading test)

Method: Use two screens with wire mesh of 1mm to sieve the soil into two piles. Crushing of clay lumps may be necessary beforehand. Then re-sieve the > 1mm pile with the 2mm mesh so that you are left with three piles.

Interpretation: Approximate proportions of material can then be determined from the sizes of the piles
- \> 2mm = gravel
- 1 - 2mm = sand
- \< 1mm = silt and clay

(viii)   Settlement test (grading test)

Method: Fill a glass jar to 1/4 full with soil and then fill the jar almost to the top with clean water. Allow the soil to soak well for an hour, then shake the jar vigorously and place on a horizontal surface. This is repeated again an hour later and the jar left standing undisturbed for at least 45 minutes but preferably longer.
Interpretation: The solid materials will have settled with the smallest at the top and largest at the bottom (after 25 seconds most of the sand and gravel portions will have settled, after 60 seconds most of the silt should have settled, and after 24 hours most of the clay should have settled). Measurement of the bands of material will give a rough estimate of quantities of the relative sized materials. Note that the values will be slightly distorted as the silt and clay will have expanded in the presence of water.

CLAY
SILT
SAND
GRAVEL

(ix)   Thread test

Method: Roll a moist ball the size of an olive on a flat clean surface forming a thread. If it breaks before the diameter of the thread is 3mm, then it is too dry and the process should be repeated with additional moisture until the thread breaks just when it is 3mm thick. This is the correct moisture content. The thread is then re-moulded into a ball and squeezed between thumb and forefinger.

3mm

Interpretation:
- if the ball is hard to crush, and does not crack or crumble, it has a high clay content
- cracking or crumbling shows a low clay content
- if it breaks before forming a ball, it has a high silt or sand content
- a soft spongy feel means organic sand

(x)   Ribbon test

Method: With the same moisture content as the thread test, form a soil sample into a cigar shape of 12 to 15mm thickness. Then progressively flatten it from one end to the other between the thumb and forefinger to form a ribbon of 3 to 6mm thickness. Keep moving the fingers along the ribbon allowing the flattened end to hang freely. Keep moving along the ribbon until the hanging end breaks off.

Interpretation:
- a long ribbon of 25 to 30cm has a high clay content
- a short ribbon of 5 to 10cm has a low clay content
- no ribbon means a negligible clay content

(xi) Water retention test (dilatency test)

Method: Using the fine material from the sieving test (vii) above, form an egg-sized ball by adding just enough water to hold it together but not stick to the hands. Press the ball gently into the curved palm of the hand while vigorously tapping this hand with the other and hence shaking the ball horizontally.

Interpretation:
- when it takes 5 to 10 taps to bring the water to the surface (a rapid reaction) and when pressed the water disappears and the ball crumbles this indicates a fine sand or course silt
- when the same result is achieved with 20 to 30 taps (a slow reaction) and the ball does not crumble but flattens on pressing then the sample is a slightly plastic or silty clay
- a very slow reaction and no change of appearance on pressing indicates a high clay content

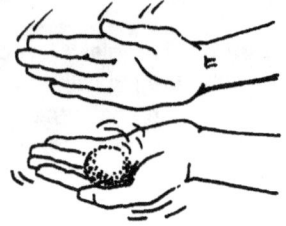

(xii) Dry strength test

Method: Take two to three moist samples from the water retention test (xi) and slightly flatten them to 1cm thickness and 5cm diameter and allow to dry completely in the sun or an oven. Then attempt to pulverize a dry piece between the thumb and index finger.

Interpretation:
- if it is broken with great difficulty and does not pulverize, it is almost pure clay
- if it can be crushed to a powder with a little effort it is a silty or sandy clay
- if it pulverizes without any effort, it is a silt or fine sand with a low clay content

Key references:

- Ayoade, 1988, pp113–30
- Brassington, 1988
- Carroll, 1991
- Davis and Lambert, 1995, pp224–56
- United States Environmental Protection Agency, 1980
- Guoth-Gumberger, 1987, pp249–54
- Hayes, 1988
- OXFAM, 1991
- Price, 1985
- Stulz and Mukerji, 1993, pp7–28
- USAID, 1982b,c,d
- Whitton and Brooks, 1975

Groundwater investigation

Groundwater levels and interaction between water sources ■

(i) Relationship between topography, geology and groundwater
- Topographic maps can be used to locate spring lines by using known 'springs' and starting points of streams shown on the maps.
- Poorly drained or marshy areas are usually underlain by low permeability materials and may mean that groundwater is discharging from an adjacent aquifer.

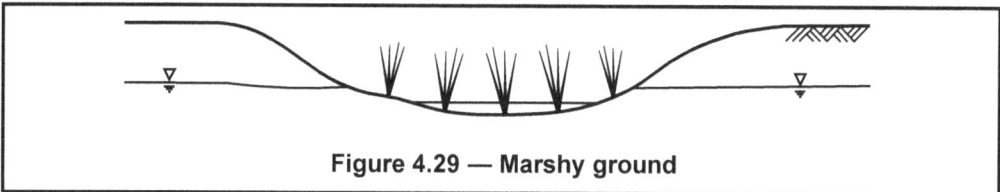

Figure 4.29 — Marshy ground

- The shape of shallow groundwater water tables usually follows the surface topography. Groundwater flows from areas of recharge to areas of discharge.
- Significant recharge can only occur at a rock outcrop or through permeable unconsolidated deposits, so by identifying these a provisional direction of flow can be determined (note that travel through fissured rocks can flow in totally different directions to those indicated by signs at the surface).

(ii) Relationship between vegetation and groundwater
- Perennial plants (all year round trees and bushes) often indicate the presence of shallow groundwater.
- Lines of vegetation in rocky, dry areas can indicate locations of faults, and hence possible areas of recharge.

(iii) Relationship between rivers and groundwater
- Rivers and lakes receive at least some or all of their water from the ground. See the following diagrams for a representation of the interactions that can occur .

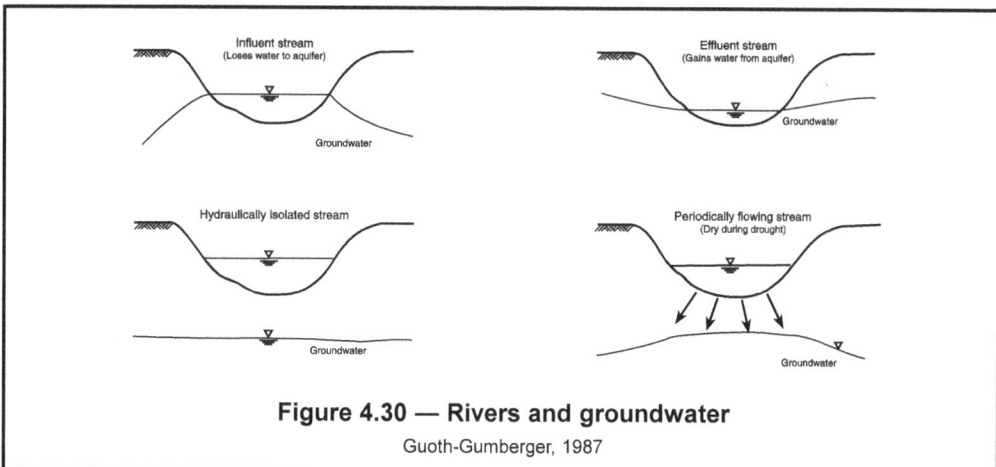

Figure 4.30 — Rivers and groundwater

Guoth-Gumberger, 1987

(iv) Relationship between springs and groundwater

Springs occur where the groundwater emerges at the ground surface. Springs can be seasonal or flow at relatively constant rates all year round. See the diagram below for alternative positions in which springs can be found and the interrelationship between water sources.

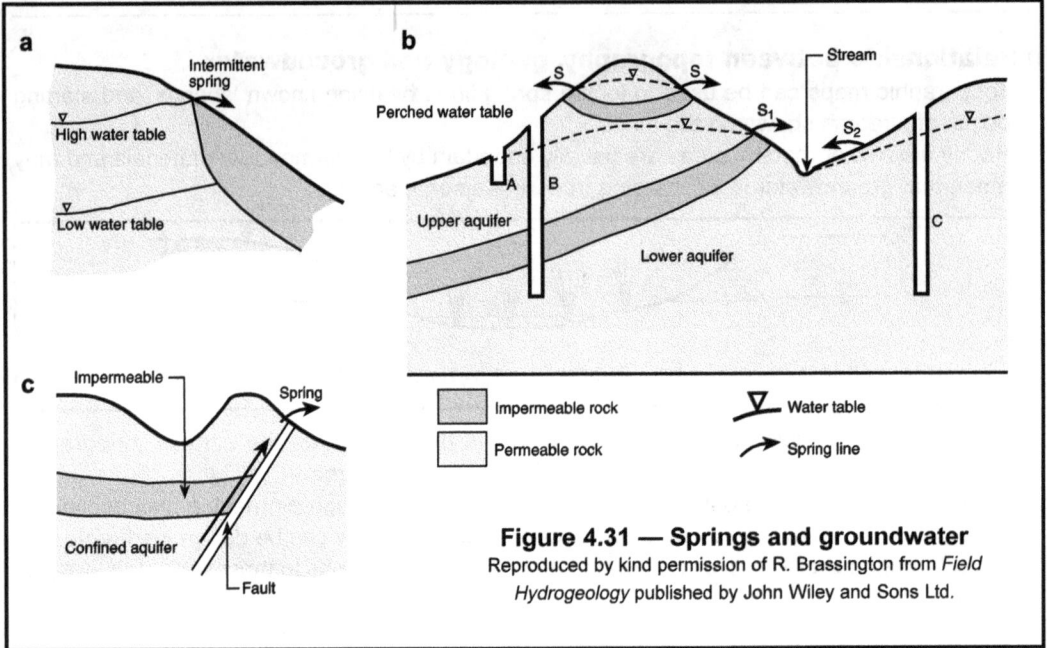

Figure 4.31 — Springs and groundwater
Reproduced by kind permission of R. Brassington from *Field Hydrogeology* published by John Wiley and Sons Ltd.

(v) Relationship between water levels in wells, boreholes and groundwater

When water is not being pumped out of a well or borehole the water becomes stable at the level of the water table (the water table level may change depending on the time of year). This is called the 'static level'. When water is pumped from a well or borehole the water level drops until it reaches a stable level for that particular pumping rate, which is the 'pumped level'. If the aquifer cannot refill the well as fast as the pumping rate then the well will pump dry and a stable level will not be reached.

The level of the water table around the borehole curves down to the pumped level to form a cone of depression. If the cone of depression of two wells overlap then the pumped level in both well and the yield will decrease. In relatively impermeable materials, such as those with clay in them, the cone will be very narrow and deep whereas for materials which are highly permeable the cone of depression will begin a long distance from the well and shallow (USAID, 1982d).

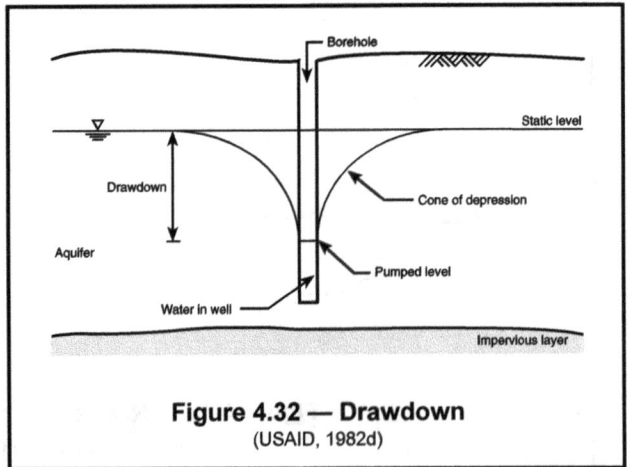

Figure 4.32 — Drawdown
(USAID, 1982d)

Static water levels in wells and boreholes are at the level of the water table and hence can be used as spot points for estimating cross-sections of groundwater levels.

Interpretation of information supplied in (i) to (v)

By noting the positions of springs, surface water sources and groundwater levels on a topographical map an attempt can be made to draw approximate groundwater level contours or cross-sections of groundwater levels. Water flows from high to low. Obviously what goes on under the ground can be very different from what is shown above ground but with the use of existing borehole logs and some knowledge of the types of rocks in the surrounding areas an initial estimation of the likelihood of available water can be made. At this point a decision can also be made on whether more detailed investigations should be requested by an experienced hydrogeologist.

Interactions between sources

See the spring diagram on p250 which indicates some interrelationships of water sources.

The interrelationship between water sources is difficult to determine as part of a rapid assessment by a non-hydrologist. The long-term effects of draining an aquifer can only be approximated by undertaking a water balance and estimating the capacity of the aquifer, the recharge and the abstraction. If large quantities of water are to be removed from a borehole or a surface lake over a long period of time then these calculations must be undertaken by a qualified hydrogeologist. Accurately estimating aquifer capacities is outside the scope of the rapid assessor untrained in hydrogeology.

However short-term effects can be observed during a period of rapid assessment by undertaking constant-rate pumping tests and monitoring other surrounding water sources (boreholes, wells, springs, streams). These tests obviously would not be undertaken in the emergency stage but could be undertaken during subsequent stages when survival supplies have already been provided. See *Measurement of yield and water levels'*, pp143–7.

Measurements should start a few weeks before the start of the test and continue for a similar period once pumping has finished to allow natural fluctuations to be identified.

Loss of yield

If a loss of yield during well use is found, this could be due to (Brassington, 1988):
- deterioration of the source itself, such as blocking up of previously permeable material by fine materials, chemical precipitation or bacterial slimes (these could be due to inadequate development of the well);
- changes in local hydrogeological conditions;
- the aquifer being of a limited capacity;
- lowered water levels through over abstraction;
- excavations into the aquifer which fill up and reduce levels of groundwater;
- mining activities with associated dewatering or provision of new water routes by opening up faults;
- civil engineering works with groundwater drains;
- land drains; and
- deterioration in the distribution system (not related to the yield), e.g. through leaking or deposits.

A useful textbook for the non-hydrologist to refer to for more detailed information on the assessment of groundwater and rainwater sources is *Field Hydrogeology* by Brassington, 1988.

Indicators of the presence of groundwater ∎

As a quick assessment of the potential of groundwater as a useful source, compare the features of the area with those noted in the table below.

If the scores are mainly 3 to 5, then groundwater could potentially be a useful source and a detailed hydrogeological study could be requested.

If the scores are mainly 1 to 3, then groundwater is less likely to be a useful source and only if there are no real alternatives should a hydrogeological study be undertaken.

Indicators of the presence of groundwater

Scores	5	4	3	2	1
Features	Positive				Negative
Geological	· Unconsolidated sands and gravels in mountain-flanked valleys or in existing river valleys	· Extensive sequences of sedimentary rocks with sandstone beds	· Igneous or metamorphic rock with faults and associated fracture zones	· Igneous or metamorphic rock outcrops with extensive weathering	· Clays and unweathered rock
Topographical and vegetation	· High mountainous areas with lush (all year round) vegetation in the valleys	→	· Undulating areas with vegetation cover	→	· Flat desert areas with negligible vegetation cover
Existing borehole information	· Large numbers of boreholes with high yields · Good quality water · Low drawdown characteristics · Insignificant seasonal variation	→	· Occasional boreholes with reasonable yields · Some seasonal variation	→	· History of unsuccessful borehole siting · Dramatic seasonal variations · Few or no wells · Saline water
Climatic and hydrogeological	· High rainfall (> 1000mm per year)	→	· Average rainfall (700mm per year)	→	· Low rainfall (< 250mm per year)
Human	· Large settlements · Successful agriculture, often large scale	→	· Scattered settlements · Medium-scale agriculture	→	· Limited settlements · No agriculture

Key references:

- Ayoade, 1988, pp113–30
- Brassington, 1993, pp136–8, p72
- Davis and Lambert, 1995, pp224–56
- Guoth-Gumberger, 1987, pp249–54
- Groundwater Survey (Kenya) Ltd., 1989
- Hayes, 1988
- Price, 1985
- USAID 1982b,c,d

Rainwater harvesting

The use of rainwater in emergencies is limited because:
- it requires significant time and capital to set up large schemes;
- it may only be available for short durations in the year;
- existing facilities will probably already be used to full capacity by local users; and
- rainfall can be unpredictable.

However, rainfall can be a useful source of water as a supplement to individual household supplies if simple catchment structures can be constructed, or for small centres such as clinics or health centres where other sources are limited. In rainwater-dependent areas techniques will already be employed on a communal or individual basis, and can therefore be replicated. Alternatively, payments can be made to use water stored in existing systems as a supplement to other supplies or for survival level in the initial stages of an emergency. In rainwater-dependent areas however, water is already scarce and therefore if water is purchased from existing storage facilities, alternatives will be required for the local communities when the supplies are used up.

Consideration should only be given for mid- to long-term projects where there is time to investigate yields and appropriate catchment structures and storage systems, or for the short-term if the affected population appears in the rainy season and there are existing structures with adequate supply.

Rainwater can be collected on corrugated sheet, tile or plastic covered roofs or on the ground with or without surface coverings or treatment. Rainwater collected on the ground can be collected either by using existing ground formations or by constructing bunds.

Techniques for storage include:
- ponds (do not tend to have isolated abstraction point);
- *birkas* (cement-lined ponds or tanks);
- *hafir* dams (artificial pond with isolated inlet and outlet structures);
- sand or sub-surface dams; and
- household or institutional tanks (ferrocement, bamboo-reinforced cement, concrete, steel, etc.)

Different geographical areas may have different names for rainwater harvesting or storage techniques.

Calculation of rainwater collection potential

$$\text{volume of water per month (l)} = \text{average monthly rainfall (mm)} \times \text{horizontal area of catchment (m}^2\text{)} \times \text{run-off coefficient}$$

Calculation of change in stored volume from uncovered storage areas such as ponds and *hafir* dams.

$$\text{Change in stored water volume} = \text{input (or monthly run-off)} - \text{output (daily water consumption)} - \text{evaporation from reservoir surface} - \text{seepage loss}$$

Annual rainfall

'In general it would seem that areas with annual rainfalls of between 200 and 1000mm are often particularly appropriate for some form of rainwater harvesting' (Skinner and Cotton, 1992). The length of the dry season also affects the appropriateness of rainwater catchment, and areas with two or more rainy seasons have an advantage.

Runoff coefficients

The run-off coefficient allows for rainfall which is lost by evaporation or seepage. The following table has been reproduced by kind permission of the publishers, Intermediate Technology Publications, from *Rainwater Harvesting: The collection of rainfall and runoff in rural areas,* by Arnold Pacey and Adrian Cullis.

Runoff coefficients

Type of catchment	Coefficients
Roof catchments	
tiles or corrugated-metal sheets	0.7-0.9
Ground surface coverings	
concrete or plastic sheeting	0.6-0.8
brick pavement	0.5-0.6
Treated ground catchments	
compacted and smoothed soil	0.3-0.5
clay / cow-dung threshing floors	0.5-0.6
soil treated with sodium salts	0.4-0.7
Untreated ground catchments	
soil on slopes less than 10%*	0-0.3
rocky natural catchments	0.2-0.5

* Sites should be individually assessed

Seepage loss in unlined reservoirs

The seepage from an engineered reservoir where the soil is relatively homogeneous and undisturbed is best approximated from laboratory tests or estimated from the soil type and its theoretical permeability. Typical values for permeability range from <0.0864mm/day in clays to 8,500,000mm/day in sands (Smith, 1990). Seepage or infiltration into the ground in areas where the soil is agricultural or where it has been disturbed by cultivation, mixed with humus and likely to be unhomogeneous is more empirical and best measured in the field (Stern, 1997). Typical values for infiltration into agricultural type soils range from 24mm/day in clays to 2400 mm/day in sands (Stern, 1979).

Simple *in situ* tests can be undertaken in the bottom of the reservoir or pond to give a rough idea of seepage loss, pp244-5.

Evaporation from surface of reservoir

Evaporation depends on humidity, wind, temperature and sunshine. In tropical conditions 4-7mm/ day is typical. Annual evaporation can vary from less than 1m in cool but humid areas to greater than 2.5m in hot desert areas (Davis and Lambert, 1995).

Key references:
- Skinner and Cotton, 1992
- Pacey and Cullis, 1986
- Stern, 1997
- Stern, 1979

5

EQUIPMENT AND ADDRESSES

Glossary

The following definitions are those used within these documents but may not be dictionary definitions.

For definitions of the following words refer to the section *Background to groundwater and aquifers pp230-5*:

aquiclude; aquifer; aquitard; artesian borehole; basement complex confined aquifer; consolidated sediments; desalination; dyke; evaporation; fault; fissure; fracture; fractures; ground water; hydraulic conductivity; igneous; infiltration; joint; laterite; loam; loess; metamorphic; mineral; perched aquifer; percolation; permeability; pores; porosity; precipitation; rock; saturated zone; sedimentary; sill; soil; specific yield; sub-soil; sub-surface water; surface water; transmissivity; transpiration; unconfined aquifer; unconsolidated sediments; unsaturated zone; voids; water table; weathering.

Accessibility	How easy something is to access or approach.
Affected population	Refugees, internally displaced persons and populations not displaced but still affected by an emergency. Where a displacement has occurred a differentiation has been made between the displaced and non-displaced or 'local population'.
Aggessivity	The carbon dioxide level in the water. Aggressive waters tend to be corrosive and hence can damage supply systems.
Agrochemical pollution	Pollution resulting from agriculture including chemicals used therein.
Assessment	Evaluation. Process of identifying and understanding a situation.
Assisted sedimentation	Sedimentation speeded up with the addition of chemicals such as alum, ferric chloride or other. Includes the processes of flocculation, coagulation and sedimentation.
Biological survey	A study of the water based biological life in an area e.g. small water animals, plants, algae, invertebrates etc.
Birka	An uncovered rainwater catchment pond / tank found in Southern Sudan and Ethiopia. Often lined with vertical concrete walls.
BOD$_5$ or BOD	The five day biochemical oxygen demand is defined as the amount of oxygen required by bacteria while stabilising decomposable organic matter under aerobic conditions (Sawyer and McCarty, 1978).

Borehole	A hole drilled to give access to an underground water source. Other names include tubewell or drilled well.
Catchment map	A diagrammatic representation of a catchment area i.e. an area of land where the natural slope of the ground leads water to be drained into a river basin or reservoir. Map should include potential sources of pollution.
Disaster	'A 'disaster' results in serious disruption of society, causing widespread human suffering and physical loss or damage, and stretches the community's normal coping mechanisms to breaking point' (Davis and Lambert, 1995).
E.coli	*Esherichia coli*, thermotolerant coliform organisms used as indicator organisms to identify the likelihood of faecal pollution.
EBCT	Empty Bed Contact Time. Calculation of time for a volume of water to pass through a filter with media, calculated ignoring the volume of the media i.e. as though the filter bed was empty.
Emergency	'A crisis that arises when a community has great difficulty in coping with a disaster. External assistance is needed, sometimes lasting for many months, perhaps years' (Davis and Lambert, 1995).
Evaluation	'An assessment at one point of time of the impact of a piece of work and the extent to which the objectives have been achieved' (Gosling and Edwards, 1995 p98).
Geomorphological analysis	The analysis, description and interpretation of landforms.
Global Positioning System (GPS)	Devise used for locating positions in the world using information from American military satellites.
Hafir **dam**	A constructed rainwater catchment pond with a settlement basin at the inlet and a separate outlet for abstraction. Found in Southern Sudan and Ethiopia.
Hydroclimatic monitoring	Monitoring of climatic changes and the effects on the hydrology of the area.
Hydrogeology	The study of geology and water in the ground.
Industrial pollution	Pollution from industrial or agricultural sources.
Internally displaced person	A person displaced within the boundary of their own country.

Invertebrates	Any animal lacking a backbone.
Landsat images	Satellite images showing thermal signatures of the ground.
Local population	Population living near to the displaced population who were there prior to the emergency or disaster.
Logistics	Planning and organisation of the provision of resources.
Morbidity data	Data relating to diseases.
Mortality data	Data relating to death.
National and local government	Central, regional and local government and, although not strictly true, authorities concerned with the supply and management of utilities.
Natural threats	Natural phenomenon which causes danger to people, facilities and the environment. May include earthquakes, volcanic eruptions, hurricanes and others.
Operation and maintenance	The activities undertaken to ensure the continued running of a process such as chemical dosing and structural repair.
Organisation	Used in this document to cover NGOs and international agencies.
Refugee	Person who has crossed an international border in genuine fear of persecution (refer to the Geneva Conventions for complete definitions).
Sanitary investigation	Survey of the sanitary or hygienic conditions of a water source.
Schmutzdecke	A layer of sediment and microbiological growth which forms on the top of a slow sand filter and breaks down pathogens by biological and chemical processes.
Seasonal yield	Volume of water obtainable from a water source during a particular season of the year.
Sedimentation	The settlement of solid matter to the bottom of a liquid.
Small water animals	Small invertebrates living in surface water, visible with the naked eye.
Socio-political consideration	A consideration related to the social or political environment.

Spring	Natural outflow of groundwater which often forms the starting point of a stream.
Survey	To look at and take a general view of.
Tankering / trucking	The transportation of water by vehicular means.
Treatability	How easy a water is to treat/ clean/ improve to a required level.
Turbidity	The murkiness of water caused by suspended materials.
Upgrading approach	Where systems are designed at a specified level of service and then subsequently improved to higher levels of service.
Water quality analysis	Evaluation of water quality using laboratory or field water testing equipment.
Water quality assessment	Evaluation of water quality using one or more of a range of methods (including water quality analysis, catchment mapping and others).
Water quality parameter	A characteristic of water quality, either chemical, physical or biological.
Water source	A water body from which water may be abstracted or obtained. Can be groundwater, surface water or rainwater. It could also be a point on an existing supply system.
Water supply	Where water is provided. It may be from a groundwater source via a borehole, shallow well or spring or from a surface water source via direct abstraction or pumped, or from rainwater collected in tanks, in ponds in the ground or sub-surface dams. Supply may be simple where the user abstracts straight from a source or it may be a complex arrangement of pumps, pipes and taps.
Well	A hole or shaft bored or dug into the earth to allow abstraction of supply of water, oil, gas etc.

Water quality analysis and surveying equipment

The types of equipment required to assess water sources in an emergency situation can be split into the following groups:
- general (including surveying, flow measurement and other); and
- water quality analysis.

Brand names and suppliers have been noted in the following listings for convenience but this does not imply endorsement by WEDC or DFID. Other brands may be just as suitable.

General equipment (surveying, yield measurement etc.) ■

General items include equipment for surveying, yield measurement, sample collection, storage, and treatability testing.

The most important items of equipment for each activity are as follows:
- **surveying** (compass; clinometer / Abney level; 3m tape; line level; altimeter / aneroid barometer; global positioning system)
- **yield measurement** (stop watch; 3m tape)
- **sample collection and storage** (sample bottles; syringes for dilutions or measurement of small volumes; sampling container and string)
- **treatability testing** (beakers (1-litre if possible); spatula / spoon; chemicals)
- **other** (sampling net for biological survey; workplace mat; tissues; marker pen; Swiss Army Knife or equivalent; torch / flashlight; survey or record book)

See the tables, pp281–2 for a detailed list of equipment.

Makes and suppliers of general equipment ■

Clinometer or Abney level

Makes and Suppliers
Clinometers and altimeters can both be purchased from surveying equipment suppliers. Their prices range from £85 (including sales tax) to several hundred pounds.

Makes (1996; Abney level):	Abney level (5.25 inch; 6.5 inch)
Makes (1996; Clinometer):	Suunto Clinometer (aluminium body with or without light illumination); Suunto Compass / Clinometers; Silva Compass / Clinometers
Example supplier:	GeoSupplies Ltd.

Altimeter or aneroid barometer

Makes and Suppliers
Altimeters are supplied by outdoor specialists and possibly surveying equipment suppliers. Their prices can range from around £100 to several hundred pounds.

Makes (1996):	Thommen Altitronic Traveller (range -500 to +6000m +/- 10m); Thommen Altitrek Altimeter (range 0 to + 5000m +/- 30m); Avocet Vertech; Silva;
Example suppliers:	Field & Trek Ltd.; Cotswolds

Global positioning system (GPS)

Makes and Suppliers

There are many suppliers and makes of GPS receivers and prices range from approximately £130 (including sales tax) to thousands of pounds. Following are a few of the makes at the lower price range and their suppliers:

Makes (1996):	Garmin (GPS 38, GPS 40, GPS 45XL); Magellan (GPS 2000, GPS 300, GPS 4000, Meridian XL, Trailblazer XL); Trimble (Scout Master (tm) GPS); Silva (GPS XL1000)
Example suppliers:	Business on the Move Ltd.; Field & Trek Ltd.; Cotswolds; Silva (UK)Ltd.

See *Catchment mapping: surveying*, pp161-8 which discusses each item of equipment and its applicability to the assessment of water sources. Also see *Useful addresses*, pp286–8 for suppliers' details.

Water quality analysis equipment ■

A range of equipment types are available for the measurement of each water quality parameter.

Physical and chemical testing equipment

The following list is a selection of equipment types.

Comparator with discs
Colorimetric method. Tablets are dissolved in the sample in a small tube. The sample in the tube is viewed in the comparator versus a graded colour on an interchangeable disc. The colour intensity / shade indicates the concentration of the parameter being tested.

Checkits / pool-testers or pocket kits
Colorimetric method. Tablets are dissolved in the sample and the resulting colour compared to a scale which is either on the sample container (checkit or pool-tester) or on a separate card (pocket kits).

Papers
Colorimetric method. Test paper strips have reactive test zones which produce colours relative to the concentration of the parameter under test. The strip is dipped into the sample and after the colour change has occurred it is compared to a scale.

Photometer
Colorimetric method. The photometer is an electronic instrument which has built in filters and a digital display. Tablets are dissolved in the sample and then the concentration of colour is measured electronically. Calibration has to be undertaken against a blank of the sample.

Electronic stick meters
Small electronic stick meters which read digitally when the enclosed electrode is submerged. They require calibrating against a standard solution periodically.

Tablet count
Titrimetric method. Tablets are dissolved one by one into a sample of known volume until a prescribed colour change takes place. The concentration of the parameter is determined from the number of tablets and the size of the sample.

Shelf-life and storage conditions for consumables:

- The **foil-wrapped tablets** (for photometer, comparator with discs and checkits) should be stored in a cool, dry place out of direct sunlight to maintain their maximum shelf-life of five years. If stored in other conditions the shelf-life reduces to two years maximum. They should always be stored out of direct sunlight.

- The **bottled tablets** (tablet count method) have a shelf-life of nine months when the seal is broken if stored in cool, dry conditions. If the seal has not been broken then they last much longer. If the seal is broken and they are stored in hot, humid conditions then the shelf-life will be six months at a maximum. They should be stored out of direct sunlight.

- The **paper strips** (as in the Merckoquant strips) will last for five years if unopened and stored in a cool, dry place (room temperature is acceptable). If opened or stored in hot and humid conditions then the manufacturer would not state time scales. They should be stored out of direct sunlight.

Microbiological testing equipment:

Several methods for the quantitative determination of indicator bacteria in a water sample are noted below with their major advantages and disadvantages.

Multiple tube (or Most probable number (MPN))
This method involves the addition of measured volumes of the sample to sets of sterile tubes or bottles each holding a suitable liquid medium (containing lactose). Thermotolerant coliform organisms (*E.coli*) produce acid and gas when incubated at 44°C for 48 hours. They then need to be incubated for a longer period for confirmative tests. This method is often used in laboratories in developing countries but is not suitable for field analysis.

Advantages:
- can be used for turbid water
- good for the detection of a small number of organisms

Disadvantages:
- result take a long time
- large volume of consumables
- training is required to carry out the test

Membrane filtration
This method involves filtering a measured volume of the sample through a membrane filter with a pore size of 45μm. Micro-organisms are retained on the surface of the filter. The filter is then placed on an absorbent pad which has been soaked in a suitable selective growth medium (containing lactose) in a petri dish and then incubated at 44°C for 24 hours. Bacteria grow into colonies on the filter paper and can be counted visually.

Advantages:
- results are quicker than from multiple tube method
- uses less consumables than the multiple tube method

Disadvantages:
- it is unsuitable for use with turbid waters or waters containing small numbers of desired organisms, as they and the undesirable bacteria grow on the same medium
- training is required to carry out the test
- there are many opportunities for contamination

Colilert / MUG

A known volume of the sample is added to pre-prepared test tubes which have then been sealed. In each tube is a mixture containing salts, nitrogen and carbon sources and a specific indicator for *E.coli* and total coliform (MUG and ONPG). Non-coliform bacteria are chemically suppressed. The tubes are incubated at 37°C. In less than 24 hours positive tubes containing total coliform turn yellow and positive tubes containing *E.coli* fluoresce in the dark. The test is confirmatory.

Advantages:
- the short time required to produce confirmed results (less than 24 hours)
- it is a simple test to undertake and does not require lengthy training
- sterilization is not necessary
- additional pieces of equipment are not needed except for an incubator, a fluorescent light (and sterile, bacteria free water and syringes if required)
- the tubes can be stored at room temperature
- the tubes can be incubated against the body in an emergency

Disadvantages:
- a large number of consumables are required
- a five tube test will only indicate up to >16 per 100ml. To determine higher levels dilution is required with bacteria-free water

Dipslides

A pre-prepared sampler, consisting of a plastic handle with a 0.45μm filter and an absorbent pad containing dehydrated nutrient medium, is immersed in the sample. 1 ml of the sample is drawn through the filter and the resulting sampler is incubated at 44 °C for 24 hours. Each colony represents 1 organism per 1ml (100 per 100ml).

Advantages:
- simple to use and no training needed
- sterilization is not required
- additional equipment is not required except an incubator

Disadvantages:
- the method is not recommended for counts of less than 10 colonies per 1ml (manufacturer's literature)
- the dipslides need to be stored at 0-2°C

Other methods:

Studies have been undertaken into alternative, non-traditional, procedures for estimating water quality. Four simple tests were studied (IDRC / CRDI / CIID, 1990) to try and overcome the problems of the present bacteriological tests. Problems with current tests are that:
- the tests are not easily portable;
- they require trained personnel; and
- they use expensive supplies;
- a long time is required to obtain the results.

Water quality analysis:
General equipment

Survey equipment

Left to right: line level, global positioning system receiver, compass / clinometer, altimeter and stopwatch

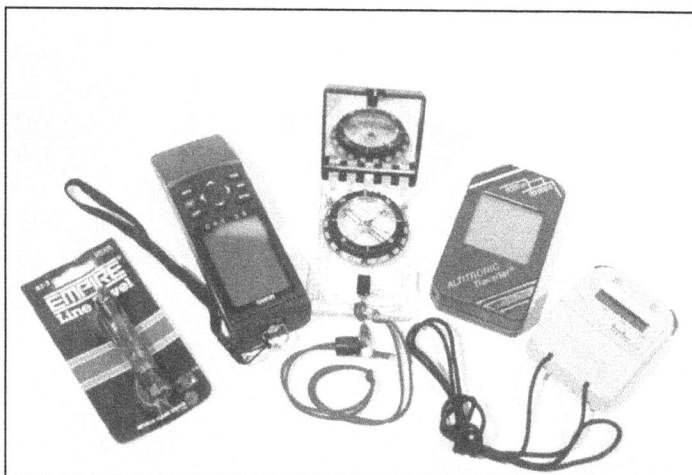

Other equipment

Left to right: 1 litre beaker, autoclavable sample containers, marker pen, spatula / spoon, tissues, 10 ml and 1 ml syringes

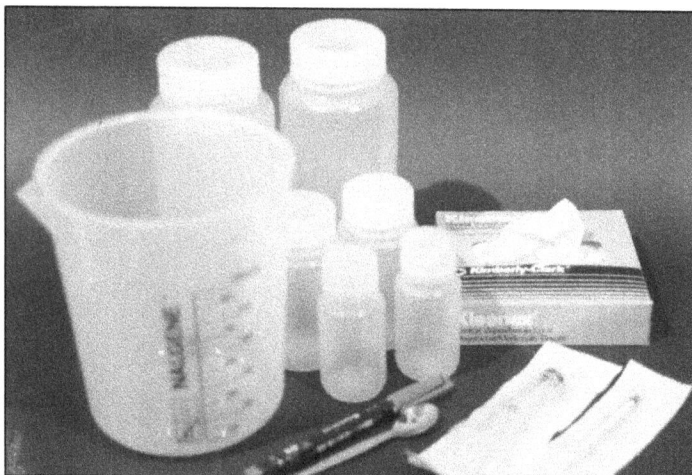

De-ionisation pack

Water quality analysis:
Physical / chemical test equipment

Comparator with disks

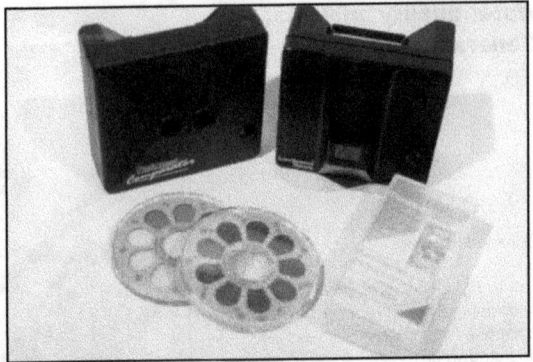

Checklists / pool testers and pocket kits

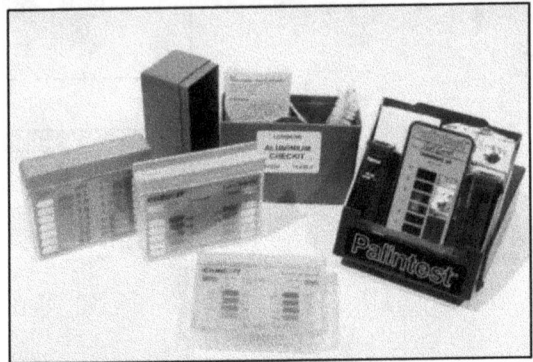

Paper strips

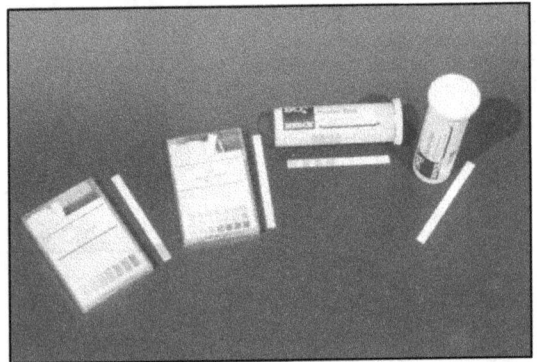

Photometer

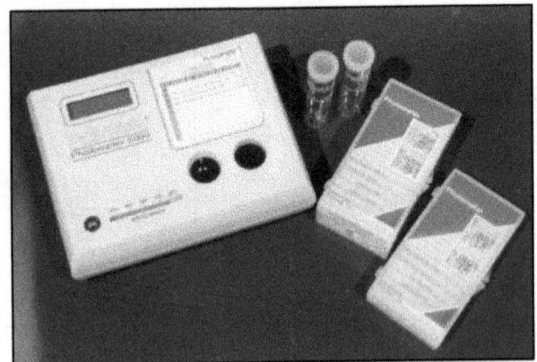

Water quality analysis:
Physical / chemical test equipment

Electric stick meters

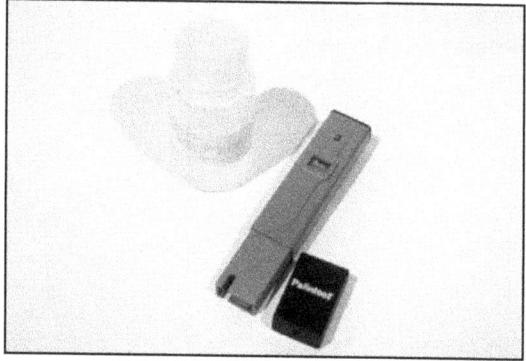

Turbidity tube

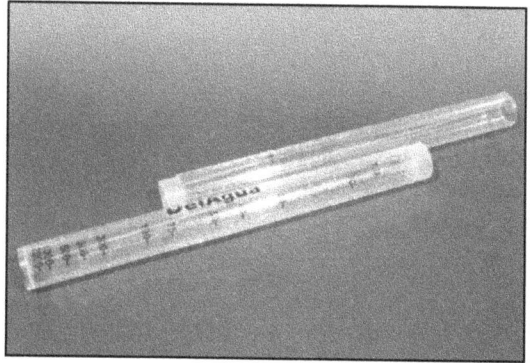

Test kits

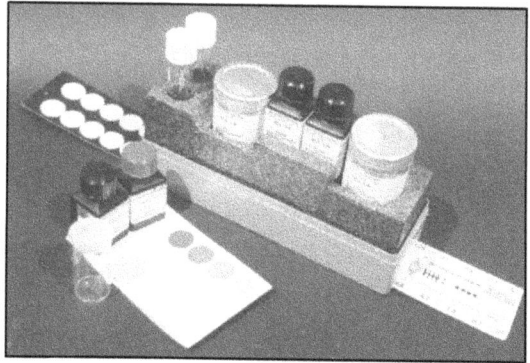

Tablet count

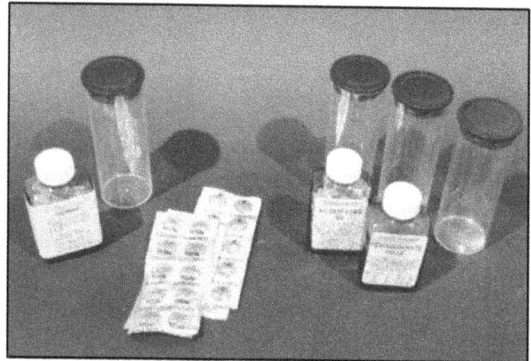

Water quality analysis: General equipment

Sampling net

Water quality analysis: Microbiological test equipment

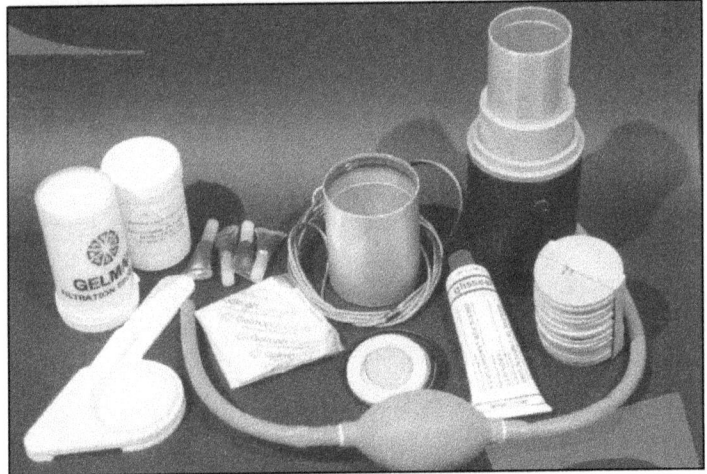

Membrane filtration apparatus (minus incubator)

Left to right: filter pads and dispenser, membrane lauryl sulphate broth and MFC broth, filter papers, sampling cup and line, spares for filtration unit, filter suction pump, grease, filter unit and petri dishes)

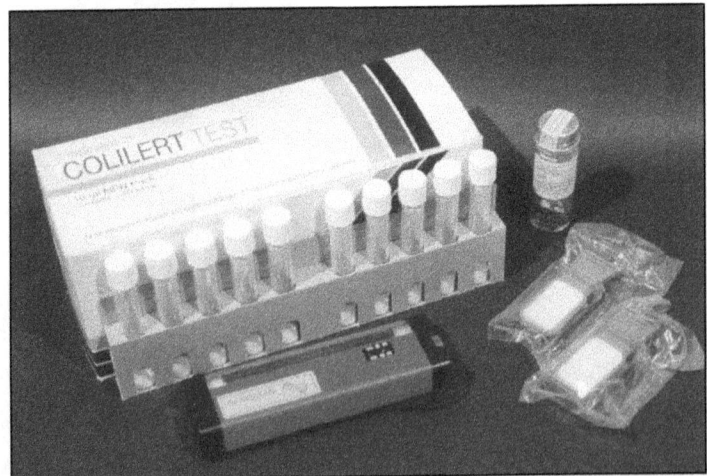

Colilert test, H_2S strip and dipslides

Left to right: Colilert test tubes, fluorescent light, H_2S strip tube and dipslides

The four tests studied were:
- Bacteriophages
- A-1 broth
- H_2S paper strip
- Presence / absence tests

The tests are not all quantitative. Further research needs to be undertaken but the tests look promising and may overcome some of the problems mentioned above. Some of the above tests are available commercially: the H_2S paper strip test is supplied as part of the All India Institute of Hygiene & Public Health and UNICEF Water Quality Field Test supplied in India. It is also supplied by the Fundaçion Zumaque in Venezuela and Premier Health Care Products in India.

Makes and suppliers of water quality testing equipment ∎

See table p270 for a selection of 'ready-made' test kits as provided by suppliers which include a microbiological component. Also see the tables pp271–276 which identify alternative items of field equipment for a range of chemical, physical and microbiological parameters and *Useful addresses,* pp286–288 for suppliers' addresses.

Notes accompanying tables pp271–276:
(i) Prices quoted are as of June 1997 and do not include sales tax or postage and packaging.
(ii) PT= Palintest; WT= Wagtech; CAM = Camlab; ELE= ELE; DEL= Delagua; MER= Merck; TINT= Tintometer
(iii) Items marked with a ✤ have chemicals which are restricted for transport by IATA regulations. Note that other items in tables pp271–276 may also be restricted in the same way. Confirmation should be sought prior to purchase.
(iv) Tables pp272–276 do not include capital costs or details for the photometer or the Lovibond or Palintest disc comparators. The basic costs for these items can be found in table p271 and should be added where necessary.

'Ready-made' test kits (including microbiological components)

Parameter	Delagua/ Oxfam	ELE '50'	ELE '25'	ELE '25l'	Wagtech 'potalab'	Wagtech 'potakit'	CAMLAB HACH, MEL presence/ absence safe drinking water lab
E.coli (includes lighter, tweezers, silicone grease, etc.)	membrane filtration - 16 test 44°C aluminum dishes {lauryl sulphate broth (lsb)} (incubator in kit box)	membrane filtration - 50 test 37 or 44°C aluminum dishes (50) or plastic dishes (16) {lsb} (incubator in kit box)	membrane filtration - 25 test 37 or 44°C aluminum dishes (25) or plastic dishes (8) {lsb} (incubator in kit box)	membrane filtration - 25 test 37 or 44 °C aluminum dishes (25) or plastic dishes (8) {lsb} (incubator in kit box)	membrane filtration - 50 / 16 test 37 or 44°C aluminum dishes (50) or plastic dishes (16) {lsb} (incubator in kit box)	membrane filtration - adjustable 25 to 50°C plastic dishes {lsb} (incubator not in kit box)	MUG reagents in disposable test tubes and fluorescent lamp (incubator included which fits in kit box)
sampling cup	yes	yes	yes	yes	yes	yes	-
turbidity	tube 5-2000 TU	meter 0-50 NTU	meter 0-50 NTU	tube 5-500 JTU	tube 5-500 JTU	tube 5-500 JTU	-
pH	comparator {phenol red 6.8-8.2}	meter 0-14	meter 0-14	photometer {phenol red 6.8-8.4}	meter 0-14	comparator 4-11{universal} ✳{other indicators available}	pH stick probe
conductivity	meter	meter 0-2000 µS/cm (temperature compensation)	meter 0-2000 µS/cm (temp. comp.)	meter 0-2000µS/cm (temp. comp.)	meter 0-1999µS/cm	pocket meter 0-199µS/cm	TDS probe
temperature	meter	meter -30 to- +150°C	meter -30 to +150°C	meter -30 to +150°C	meter 0-100°C	thermometer	thermometer
redox	-	meter 0-1999 mV	meter 0-1999mV	meter 0-1999 mV	meter 0-1999 mV	-	-
nitrates	-	photometer 0-1.0mg/l (as NO₃-)	photometer 0-1.0mg/l as NO₃-)	✳ photometer 0-1.0mg/l	photometer 0-20 (as N)mg/l	✳ comparator 0- 15 (as N)mg/l	comparator 0-50mg/l as ?
nitrites	-	photometer 0-0.5 (as N) mg/l	photometer 0-0.5 (as N)mg/l	✳ photometer 0-0.5 (as N)mg/l	photometer 0-0.5 (as N)mg/l	✳ comparator 0-0.4 (as N)mg/l	-
ammonia	-	photometer 0-1.0mg/l	photometer 0-1.0mg/l	✳ photometer 0-1.0mg/l	photometer 0-1.0mg/l	✳ comparator 0-1.0mg/l	-
aluminium	-	✳ photometer 0-0.5mg/l	✳ photometer 0-0.5mg/l	✳ photometer 0-0.5mg/l	✳ photometer 0-0.5mg/l	✳ comparator 0-0.5mg/l	-
fluoride	-	✳ photometer 0-1.5mg/l	✳ photometer 0-0.5mg/l	✳ photometer 0-0.5mg/l	✳ photometer 0-1.5mg/l	✳ comparator 0-1.5mg/l	-
iron	-	✳ photometer 0-10mg/l	✳ photometer 0-10mg/l	✳ photometer 0-10mg/l	✳ photometer 0-1.0 / 10mg/l	✳ comparator 0-1.0 / 10mg/l	-
manganese	-	✳ photometer 0-0.03 mg/l	✳ photometer 0-0.03mg/l	✳ photometer 0-0.03mg/l	✳ photometer 0-0.03mg/l	✳ comparator 0-0.03mg/l	-
chlorine	comparator {DPD1 & DPD3}	photometer 0-5.0mg/l	photometer 0-5.0mg/l	photometer 0-5.0mg/l	photometer {DPD} 0-5mg/l	comparator {DPD} 0 to 1, 2, or 5mg/l	comparator 0-3.5mg/l
case supplied	yes	yes	yes	no (carrying bag can be bought)	yes	no	yes
weight	6 kg	20kg	16kg	9kg			
Notes: (✳ indicates optional extra)		28 parameters can be tested with the photometer	as ELE 50	as ELE 50	36 parameters can be tested with the photometer Also stopwatch and deionised water pack	19 parameters can be tested with the comparator Also stopwatch and deionised water pack	Only indicates presence/ absence of *E.coli*. It is not quantitative

Microbiological tests — field equipment alternative

	Equipment / consumable	Supplier	Code	Capital cost (£)	Consumables cost (£)
Dipslides	Incubator	WAG	WAG8000	603.98	-
	Dipslides	PT (or Millipore)	PT 710	-	16.40 for 10
	Consumable cost per test = £1.648 (for 100 when purchasing more than 100)				
Colilerts	Incubator	WAG	WAG8000	603.98	-
	Colilert tubes	PT	CT010	-	45.25 for 50 tubes
for dilutions:	Plastic syringes (1ml and 10ml)	BDH / Merck	-	-	19.86 & 16.19 per 100
	UV lamp	PT	CT102	25.25	-
	Consumable cost per test = £13.95 (for 15 tubes and count to >1600 / 100ml)				
Membrane filtration	Delagua kit includes filtration unit, incubator, physical / chemical test equipment (pH, chlorine and turbidity) and consumables for 200 tests	DEL	-	1050	-
	MLS broth	DEL	-	-	3.00 for 38.1g tub (200 tests)
	Pads and filter papers	DEL	-	-	20.00 for 200
	Pad dispenser	DEL	-	-	6.11
	Consumable cost per test = £0.15 for one filtration without wastage (for 6 filtrations using syringes for dilutions then cost = £1.23 without wastage)				

Photometer and Comparator costs

Equipment	Code (*, **, or *** are high-lighted in tables pp272–276 when appropriate)	Supplier	Capital cost (£)
Photometer (as Palintest but also supplied by others)	PT250 *	PT (also supplied by ELE and WT)	480.00
Disc comparator (as Lovibond but also supplied by others)	142000 **	TINT (also supplied by ELE and WT)	31.50
Set of five No. 13.5mm cells (10ml) cells for Lovibond disc comparator	354243 **	TINT (also supplied by ELE and PT)	16.00
Disc comparator 'standard kit' includes comparator, cells, dilution tube, case (Palintest)	PT220 ***	PT	54.60

Core water quality parameters — field equipment alternatives

Parameters	Range and accuracy required	Field equipment available	Range and accuracy of equipment	Supplier	Code capital equip.	Capital cost (£)	Code consumables	Consumables cost (£)
Turbidity	<5, 5, 10, 20, 50, 100, 200 NTU	Turbidity tube	5-500 TU	DEL	-	-	-	-
		Photometer	5-400TU	PT (or ELE, WT)	*	*	-	-
pH	4-10 +/- 0.5	pH sensor		PT	PT151	39.30	PT105/S	16.20 Buffer pack for pH 4,7,10
		pH sensor (self-calibrating)	-2 to 16 +/- 0.1	MER	309/0178/03	40.75	-	-
		Papers	1-12 +/- 1 Pehanon indicator papers	CAM	-	-	mn/90401	10.80 for 200
		Papers	4-9 +/- 0.5 Pehanon indicator papers	CAM	-	-	mn/90424	9.30 for 200
		Papers	4-7 +/- 0.2 non-bleeding stips	MER	-	-	315022D	10.40 for 100
		Papers	6.5-10 +/- 0.2 non-bleeding strips	MER	-	-	315062L	10.40 for 100
		Papers	0-14 non-bleeding strips	MER	-	-	315082P	10.40 for 100
		Checkit	6.0-9.2 +/- 0.4	TINT	155280	19.95	-	6.30 for 100
		Checkit	6.0-8.2	DEL	-	10.50	-	9.00 for 250 phenol red
		Pocket kit	4-10	PT	-	-	PK136	14 for 50
		Disc comparator	4-10	PT	CD136	28.25	AK136	11.95 for 200 universal
		Disc comparator	6.8-8.4 +/- 0.2	TINT	**2/1J	**36.50	511750	5.20 for 100 phenol red
Odour	not objectionable to consumers	Sample containers with lids	-	see general equipment	-	-	-	-
Conductivity	Conductivity < 450, 450 to > 1300µS/cm +/- 100µS/cm	Conductivity meter / TDS sensor		PT	PT159 cond PT152 TDS	46.55	PT156 cond PT155 TDS	7.85 standard conductivity solution 7.85 standard TDS solution
	TDS < 300, 300 up to 1000mg/l +/- 100mg/l	Conductivity meter / TDS sensor	0-1990 µS/cm +/- 10 0-1990mg/l +/- 10	MER	309/0782/ 01 or 03	40.00	309/0741/14 cond	10.50 standard conductivity solution
		Portable conductivity meter	0-1990µS/cm +/- 10 0-1990mg/l +/- 10	DEL	-	220.50	-	-

Secondary water quality parameters — field equipment alternatives

Parameter	Range and accuracy required	Field equipment available	Range and accuracy of equipment	Supplier	Code capital equipment	Capital cost (£)	Code consumables	Consumables cost (£)
Chloride	100, **250**, 500 +/- 50	Tablet count	0-1000	PT	-	-	AS079	7.55 for 50
		Tablet count	0-5000	TINT	-	-	414180	17.50 for av 40
		Pocket kit	0-1000	PT	-	-	PK079	14 for 50
		❖Drop count titration	20-400	CAM	-	-	HH/01440-01	39.30 for 100
		Disc comp (LB)	0-200	TINT	**3/71	**60.00	464801	5.75 for 100ml reagent
		Photometer	0-50 to 0-50,000	PT	*	*	PM268	13.50 for 50
Flouride	0.5, **1.5**, 3.0 +/- 0.5	❖Disc comp. (LB) + Nessler attachment	0-1.6	TINT		too bulky and fragile		-
		Photometer	0-1.5	PT	*	*	PM179	14.05 for 50
		Disc comp (PT) + Nessler attachment	0-1.5	PT		too bulky and fragile		
		❖Colorimeter	0-2	CAM	HH/46700-05	350.00 (includes 50 tests)	-	-
Iron	0.1, **0.3**, 1.0 +/-0.1	Aquaquant, simple	0-1.0	MER	-	-	166052D	25.00 for 50
		Checkit	0-10.0 +/- 0.2 up to 1.0 +/- 2.0 up to 10	TINT	155240	19.95	515370	16.80 for 100
		Cube comparator	0-5.0 +/-1	CAM	HH/14008-00	18.60 (inc I50 tests)	-	-
		Pocket kit	0-1.0	PT	-	-	PK155	14 for 50
		Disc comp (LB)	0.1-1.0 +/-0.1	TINT	**3/116	**36.65	NOL 515370	16.80 for 100
		Disc comp (PT)	0-1.0	PT	***CD155	***28.25	AK155	32.40 for 250
		Photometer	0-1.0	PT	*	*	PM155	11.90 for 50
Manganese	0.05, **0.1**, 0.3 +/-0.05	Disc comp (LB) + Nessler attachment	0.0025-0.5	TINT		too bulky and fragile		
		Photometer	0-0.03	PT	*	*	PM173	11.90 for 50
		❖Disc comp (HACH)	0-0.7 +/-0.05	CAM	HH/23508-00	160 (includes 50 tests)	-	-
		Disc comp (PT)	0-0.03	PT	***CD173	***28.50	AK173	26.90 for 250
		Aquaquant	0-0.5	MER	-	-	165442J	88.26 for 110

Parameter	Range and accuracy required	Field equipment available	Range and accuracy of equipment	Supplier	Code capital equipment	Capital cost (£)	Code consumables	Consumables cost (£)
Nitrates	30, **50**, 80, 100 as NO_3^- (6.8, **11.4**, 18.8, 22.8 as N)	❖Disc comp (LB)	0-100 as NO_3^-	TINT	**3/142	**36.65	513111 & 513121	15 for 250 (x2)
		❖Pocket kit	0-75 as NO_3^-	PT	-	-	PK184	14 for 50
		❖Photometer	0-20 as N	PT	*	*	PM163	17.05 for 50
		Disc comp (HACH)	0-50 +/- 1 as N	CAM	HH/01468.03	63.20 (includes 100 tests)	-	-
		Cube comp	0-50 +/- 10 as N	CAM	HH/14037.00	18.60 (includes 50 tests)	-	-
		Merckoquant strips	0-10-30-60-100-250-500 as NO_3^-	MER			315244P	16.60 for 100
		❖Checkit	(0.2-20mg/l as N)	TINT	155250	44.90	513111 & 513121	15.00 & 12.50 for 250
		Nitrate test tube	required with LB disc comparator and photometer	TINT	366220	1.35 (x2)	-	-
Nitrites	1, 2, **3**, 5 as NO_2^- +/- 1 (0.3, 0.7, **0.9**, 1.5 as N)	Disc comp (LB)	0-0.5 as N	TINT	**3/103	**36.50	512310	7.75 for 100
		Pocket kit	0-2.0 as NO_2^-	PT	-	-	PK109	14 for 50
		Photometer	0-0.5 as N	PT	*	*	PM109	6.25 for 50
		Disc comp (HACH)	0-0.5 as N	CAM	HH/21820-00	63.20 (includes 100 tests)	-	-
		Cube comp	0-1.0 +/- 0.2 as N	CAM	HH/20596-00	18.60 (includes 50 tests)	-	-
		Merckoquant strips	0-1-5-10-40-80 as NO_2^-	MER	-	-	315202F	23.40 for 100
		Checkit	0-1.6 as NO_2^-	TINT	155260	19.95	512310	7.75 for 100
		Disc comp (PT)	0-15 as N	PT	***CD109	***28.25	AL109	15.05 for 200
Sulphates	100, **400**, 600 as SO_4 +/- 50	Photometer	0-200	PT	*	*	PM154	5.15 for 50
		Tablet count	0-200	TINT	-	-	414320	20.50 for av. 40
		❖Turbidimetric	50-200 +/-50	CAM	HH/02251.00	53.90 (includes 100 tests)	-	-
		Merckoquant strips	200-300, 400-500, 800-900, 1400-1600	MER	-	-	315212H	23.40 for 100
Taste	local reports	local reports	-	-	-	-	-	-
Temp	e.g. -10 to 100°C	Thermometer in brass case	-10 to 50°C	PT	PT684	17.10	-	-
		Pocket thermometer in aluminium case	-10 to 250°C	PT	PT689	11.55	-	-

Treatability tests - field equipment alternatives

Parameter	Range and accuracy required	Field equipment available	Range and accuracy of equipment	Supplier	Code capital equipment	Capital cost (£)	Code consumables	Consumables cost (£)
Chlorine residual	0, 1, 2 +/- 0.2	Checkit	0.2-8.0 +/- 0.2 to 1.0 then various to 8.0	TINT	155300	19.95	511310 & 511290	5.10 for 100 (x2) rapid dissolving
		Disc comp (LB)	0.1-2.0	TINT	3/4OJ	30.30	511310 & 511290	5.10 for 100 (x2) rapid dissolving
		Disc comp (PT)	0-2.0 free combined and total	PT	CD011/5	28.25	AK031	17.60 for 200
		Photometer	0-5.0 free combined and total	PT	*	*	AP031	20.30 for 200
		Pocket kit	0-2.0	PT	-	-	PK011	14 for 50
		Disc comp (HACH)	0-3.5 +/- 0.1 (free and total)	CAM	HH/02231-01	48.30 (includes 50 tests)	-	-

Industrial / agrochemical — field equipment alternatives

Parameter	Range and accuracy required	Field equipment available	Range and accuracy of equipment	Supplier	Code capital equipment	Capital cost (£)	Code consumables	Consumables cost (£)
Aluminium	0.1, **0.2**, 0.5	Disc comp (LB)	0.1-0.5 +/-0.5	TINT	✱✱ 3/127	✱✱ 36.50	515461 & 515471	13.40 for 250 (x2)
		Photometer	0-0.5	PT	✱	✱	PM166	10.55 for 50
		Pocket kit	0-0.5	PT	-	-	PK166	14 for 50
		Aquaquant	0-0.8	MER	-	-	165562Q	94.70 for 185
		Checkit	0-0.5	TINT	155200	19.95	515461 & 515471	13.40 for 100 (x2)
		Disc comp (PT)	0-0.5	PT	✱✱✱ CD166	✱✱✱ 36.55	AK166	7 for 250
Arsenic	0.005, **0.01**, 0.03	Merckoquant strips	0-0.1-0.5-1.0-1.7-3.0	MER	-	-	315292A	76.20 for 100
Cadmium	0.001, **0.003**, 0.005	none	-	-	-	-	-	-
Chromium	0.01, **0.05**, 0.1	Disc comp kit (LB)	0.01-0.1	TINT	413630	260.00	-	-
		Photometer	0-1.0 (vi & iii)	PT	✱	✱	PM281 (vi) & PM281S (iii)	17.05 for 50 & 47.35 for 50
		❖Colorimeter	0-0.5 (vi)	CAM	HH/41100-03	450.00 (includes 100 tests)	HH/25050-25	19.50 for 25
		❖HACH cube	0-1.0 +/- 0.2 (iv)	CAM	HH/12527-00	18.60 (includes 50 tests)	-	-
Copper	1, **2**, 5 +/- 1	❖Disc comp	0.5-5.0 +/-0.5	TINT	✱✱ 3/149	✱✱ 30.80	513550 & 513560	21.90 & 10.00 for 100
		Photometer	0-5.0	PT	✱	✱	PM186	16.25 for 50
		Aquaquant	0-5.0	MER	-	-	165281K	88.26 for 100
		❖Disc comp (HACH)	0-5.0 (free & total)	CAM	HH/21941.00	66.80 (includes 50 tests)	-	-
		Disc comp (PT)	0-5.0	PT	✱✱✱ CD186	28.25	AK186	39.75 for 50
		Pocket kit	0-5.0	PT	-	-	PK186	14 for 50
		Checkit	0-5.0 (free & total)	TINT	155420	19.95	513550 & 513560	21.90 & 10.00 for 100
Detergents	visual, odour	visual, odour	-	-	-	-	-	-
Lead	0.005, **0.01**, 0.03	❖Colorimeter	0-0.15	CAM	HH/41100-48	570 (includes 20 tests)	-	-
Mercury	0.005, **0.01**, 0.03	none	-	-	-	-	-	-
Pesticides	varies	none	-	-	-	-	-	-
Petroleum products	visual and odour	none	-	-	-	-	-	-

Equipment selection ■

The ideal equipment requirements for assessing emergency water sources are:

Individual items:
- easy to use with simple instructions
- small and easily transportable
- no restrictions on air transport
- fast and easy to produce results
- covers range and is accurate enough
- limited requirement for distilled / deionized water
- dilutions not necessary
- does not require calibration (or then calibration to itself, or then calibration to deionized water)
- robust — limited effects from: U.V.light; shock; humidity; temperature
- can test several parameters
- easy to repair or replace
- limited consumables or consumables easy to obtain
- reasonable cost of equipment and consumables
- microbiological test equipment - limited need for sterilization

Whole kit:
- can be packed into a durable case; and
- possible to carry the kit over long distances by hand or using a shoulder strap.

There are very few items of equipment which are perfect for the task as most items have both positive and negative features. Examples of negative features of the equipment include:
- the ranges measured by the equipment are not appropriate and hence dilutions are required to measure the parameter to the World Health Organisation guideline value;
- the equipment is bulky, heavy, expensive or fragile; or
- some of the test reagents are restricted for air transportation by IATA regulations.

Example total kit list ■

The following kit has been identified as suitable for **assessing emergency water sources and treatment processes in the field**. *Modifications to this kit list would be required for a monitoring programme.*

The kit has been divided into three sections:
- Core tests
- Secondary tests
- General and treatability tests

When packaging the kit it can be divided into the following parts:
1. The Delagua kit has all of the equipment to undertake the core tests (including microbiological analysis) if the conductivity stick / sensor, standard solution for calibration and the pH non-bleeding sticks (to widen the pH measurement range of the pool-tester included in the kit) are added.
2. The secondary tests would need to be packed separately to the core tests if the Delagua kit is used. They include paper strips, a photometer, and tablet count methods. A deionized water

pack would be required to provide dilution water for the manganese test as the photometer measures a range below the WHO guideline level. It can also be used to provide dilution water when one of the parameters is found to be unusually high. The general items for survey and yield measurement, sample collection and storage, and treatability can be packed with the secondary test equipment.

Alternatively, if the Delagua kit is not selected and an alternative incubator is used then the whole kit could be packed into a single case.

Reasons for choice

When identifying suitable physical / chemical test equipment the aim was to identify a single, simple, small but robust item of equipment covering the required range for measurement without the need for dilution. The ideal requirements for equipment have been noted earlier on p227. Laboratory trials, field trials and personnel preferences were also used to assess the alternative options.

The final choice of equipment was partially directed by the difficulty of measuring fluoride in the field. The photometer has been included in this kit list to measure several of the parameters simply due to its ability to measure fluoride to WHO guideline levels. The only other simple item of equipment identified as potentially suitable for field analysis of fluoride was the disc comparator. However Nessler attachments are required for the measurement of fluoride, and this consists of long glass tubes which are not suitable for a portable field kit. Although the photometer can measure several parameters and, therefore, is favorable in this way, it is electronic and hence not always trusted by fieldworkers. Some of the reagents required to measure the secondary parameters (e.g. nitrates and nitrites) are also restricted by IATA transport regulations. Some of the parameters require dilution to measure at WHO guideline levels (e.g. manganese).

Should fluoride measurement not be required the following items of equipment can be interchanged with the photometer:

- Iron: - Lovibond checkit
- Manganese: - Aquaquant manganese kit (easy to use and samples do not require dilution but it has liquid reagents and is bulky)
- Aluminum: - Lovibond checkit
- Chlorine: - Checkit

The photometer would not be suitable for daily monitoring of chlorine or aluminium residual on site. The checkits are much more suitable for this purpose.

Simple field equipment for the measurement of arsenic to WHO guideline levels was not identified.

The next best alternative to the membrane filtration test (for a quantitative measurement of *E.coli*) was found to be the Colilert test. The main problem with this test is the volume of consumables it requires, it's cost, and the need for sterile dilution water. However the test is simpler to undertake and incubates at 37°C which is advantageous in the field. The main disadvantage of the Delagua kit is its weight.

Core tests — example field kit list

Parameter / purpose	Equipment type / method	Supplier	Order number capital	Capital cost (£)	Order number consumables	Consumables cost (£)	Total kit	Total cost (£)
Turbidity	Turbidity tube (5-500 TU)	DEL	-	36.28	-	-	In Delagua kit	-
pH	BDH non-bleeding strips	MER	-	-	315022D (4-7 pH) & 315062L (6.5-10 pH)	10.40 for 100 (x2)	2 con	20.80
Conductivity	Conductivity / TDSsensor	PT	PT159	46.55	PT156	7.85 standard solution	1 cap / 1 con	46.55 / 7.85
E.coli (Sterilisation)	✦Methanol / ethanol / alcohol	buy in field	-	-	-		-	
E.coli (Stabilisation of chlorinated samples)	Sodium thiosulphate (hydrated)		-	-	-		-	
E.coli (Incubator)	Delagua kit (includes items below)	Del	-	-	-	-	1 cap & cons	1050.00
	Charging unit, leads, battery							
	Filter unit including funnel and collar, vacuum cup, vacuum pump, sample cup, cable for sample cup, bronze disc, sealing gasket and rubber o-ring							
	Petri dishes x 16							
	MLS broth (38.1g)	Del	-	-	-	3.00	4 con	12.00
	Pad dispenser	Del	-	6.11	-	-	1 cap	6.11
	Pads and filter papers (200)	Del	-	-	-	20.00	1 con	20.00
	Tweezers							
	Screwdriver							
	Lighter							
	Lubricating grease							

Secondary tests — example field kit list

Parameter / purpose	Equipment type / method	Supplier	Order number capital item	Capital cost (£)	Order number consumables	Consumables cost (£)	Total kit	Total cost (£)
Chloride	Tablet count	PT	-	-	PK079	7.55 for 50	1con	7.55
Fluoride	Photometer	PT	PT250	480.00	pm179	14.05 for 50	1 cap 1 con	480.00 14.05
Iron	Photometer	PT	PT250	included in fluoride price	pm155	11.90 for 50	1 cap 1 con	- 11.90
Manganese	Photometer	PT	PT250	included in fluoride price	pm173	11.90 for 50	1 cap 1 con	- 11.90
Nitrates	Merckoquant strips	MER	-	-	315244P	16.60 for 100	1 con	16.60
Sulphates	Merckoquant strips	MER	-	-	315212H	23.40 for 100	1 con	23.40
Permanganate value	Tablet count	PT	-	-	CP113	33.55 (inl. 50 tests)	1 con	33.55
Deionized water packs	water pack	PT	PT500		-	8.15	2con	16.30

General and treatability tests — example field kit list

Parameter/ purpose	Equipment type /method	Supplier	Order number capital item	Capital cost (£)	Order number consumables	Consumables cost (£)	Total kit	Total cost (£)
Yield measurement and survey								
Measurement	stop watch						1 cap	
	GPS (Garmin 38)	Internet - Business on the move	-	126.80		-	1 cap	126.80
	compass	Geo Supplies	SV15TDCL	44.95	-	-	1 cap	44.95
	altimeter	Field & Trek	25075	119.11	-	-	1 cap	129.00
	float and weight	Use 110 ml bottles + sand					1 cap	
	calculator						1 cap	
	Swiss Army-type pen knife		1-09-01	19.92		-	1 cap	19.92
	pencil, pen and ruler						1 cap	
	paper						1 con	
	3m tape		-	2.99	-	-	1 cap	2.99
	torch	PT	CT102	25.25	-	-	1 cap	24.25
	batteries						2 cons	
	geo lens	Geo Supplies	GLx10	2.50	-	-	1 cap	2.09
	line level		-	1.39	-	-	2 cap	2.78
	survey book	Geo supplies	CW2256	7.36	-	-	1 cap	7.36
	electrical tape						1 con	
Other								
Sample collection and storage	sample bottles 60ml x 12	MER	215/0399/02	5.88	-	-	1cap	5.82
	sample bottles 110ml x 12	MER	215/0399/04	9.12	-	-	1cap	9.73
	bottles 500ml x 12	MER	215/0399/16	20.37	-	-	1 cap	21.75
	syringes 1ml	MER	-	-	406/0375/11	19.86 for 100	1 cons	36.18
	syringes 10ml	MER	-	-	406/0375/14	16.19 for 100	1 cons	16.00
	sampling cup	included with filtration kit						
	sampling line	included with filtration kit						
	biological sampling net (1 mm mesh bag for 200mm frame)	GB nets		6.85		-	1 cap	6.85
Cleaning	glassware wipes (or tissues)	PT	-	-	PT619	2.00	1con	2.10

Parameter / purpose	Equipment type /method	Supplier	Order number capital item	Capital cost (£)	Order number consumables	Consumables cost (£)	Total kit	Total cost (£)
Working surface	workplace mat	PT	PT525	5.25	-	-	1 cap	5.25
Marker	marker pen						1 cap	
Treatability	spatula/spoon (120ml)	MER	2600140/01	5.76	-	-	2 cap	11.52
	beakers 11 x 5	MER	2090730/39	10.97	-	-	1 cap	12.48
(Alkalinity)	Tablet count (Total, M or T) (Caustic, P)	TINT	-	-	414130 414140	(for 20-100 tests) 14.10 15.40	1 cap 1 cap	29.50
(Temperature)	Thermometer in case	PT	PT684	17.10	-	-	1 cap	17.10
(Aluminium)	Photometer	PT	PT250	included in fluoride price	PM 166	10.55 for 50	1 cap	-
(Residual chlorine)	Photometer	PT	PT250	included in fluoride price	PM 031	20.30 for 200	1 con	10.55
	Aluminium sulphate (18 hydrate)	buy in-country	-	-	-	-	1 cap 1 con	20.30
	HTH 65%	buy in-country						
	35 % chlorine	buy in-country						
	ferric chloride	buy in-country						
Kit box								

Water treatment: Mobile treatment units and modular kits

Details ■

Mobile treatment units are self-contained and portable. Modular kits come in pieces and are fitted together on location. The following table identifies a selection of mobile units and two modular treatment kits. Most of the larger relief organizations have their own selection of modular kits which are ordered through their logistics departments. Items such as water storage tanks have not been included in this table. For information on Oxfam tanks, bladder tanks, fast tanks, modular distribution kits, pumping units, etc. contact the relief organizations directly.

Nothomb (1995, p8), referring to mobile treatment units states that 'The uses are still not clearly defined, nor are the specifications. No unit seems to live up to the high expectations. The performances have not been properly and independently evaluated, as neither the indicators of performance nor test protocols are defined.'

Water treatment: Mobile treatment and modular kits

Description	Performance (details taken from manufacturers' literature or from Nothomb, 1995)	Supplier	Approximate cost (1995)
Modular kits			
Treatment unit for water for emergency situations {includes: Four containers mounted on 'euro-palettes' weighing a total of 500kg. Contains all material for approx. 1.5 months of treatment (except fuel). Includes pumps, feed controls, piping, etc.} .	30 m³/h max. Used at 5 to 8m³/h at a pressure of approx. 1 bar produces an effluent of 5 NTU from water of 50 - 200 NTU. Uses coagulation with ferric chloride (or alternatively aluminium sulphate with pH adjustment), and rapid sand filtration with chlorination to complete. Storage tanks are not part of the kit.	MSF Belgium	250,000 fb (8000 ecus)
Oxfam slow sand filter kit {includes 2 x 95,000 litre and 2 x 75,000 litre tanks and fittings including underdrainage, but does not include treated water tanks}	Will supply 3.2m³/hour	Oxfam (UK & Ireland)	£16,310 (US$26,000)
Mobile units			
Self-contained water purification kit {includes: 1 trailer-mounted water purification unit, 1 steel tank 40m³, six water distribution kits with six taps each, piping, tools, necessary accessories such as monitoring tools and consumables for min six months (excluding gasoil)}	Can fulfil daily water requirement of 10,000 people. Slotted well PVC pipe is provided with 6m-long perforated water collection pipe to construct an infiltration gallery to reduce turbidity. Sand and gravel required locally. Main treatment process of unit is rapid sand filtration.	UNICEF	$US29,000
Portable water purifier {includes: purification unit only with cartridge for 25 to 5000 litres depending on size of unit}	Small-scale use only. Up to a maximum of 1500 litres / day. Uses coarse filtration, absorption filtration with activated charcoal cloth, primary disinfection and secondary disinfection with an iodine-resin complex. Can also have post filtration to remove iodine residual. Tests have indicated > 99.9% of virus removal.	Pre-Mac, Kent, UK	
Aquarius 150 * water purification unit	Uses pre-chlorination, coagulation and flocculation, horizontal sand filters and an activated carbon filter. Flow rate of 0.6m³/hr at 75 NTU. (Sizes vary from 0.18 - 6m³/hr). 90kg. US$200 consumables for 90 days. Disinfection capacity not consistent.	Water International Ltd. UK	US$3000

Description	Performance (details taken from manufacturers' literature or from Nothomb, 1995)	Supplier	Approximate cost (1995)
GB13000D* water purification unit	Uses diatomaceous earth coated filter. Chlorination. Flow rate of 4.3m³/hr at 75 NTU. (5-7m³/hr) 350kg. US$20,900 consumables for 90 days. Can reduce max. turbidity of 200 NTUto 5 NTU. Disinfection capacity not consistent.	Goodmann Ball Inc. USA	US$37,000
LMS* water purification unit	Uses course straining. Sand and activated carbon filtration and optional microstrainer. Venturi chlorine doser. Flow rate of 8.0m³/hr at 75 NTU.1600kg. US$270 consumables for 90 days. Can reduce max. turbidity of 50 NTU to 5 NTU. Disinfection capacity not consistent.	LMS Industries, France	US$18,000
Berkefeld* water purification unit	Uses pre-chlorination, coagulation with ferric chloride, adsorption with powdered activated carbon, flocculation with lime, filtration (using candle filters pre-treated with diatomite and activated carbon). Flow rate of 5.4m³/hr at 75 NTU. 3000kg (includes weight of vehicle). US$33,500-93,000 consumables for 90 days. Can reduce max. turbidity of 500 NTU to 5 NTU. Good disinfection to WHO recommended levels.	Berkefeld Anlagebau GmbH, Germany	US$87,000
CLM5000* water purification unit	Pre-chlorination, pH correction, coagulation and flocculation with polychlorate aluminium sulphate and then filtration on a foam medium. Activated carbon filtration. UV disinfection and / or chlorination. Flow rate of 4.0m³/hr at 75 NTU. 1600kg. US$2680 consumables for 90 days. Can reduce max. turbidity of 200 NTU to 5 NTU. Good disinfection but to < 30 min contact time.	Sulzer Chemtech Ltd., Switzerland	US$56,000
Conniston* water purification unit	Filtration in filter coated with diatomaceous earth and chlorination via a venturi chlorine doser. Flow rate of 4.0m³/hr at 75 NTU. 250kg. US$200 consumables for 90 days. US$24,300 consumables for 90 days. Can reduce max. turbidity of 200 NTU to 5 NTU. Disinfection capacity not consistent.	Stella-Meta, UK	US$21,000
Lightweight water purification unit (WPU(L)) portable*{strainer, pump unit, filter, chlorinator and fittings, two tanks capacity 1,550 l }	Average 1.36 m³/h. Unit will filter 95% of all particles greater than 0.005 mm. Raw water is passed through a floating suction strainer and pumped into a Vokes filter unit (diamotaceous earth) and then it is chlorinated using a venturi feed system. Uses liquid chlorine. Flexible water tanks.	Refer to British army	
Standard Water purification unit (WPU(S)) portable*{strainer, pump unit, filter, chlorinator and fittings, two tanks capacity 8,000 l }	Average 6.8m³/h. Unit will filter 95% of all particles greater than 0.005mm. Raw water is passed through a floating suction strainer and pumped into a Vokes filter unit (diamotaceous earth) and then it is chlorinated using a venturi feed system. Uses liquid chlorine. Flexible water tanks. Total weight 540kg.	Refer to British army	
Reverse Osmosis Plant (Weir Westgarth) containerised*	Average 4.15m³/h.	Refer to British army	
Water purification unit (NBC)*{All equipment mounted in a trailer. pumpset, filtration unit, high pressure pumps set, reverse osmosis units, carbon absorption columns, chlorine dosing, two 13,640 l fabric water storage tanks and relative fittings}.	Average 6.8m³/h in non-NBC mode or 2.28m³/hr in NBC mode. Can supply water from brackish sources, or water contaminated by sewage, nuclear, biological or chemical substances but not sea water. Process involves filtration, reverse osmosis, activated carbon absorption and chlorination. There are four eight inch diameter reverse osmosis modules and four stellacarb carbon absorption columns. Total weight for towing is 3300kg.	Refer to British army	
Water purification unit (NBC) Desalination version: Trailer mounted *	Average 1.9m³/h	Refer to British army	

---

* Information on these units was taken directly from Nothomb (1995) and the results of an interagency collaborative testing meeting in Geneva, Switzerland on June 12-20, 1995. For further direct comparisons refer to Nothomb (1995).
** Units used by the British Army

Useful addresses

Organizations which may be able to interpret industrial pollution data ■

Should you not be able to interpret industrial pollution laboratory data yourself, or you are not able to find an organization in the vicinity to do it then the following organizations may be able to assist. They should either have the capacity to interpret the data or will be able to provide alternative contacts. There is likely to be a charge for any interpretation work and this should be discussed with the organiation when you first contact them.

This study does not have the capacity to confirm the skill of the organizations or the personnel responding to requests and so further investigations should be undertaken where necessary.

Details of organizations and contacts

The National Centre for Environmental Toxicology
Water Research Centre (WRc plc)
Henley Road
Medmenham
Marlow, Bucks
SL7 2HD
UK

Tel: +44 1491 571 531
Fax: +44 1491 579 094
e.mail cet@wrcplc.co.uk

Office of Science and Technology
United States Environmental Protection Agency
Washington DC 20460
USA

Contact for accidental spills of contaminants: Mr Jim Taft of the Office of the Ground Water and Drinking Water (OGWDW)
Tel: +202 260 5519

Contact for treatment and removal of contaminants: Dr Krishan Khanna of the Health and Ecological Criteria Division (HECD)
Tel: +202 260 7588

Umweltbundesamt Institute for Water, Soil and Air Hygiene
PO Box 33 00 22
14191 Berlin
Germany

Tel: +49 30 8903 1400
Fax: +49 30 8903 1830

Contact: Director and Professor H.H. Dieter

WELL
Water and Environmental Health at London and Loughborough
London School of Hygiene & Tropical Medicine (University of London)
Keppel Street
London
WC1E 7HT
UK

Tel: +44 171 927 2211
Fax: +44 171 636 7843
e.mail: scairncr@lshtm.ac.uk

Department of Urban Environmental Health,
World Health Organisation,
CH-211, Geneva 27
Switzerland

Tel: +41 22 791 2111
Fax: +41 22 791 0746
Telerg: UNISANTE-GENEVA
Telex: 415416OMS

Equipment manufacturers and suppliers ■

International suppliers

Company	International head office	Africa, Asia, Middle East	European Office	The Americas & Australasia
Berkefeld Anagebau GmbH	Luckenweg, 5 Postfach 3202 29227 CELLE Germany		as international	
Business on the Move Ltd.	2, Woodhill, Kentish Lane, Hatfield, Herts. AL9 6JY, UK Tel: +44 1707 663533 Fax: +44 1707 645976 internet location: www.21store.com/botm/ botm.htm		as international	
Camlab Limited (Hach products)	HACH Company International Marketing Department, PO Box 389 Loveland, Colorado 80539 USA Tel: +1 303 669 3050 Fax: +1 303 669 2932 Telex: 160840	HACH distributes through a network of dealers and distributors. Details can be obtained from the head office.	Camlab Limited, Nuffield Road, Cambridge CB4 1TH, UK Tel: +44 1223 424222 Fax: +44 1223 420856	as international
Cotswold	Contract Department tel: +44 1277 224647 fax: +44 1277 260 789		as international	
ELE International Limited	Eastman Way Hemel Hempstead Hertfordshire HP2 7HB, UK Tel: +44 1442 218355 Fax: +44 1442 252474 / 219045 Telex: 825239 ELELTD G		as international	
Field & Trek Plc.	Contracts Department Unit 3 Wates Way Brentwood, Essex CM159TB, UK Tel: +44 1277 263 554		as international	
GB Nets	Linden Mill Hebden Bridge West Yorkshire, HX7 7DP, UK Tel: +44 422 845365		as international	
Geosupplies Ltd.	16, Station Road Chapeltown Sheffield, S30 4XH, UK Tel: +44 114 245 5746 Fax: +44 114 240 3405		as international	
Goodman Ball Inc.	3639, Haven Avenue Menlo Park CA 94025, USA		as international	
LMS Industries	73100 Aix-les-Bains, France		as international	
Merck Ltd. (BDH Products)	PROMOCHEM GMBH POB 101340 Mercatorstrasse 51 D46469 Wesel Germany Tel: +49 281 98 87 0 Fax:+49 281 9887199 Telex: 812741 Promo D	Howse & McGeorge Ltd. Laboratory Division PO Box 72030 Nairobi, Kenya Tel: +254 2553064 / 2553154 Fax: +254 2601345 Telex: 21554 Arabco JO	Merck House Poole, Dorset BH15 1TD, UK Tel: +44 1202 664 778 Sales tel (freephone): +0800 223 344 Fax: +44 1202 666536 Telex: 411 186 TETRA G	MERCK PTY LTD 207 Colchester Road, Kilsyth, Victoria 3137, Australia Tel: +61 03 97285855 Fax: +61 03 97287611

There are many other distributors in Africa, Asia, the Middle East, Europe, USA and Australasia other than those noted here.

Company	International head office	Africa, Asia, Middle East	European Office	The Americas & Australasia
Merck Ltd. (BDH Products) (cont.)		E MERCK (INDIA) Limited Shiv Sagar Estate 'A' Dr Annie Besant Road PO Box No. 16554 Worli, Bombay 400 018 Tel: +91 22 4922855 Fax: +91 22 4950307 Telex: 1173756		Gallard Schlesinger Industries Inc. 584, Mineola Avenue Carle Place New York, 11514-1731 USA Tel: +1 516 333 5600 Fax: +1 516 333 5628
				Quimibras Industrias Quimicas SA Praca de Bandeira 141, GR 201, Rio de Janeiro RJ 20220, Brazil Tel: +55 21 273 2022 Fax: +55 21 293 3291 Telex: 30083 REDY
Millipore Corporation	80, Ashby Road, Bedford, MA 01730, Massachusetts, USA Tel: +1 800 645 5476 Fax: +1 617 275 5550	For Austria, Central Europe, Africa, Middle East and the Gulf: Millipore Ges.m.b.H. A-1130 Wein, Austria, Tel: +43) 1 877 8926 Fax: +43 1 877 1654 Telex: + 43 1 877 1654 Millipore also has subsiduaries in many other countries including: China, India, Japan, Malaysia, Taiwan etc.	Millipore (U.K.) Ltd. 'Tehe Boulevard' Blackmore Lane, Watford Hertfordshire, WD1 8YW,UK Tel: +44 923 816 375 Fax: +44 923 818 297 Telex: 24191 milipor g Millipore S.A. BP 307, F-78054 Saint-Quentin Yvelines Cedex, France Tel: +33 1 30 12 7000 Fax: +33 1 30 12 7180 Telex: 698371 F Millipore has many other subsiduaries across Europe.	As international office
MSF Belgium	Logistics Department Duprestr 94 B-1090 Jette Brussels Belgium Tel: +32 2 474 7474 Fax: +32 2 474 7575		as international	
OXFAM (UK and Ireland)	Public Health Team OXFAM (UK and Ireland) 274, Banbury Road Oxford OX2 7DZ, UK Tel: +44 1865 312 135 Fax: +44 1865 312 600 Telex: 83610 OXFAM G		as international	
Palintest Ltd.	Palintest House Kingsway Team Valley Gateshead Tyne & Wear NE11 ONS, UK Tel: +44 191 491 0808 Fax: +44 191 482 5372		as international	21, Kenton Lands Road PO Box 18733 Erlanger, Kentuky 41018 USA Tel: +1 606 341 7423 Fax: +1 606 341 2302 4/84-88 Riverside Road, Chipping Norton, PO Box 318, Padstow, NSW 2211, Australia Tel: +61 2 755 3486 Fax: +61 2 755 3491
Pre-Mac (Kent) Ltd.	40, Holden Park Road Southborough, Tunbridge Wells, Kent TN4 OER, UK Tel: +44 1892 534 361 Fax: +44 1892 515 770		as international	
Robens Institute (Delagua)	Robens Institute University of Surrey Guildford, Surrey GU2 5XH, UK Tel: +44 1483 509 203 Fax: +44 1483 503517 Telex: 859331		as international	

Company	International head office	Africa, Asia, Middle East	European Office	The Americas & Australasia
Silva (UK) Ltd.	Unit 10 Sky Business Park Eversley Way Egham, Surrey TW20 8RF, UK Tel: +44 1784 471 721 Fax: +44 1784 471 097		as international	
Stella-Meta	Laverstoke Mill Whitchurch Hampshire RG28 7NR, UK		as international	
Sulzer Chemtech Ltd.	PO Box 65 8404 Winterthur Switzerland		as international	
The Tintometer Ltd. (Lovibond products)	Waterloo Road Salisbury SP1 2JY UK Tel: +44 1722 327242 Fax: +441722 412322 Telex: 47372		Tintometer GmbH Schleefstraße 8a D-44287 Dortmund Germany Tel: +49 231 94510 0 Fax: +49 231 94510 20 Tintometer AG Hauserstauâe 53 CH-5200 Windisch Switzerland Tel: +41 56 422829 Fax: +41 56 424121	
UNICEF	UNICEF Supply Division UNICEF Plads Freeport DK-2100 Copenhagen Denmark Tel: + 45 27 35 27 Fax: + 45 26 94 21			
Wagtech International Limited	10, Thatcham House Turners Drive Thatcham, Berkshire RG13 4QD UK Tel: +44 1635 872929 Fax: + 44 1635 872808 Telex: +846256 wagtec g	Kitgum House 103, Jinja Road P.O.Box 3218 Kampala Uganda Tel: +256 41 232100 / 259646 Fax: +256 41 244606 Telex: 61208 magric uga	as international	
Water International Limited	The Atrium, Mercury Court Tithebarn Street Liverpool L2 2QP, UK		as international	

Equipment manufacturers and suppliers — Local

Company	Address
Fundacion Zumaque	Oficina: Edificio Maraven, Piso 6o, Chuao-Apartado 829 - Caracas 1010A, Venezuela Telefono: +58 2 908.22.06
Premier Health Care Products	41 & 42, S.V. Co-op, Ind. Estate, Balanagar, Hyderabad 500 037, A.P. India Tel: +91 40 273515 / 273525, Fax: +91 40 271879
All India Institute of Hygiene & Public Health and UNICEF, Calcutta	Contact either of the organizations noted on the left

General ■

The addresses which follow are only a few of the many which could be useful for obtaining information on water sources around the world. The **embassy of the country of concern** or your **home country government survey department** may be able to provide relevant addresses for the country under consideration.

General addresses

Address	Information
Ordnance Survey RomseyRoad Maybush Southampton SO9 4DH UK	Topographic maps, geological maps
British Geological Survey Keyworth Nottingham NG12 5GG, UK or Hydrogeology unit Macclean Building Crowmarsh Gifford Wallingford Oxfordshire OX10 0RA UK	Geological maps, hydrogeological maps, reports, satellite imagery and general data for Great Britain and Overseas. BGS also have a system under trial where they answer any request made for hydrological information for any area to be used in an emergency response, and they are attempting to respond using interpretations of satellite imagery and other data within two to five weeks.
Spot image 16, Bis Avenue Edourd Belin BP 4359 31030 Toulouse, Cedex France	Satellite imagery
National Cartographic Information Center (NCIC) US Geological Survey, 507 National Center, Reston Virginia 22092, USA	Free information on national state topographic maps and information and remote sensing.
Operations section WRD US Geological Survey 405, National Center, Reston Virginia, 22092, USA	Data on surface water, groundwater and water quality collected by the US Geological Survey
United States Geological Survey Box 25425 Federal Center Denver, Colorado 80225, USA	USGS maps, books, professional papers and other publications on the geology of the USA and overseas

United Nations addresses

Address	Information
United Nations Environment Programme (UNEP) PO Box 30552, Nairobi, Kenya Tel: +254 2 230 800 Fax: + 254 2 226 886 IPAUNEP@lgc.apc.org	Responsible for the Global Environmental Monitoring System (GEMS)
World Meterological Organisation World Weather Watch Department WMO/OMM, Case Postale No.2300 CH-1211 Geneva 2 Switzerland Tel: +41 22 730 8333 email: nkootval@www.wmo.ch	In case of emergency, natural disaster or other crises for which UN assistance has been requested and in which meterology or hydrology may affect the process of providing humanitarian relief, 24-hour operational contacts through DHA's emergency number +41 22 917 2010
Department of Humanitarian Affairs (DHA) Vienna International Centre PO Box 500 1400 Vienna Austria Tel: +43 1 21131 Fax: +43 1 232156 Telex 135 612 and Palais des Nations CH–1211 Geneva 10 Switzerland Tel: +4122 9171234 Fax: +4122 9170023 e.mail: DHAGVA@DHA.UNICC.ORG	Assists the UN system in co-ordinating humanitarian assistance
United Nations High Commissioner for Refugees (UNHCR) Centre William Rappard 154, rue de Lausanne 1202 Geneva 21 Switzerland Tel: +41 22 739 8111 Fax: +41 22 731 9546 Telex: 415 740	Concerned with the international protection of refugees and the promotion of durable solutions for their problems. Often acts as the co-ordinating organization in the field.
Food and Agriculture Organisation (FAO) via delle Terme di Caracalla 00100 Rome, Italy Tel: +39 6 579 73152 Fax: +39 6 579 75155	Soils, vegetation cover and other aspects of land use around the world.

Bibliography

Adams, J. (1995) 'Environmental health and environmental impact: Policy and practice in emergency water supply and sanitation', in: *OXFAM, Sanitation Workshop,* 11-14 December.

Anderson, M.B., Howarth, A.M. and Overholt, C. (1992) *A Framework for People — Orientated Planning in Refugee Situations Taking Account of Women, Men and Children: A practical tool for refugee workers,* Geneva.

Assar, M. (1971) *Guide to Sanitation in Natural Disasters,* WHO, Geneva.

Ayoade, J.O. (1988) *Tropical Hydrogeology and Water Resources,* Macmillan Publishers, Hong Kong.

Bahu, B., Crittenden, B., and O'Hara, J. (1997), *Management of Process Industry Waste,* Institution of Chemical Engineers, UK.

de Barg, L. (1995) *Water Quality Monitoring and Watershed Management,* Step by Step, USA

Bartram, J. (1990) *Drinking Water Supply Surveillance,* Robens Institute, Guildford,UK.

BDH, (1997) 'Safety data sheets', BDH, UK.

Bell, G.R. (1992) *Oxfam Emergency Water Supply Program, Rohingya refugee camps, Bangladesh.*

Bhalla, D.K. and Majumdar, K.M., (1996) 'Deteriorating ground water quality', in Pickford, J. (ed) *Proceedings of the WEDC 22nd Conference, Reaching the Unreached: Challenges for the 21st Century,* New Delhi, India, Septmber.

Bouvier, A. (1991) 'Protection of the environment in times of armed conflict', *International Review of the Red Cross,* Nov-Dec.

Bouvier, A. (1992) 'Recent studies on the protection of the environment in times of armed conflict', *International Review of the Red Cross,* Nov-Dec.

Brassington, R. (1988) *Field Hydrogeology,* John Wiley & Sons, UK.

Bridgewater A.V. and Mumford, C.J. (1979), *Waste Recycling and Pollution Control Handbook,* George Goodwin Ltd., London, UK.

Brikke, F., Bredero, M., De Veer, T. and Smet, J. (1995) Draft - *Linking Technology Choice with O&M in the Context of Rural and Low-income Urban Water Supply and Sanitation,* IRC, O&M Working Group, WS&S Collaborative Council

Brink, A.B.A., Partridge, T.C. and Williams, A.A.B. (1984) *Soil Survey for Engineering.* Clarendon Press, Oxford, UK.

British Army, Field Manual Extracts

British Standards Institution, (1988), *Draft for Development, Code of Practice for the Identification of Potentially Contaminated Land and its Investigation* DD 175. British Standards Institution.

BS 5930:1981 Code of Practice for Site Investigations, HMSO.

Cairncross, S. and Feachem, R. (1978) *Small Water Supplies*, Bulletin No 10. Ross Institute, London.

Cairns, J., Albaugh, D.W., Busey, F. and Duane Chanay, M. (1968) 'The sequential comparison index: A simplified method for non-biologists to estimate relative differences in biological diversity in stream pollution studies', *Journal WPCF*, 10(9) pp1607–13

Campbell, G.R. (1996) Personal Communication, Addis Ababa, Ethiopia.

Carroll, R.F. (1991) *Disposal of Domestic Effluents to the Ground*, Overseas Building Note 195, Building Research Establishment, UK.

CEHA, (1991) *Manual on Water and Sanitation for Health in Refugee Camps*, CEHA & UNEP, Jordan.

Chalinder, A. (1994) *Water and Sanitation in Emergencies,* Relief and Rehabilitation Network, UK.

Choveaux, N. (1991) *Hands-on Stream and Pond Life: A Field Guide*, Umgeni Valley project, Sahre-Net, South Africa.

Clegg, J. (1986) *Observers Pond Life*, Penguin Group, South Africa.

Coad, A. (1995) *Water Treatment Lecture Notes*, WEDC.

Collins, C.J.L. (1996) 'Refugee crisis around the Great Lakes', *Africa Recovery*, May.

Conti, R., (1997) Personal Communication, ICRC, Geneva

Dahi, E. (1996) 'Contact precipitation for defluoridation of water', in *WEDC 22nd Conference, Reaching the Unreached: Challenges for the 21st Century,* New Delhi, 9-13th September.

Dahi, E., Mtalo, F., Njau, B., and Bregnhj, H. (1996) 'Defluoridation using the Nalgonda Technique in Tanzania', in *Pickford, J. (ed) WEDC 22nd Conference, Reaching the Unreached: Challenges for the 21st Century*, New Delhi, 9-13th Sept. 1996

Davies, A. and Barclay, J. (1996) *Silva GPS and Electronic Compass*, Silva, UK Ltd., UK.

Davies, T.T. (1997) Personal communication.

Davis, J. (1988) 'From emergency relief to long term development', *Waterlines*, 6 (4) pp29-31.

Davis, J. and Brikke, F. (1995) *Making Your Water Supply Work: Operation and Maintenance of Small Water Systems*, Occasional Paper Series 29, International Reference Centre for Community Water Supply and Sanitation, The Netherlands.

Davis, J. and Lambert, R. (1995) *Engineering in Emergencies: A Practical Guide for Relief Workers.* Intermediate Technology Publications, London.

Degremont. (1979) *Water Treatment Handbook,* 5th Edition. John Wiley and Sons, New York.

Dickinson, G.C. (1969) *Maps and Air Photographs,* Edward Arnold (Publishers) Ltd., UK.

Disaster Relief Agency (1995) *Proposal for Stand-by Quick Response Mobile Water Transport System for Emergency Situations,* Disaster Relief Agency, The Hague, The Netherlands.

van Dongen, Pieter and Woodhouse, M. (1994) *Finding Groundwater: A Project Managers Guide to Techniques and How to Use Them,* UNDP - World Bank Water and Sanitation Program, Washington.

Economic and Social Commission for Asia and the Pacific (1990) *Water Quality Monitoring in the Asian and Pacific Region,* Water Resources Series No 67. UN, New York.

Ellet, K.K. (1993) *An Introduction to Water Quality Monitoring Using Volunteers: A Handbook for Co-ordinators,* Alliance for the Chesapeake Bay Inc., USA.

Fell, N. (1996) 'Outcasts from Eden', *New Scientist,* 31 August, pp24–27.

Flemming, G. (1991) *Recycling Derelict Land,* Institution of Civil Engineers, UK.

Foerster, J. (1996) *'Uvira Water Supply Project',* Internal Report, ICRC /ARC, Melbourne, Australia.

Galvis, G., Visscher, J.T., Fernandez, J., and Beron, F. (1993) *Pre-treatment Alternatives for Drinking-water Supply Systems.* Occasional Paper Series, International Reference Centre for Community Water Supply and Sanitation, The Netherlands.

Gosling, L. and Edwards, M. (1995) *A Practical Guide to Assessment, Monitoring, Review and Evaluation.* Development Manual 5, Save the Children, London.

Gould, T.J. (1992) 'Sustainable Refugee Participation in Water Supply and Sanitation Schemes'. MSC thesis, WEDC, UK.

Grabow, W. (1996) 'Waterborne Diseases: Update on Water Quality Assessment and Control', *Water South Africa,* 22,(2), April.

Green, D.R., (1991) *Field Kits and Associated Training for Monitoring Drinking Water Quality in Pacific Island Countries.* Institute of Natural Resources, University of the South Pacific, Fiji.

Greensmith, J.T., (1967) *Practical Geology for Schools,* Leonard Hill, London.

Groundwater Survey (Kenya) Limited, (1989) *Well Siting for Low-cost Water Supplies* (Vol.2). Groundwater Survey (Kenya) Ltd., Nairobi.

Guoth-Gumberger, Marta and Rueh, (1987) *Small Projects, Training Manual, Vol II Water Supply,* Sudan Council of Churches, Munuki Water and Sanitation Project, Sudan.

Hansch, S. (1995) *How Many People Die of Starvation in Humanitarian Emergencies,* Refugee Policy Group, Washington, USA.

Hansch, S. (1996) *Operational Lessons of NGO Assistance to Rwandan Refugees: Experiences from Zaire, Tanzania and Burundi,* The Refugee Policy Group, Washington USA.

Hawkes, H.A. (1957) 'Biological Aspects of River Pollution' in L. Klein *Aspects of River Pollution.* Butterworths Scientific Publications, London.

Hayes, A. (1988) 'Drilling water wells in disaster areas', *Waterlines,* 6(4) pp10–12.

Hellawell, J.M. (1978) *Biological Surveillance of Rivers,* WRC, Stevenage.

Hilton, T.E., (1964) *Practical Geography in Africa,* Longmans, Green & Co. Ltd., UK.

HMSO, (1996) *The Special Waste Regulations,* No. 972. HMSO, London.

Hodgkiss, A.G. (1970) *Maps for Books and Theses,* David Charles, UK.

Hodgson, R. and Tannock, S. (no date) 'Water and Environmental Sanitation in Urban Emergencies'. a note prepared for UNICEF.

Hofkes, E.H. (ed.) (1983) *Small Community Water Supplies. Technology of Small Water Supply Sytems in Developing Countries,* Technical Paper Series 18. International Reference Centre for Community Water Supply and Sanitation, The Netherlands.

Howard, J. (1979) *Safe Drinking Water. Information and Practice When Treatment of Drinking Water Supplies is Necessary.* Oxfam, Oxford.

Hutton, L.G., (1983) *Field Testing of Water in Developing Countries,* Water Research Centre, UK.

Hynes H.B.N. (1974) *The Biology of Polluted Waters.* Liverpool University Press, Liverpool, UK.

ICRC (1994) *Water and War: Symposium on Water in Armed Conflicts,* Montreux, 21-23, November, ICRC.

IDRC, CRDI, CIID (1990) *Use of Simple, Inexpensive Microbial Water Quality Tests, Results of a Three Continent, Eight Country Research Project,* eds. B.J Dukta and A.H. El Shaarani. IDRC, Canada.

IFRC (1995) *World Disasters Report,* Martinus Nijhoff Publishers, The Netherlands.

IIED (1991) 'Participatory Rural Appraisal of the Feb 91 Bangalore PRA Trainers Workshop, IIED, London'. MYRADA, Bangalore.

Intertect,(1971) *Refugee Camps and Camp Planning, Report I: Camp planning.* Intertect, Dallas, Texas.

Intertect (1971) *Refugee Camps and Camp Planning, Report II: Camp improvements,* Intertect,. Dallas, Texas.

Interdepartmental Committee on the Redevelopment of Contaminated Land (ICRCL) (1983), *Notes on the Redevelopment of Scrap Yards and Similar Sites*, Guidance Note 42/80.

Interdepartmental Committee on the Redevelopment of Contaminated Land (ICRCL) (1986), *Notes on the Redevelopment of Gas Work Sites*, Guidance Note 18/79.

International Reference Centre for Community Water Supply and Sanitation (1976) *Prediction Methodology for Suitable Water and Wastewater Processes*, Technical Paper No.8. WHO International Reference Centre for Community Water Supply and Sanitation, The Netherlands.

Jagour, M., (1996) Personal Communication, MSF France, Bujumbura, Burundi

Jahn, Al.A.S. (1981) *Traditional Water Purification in Tropical Developing Countries: Existing methods and potential application.* GTZ, Germany.

Jordan Jnr, T.D. (1984) *A Handbook of Gravity Flow Water Systems*, Intermediate Technology Publications, London.

Kawamura, S. (1991) *Integrated Design of Water Treatment Facilities*, John Wiley and Sons, UK.

Keller, A.Z. and Wilson, H.C. (1992) *Hazards to Drinking Water Supplies*, Springer–Verlag, Germany

Klein, L. (1957) *Aspects of River Pollution.* Butterworths Sceintific Publications, London.

Lambert, B. (1994) 'Engineers humanitarian relief and water supplies', *Waterlines,* 13(1) pp2–3.

de Lange, E. (1994) *Manual for Simple Water Quality Analysis,* IWT Foundation, The Netherlands.

Larcher, P. (1997) Personal Communication, Construction Enterprise Unit, Loughborough University, UK.

Lashley, D.A. (1997) *Vulnerability Assessment of Drinking Water Supply Infrastructure of Montserrat*, Pan American Health Organization

Leurs, R. (1993) *A Resource Manual for Trainers and Practitioners of Participatory Rural Appraisal (PRA),* Development Administration Group, UK.

Lloyd, B. and Helmer, R. (1991) *Surveillance of Drinking Water Quality in Rural Areas,* Longman Scientific & Technical, United States.

Maier, F.J. (1963) *Manual of Water Fluoridation Practice,* McGraw-Hill Book Company Inc., USA.

Manja, K.S., Maurya, M.S., and Rao, K.M. (1982) 'A simple field test for the detection of faecal pollution in drinking water', *Bulletin of the WHO* 60(5) pp797–801.

Mann, H.T. and Williamson, D. (1973) *Water Treatment and Sanitation: Simple Methods for Rural Areas,.* Intermediate Technology Publications, London.

Martin, F.W., Lippilt, J.M., and Prothero, T.G. (1992) *Hazardous Waste Handbook for Health and Safety*, 2nd Edition. Butterworth-Heinemann, UK.

Masschelein, W.J. (1992) *Unit Processes in Drinking Water Treatment*, Marcel Dekker Inc., Basal, Switzerland.

Mbugua, J. and Nissen-Petersen, E. (1995) *Rainwater an Under-Utilized Resource*, Swedish International Development Authority, Nairobi.

McCaffrey, S.C., (1993) 'Water, politics and International Law' in Gleich, P.H. *Water in Crisis, A Guide to the World's Freshwater Resources*, Oxford University Press, New York.

McKensie, S. and de la Haye, Renee. (1996) 'Interim Evaluation of OXFAM's Environmental Health Programme in the Goma Refugee Camps', OXFAM.

Miller, G.T. (1994) *Living in the Environment* (8th Edition). Wadsworth Publishing Company, Belmont, California.

Ministry of Defence, (1970) *Manual of Map Reading, Air Photo Reading and Field Sketching, Part III*, 3rd Edition. Ministry Of Defence, UK.

Moro-Castro, D. (1996) Personal Communication, UNHCR

MSF, (1994) *Public Health Engineering in Emergency Situations*. MSF Paris, France.

MSF Holland, (1995) (Draft) *Operational Policies for Watsan Programmes*. TSG MSF Holland.

MSF Belgium, (1996a) *Eau, Hygiene et Assainissement, Chemie des Eaux Guideline*. MSF Belgium.

MSF Belgium (1996b) *Log-News no 11*. Departement Logistique, MSF Belgium.

MSF Holland (undated) Early Assessment Forms, Old and New Versions. MSF Holland.

Mundo, D. F. (1995) 'Money isn't everything', *Refugees 4*.

Nair, K.S. (1996) Personal communication, CARE, Jijiga, Ethiopia.

National Rivers Authority (1994) *Abandoned Mines and the Water Environment*, London, HMSO.

Nemerow, N.L. and Dasgupta, A. (1991) *Industrial and Hazardous Waste Treatment*. Van Nostrand Reinhold, New York.

Nembrini, P.G. and Etienne, Y. *(no date) Water, Sanitation and the Environment in Conflict Situations*. ICRC, Genève, Switzerland.

Nixon, S.C. (1993) 'Bankside Storage and Infiltration Systems' (ENV 9037): Final report to the department of the environment, DOE 3266 (P).

Nothomb, C. (1995) 'Portable Water Treatment Units for Emergency Situations', MSc thesis, WEDC, UK.

Ockelford, J.J. (1989) 'An Expert System for Water Supplies in Disaster Relief', MSc thesis, WEDC, UK.

Ockwell, R. (1986) *Assisting in Emergencies. A Resource Handbook for UNICEF Field Staff.* UNICEF, Genèva, Switzerland.

ODA (no date) *Manual of Environmental Appraisal*, Overseas Development Administration, UK.

Oxfam (1991) *Oxfam Water Supply Scheme, Well Digging Pack: Survey Auger Kit (For Investigating Possible Sites for Hand Dug Wells).* OXFAM Technical Unit, Oxford, UK.

Oxfam (1995) *The Oxfam Handbook of Development and Relief.* Oxfam (UK and Ireland), Oxford, UK.

Oxfam, *Oxfam Water Supply Scheme for Emergencies: filtration pack, distribution pack, water pumping pack.* OXFAM, Oxford, UK.

Pacey, A. and Cullis, A. (1986) *Rainwater Harvesting: The Collection of Rainfall and Run-off in Rural Areas.* Intermediate Technology Publications, London.

PAHO (1997) *Draft Guidelines for the Preparation of the Vulnerability Analysis of the Drinking Water supply and Sewerage System, PAHO (restricted document)*

Palintest Ltd. (1989) 'Rapid Methods for the Bacteriological Testing of Water', Oxford Conferences, Sutton Coldfield, UK, Monday 5th June.

Pollard, S.J., Harop, D.O., Crowcroft, P., Mallett, S.H., Jeffries, S.R., and Young, P.J., (1995) 'Risk assessment for environmental management: Approaches and applications', *Journal of the Chartered Institution of Water and Environmental Management,* 9(6).

Pre-Mac Water Filters (1995) Suppliers Information, Pre-Mac (Kent) Ltd.

Premier Deepwell Handpumps (P) Ltd., Domestic Defluoridation Unit, India.

Premier Health Care Products (no date) *Water Testing Kit. A Simple Field Test for the Detection of Faecal Pollution in Drinking Water*, India.

Price, M. (1995) *Introducing Groundwater.* George Allen & Unwin (Publishers) Ltd., UK.

Reed, R. and Dean, P.T. (1995) 'Recommended methods for the disposal of sanitary wastes from temporary field medical facilities', *Disasters* 18,(4).

Renchon, Bridgette, and Smith, M.D. (1986) *L'eau dans les Camps de Personnes Deplaces,* MSF, Universite Catholique de Louvain.

Sandler, R.H. and Jones, T.C. (1987) *Medical Care of Refugees.* Oxford University Press, New York-Oxford.

Sakharwarz, B. (1994) 'Planning for the long-term in Cambodia', *Waterlines* 13,(1) pp19–21.

Sawyer, C.N. and McCarty, P.L. (1989) *Chemistry for Environmental Engineering,* 3rd Edition.

McGraw Hill Int.

Schulz, C.R. and Okun, D.A. (1984) *Surface Water Treatment for Communities in Developing Countries.* Intermediate Technology Publications, London.

Seaman, J. (ed.) (1981) 'Medical care in refugee camps', *Disasters* 5(3).

Semat Technical (UK) Ltd., *Everything You Want to Know About Coagulation and Flocculation,* Semat Technical (UK) Ltd.

Sewell, R. (1988) 'The software of emergency water supplies', *Waterlines,* 6(4) pp2–5.

Shelembe, E.B. (1995) *Monitoring Visible Water Life.* Share-Net, Umgeni Valley Project, South Africa.

Shelley, C. (1994) 'Refugee water supplies: Some political considerations', *Waterlines* 13(1).

Shen, T. (1995), *Industrial Pollution Prevention.* Springer-Verlag, Berlin.

Sherlock, P. (1988) 'Coping with equipment in emergencies', *Waterlines,* 6(4) pp26–8.

Shook, G.A. and Englande, A.J. (1992) 'Environmental health criteria for disaster relief and refugee camps', *International Journal of Environmental Health Research* 2, pp171–83.

Shook, G.A. (1983) 'Developing a sanitary survey form for evaluating refugee camp locations, *Journal of Environmental Health* 45(6) pp295–8.

Sigma Chemicals Co. (1997) Material Data Sheets, Sigma Chemical Co., UK.

Silley, P.T. (1955) *Topographical Maps and Photographic Interpretation.* George Philip & Son Ltd., UK.

Simmonds, S., Vaughan, P. and Gunn, W. (1985) *Refugee Community Health Care.* Ross Institute, Oxford University Press, Oxford.

Siru, D. (1992) 'Sanitary Survey Training in Malaysia', MSc thesis, WEDC, UK.

Skinner, B. and Cotton, A. (1992) *Community Rainwater Catchment.* International Labour Office, UK / Geneva.

Smethurst, G. (1992) *Basic Water Treatment for Application WorldWide*, 2nd Edition. Thomas Telford, London.

Smith, G.N. (1990) *Elements of Soil Mechanics*, 6th Edition. BSP Professional Books, Oxford, UK.

Smith, M. (1995) 'Sanitary Survey Lecture Notes', WEDC, UK.

Stern, P. (ed), from an original work by F. Layland (1983) *Field Engineering: An Introduction to*

Development Work and Construction in Rural Areas. Intermediate Technology Publications, UK.

Stern, P. (1979) *Small Scale Irrigation: A Manual of Low-Cost Water Technology.* Intermediate Technology Publications Ltd., London.

Stern, P. (1997) Personal communication.

Sterritt, R.M. and Lester, J.N. (1988) *Microbiology for Environmental and Public Health Engineers.* E. & F.N. Spon, London.

Stulz, R. and Mukerji, K. (1993) *Appropriate Building Materials: A Catalogue of Potential Solutions,* 3rd Edition. SKAT & IT Publications Ltd.,St. Gallen, Switzerland and London.

SUUNTO (no date) Manufacturer's instructions for SUUNTO PM–5 Clinometer.

Sylvester, D. (1952) *Maps and Landscape.* George Philip & Son Ltd., UK.

Tearle, K., (1973), *Industrial Pollution Control.* Business Books Ltd, London.

Tebbutt, M. (1994) *Camp Assessment, Technical Fact Sheet.* Concern, Burundi.

Tebbutt, T.H.Y. (1992) *Principles of Water Quality Control*, 4th edition. Pergamon Press, Oxford.

Tilley, M.N. (1995) 'Military Water Treatment Systems', *Water Supply*, 14 (3 / 4) pp439–52.

Twort, A.C., Law, F.M., Crowley, F.W. and Ratnayaka, D.D. (1994) *Water Supply*, 4th Edition. Edward Arnold, London.

Ulens, H. (1992) 'Water Field Testing in Emergency Situations', MSc thesis, WEDC, UK.

Umgeni Valley Project (undated), Water Quality Slide, South Africa.

United States Environmental Protection Agency, (1980) *Design Manual On-site-wastewater Treatment and Disposal Systems.* USEPA, Washington.

United States Environmental Protection Agency (1991) *Volunteer Lake Monitoring: A Methods Manual.* USEPA, Washington.

United States Environmental Protection Agency (1990) *Volunteer Water Monitoring: A Guide for State Managers.* USEPA, Washington.

UNCHS (Habitat), (1987) *Water Supply and Waste Disposal Management: Impact-Evaluation Guidelines.* UNCHS, Nairobi, Kenya.

UNDP & IAPSO (1995) *Emergency Relief Items Compendium of Generic Specifications.* UNDP / IAPSO, Geneva.

UNDP - World Bank (1991) 'Information and Training for Low-Cost Water Supply & Sanitation: Water treatment', Participant's notes. UNDP - World Bank, Water and Sanitation Programme 4.5, Washington, USA.

UNDTCD (1991) *Criteria for Approaches to Water Quality Management in Developing Countries*, Natural Resources Water series No 26. UN, New York.

UNESCO and WHO (1978) *Water Quality Surveys: A Guide for the Collection and Interpretation of Water Quality Analysis Data*. United Nations Educational, Scientific and Cultural Organisation and WHO, UK.

UNHCR (1982) *Handbook for Emergencies*. UNHCR, Geneva.

UNHCR (1992) *Water Manual for Refugee Situations*, Programme & Technical Support Section, Geneva, Switzerland.

UNHCR (1996a) *Inventories for Water Supply Systems*, UNHCR Regional Liaison Office, Addis Ababa, Ethiopia

UNHCR (1996b) *Refugees* 3(105).

UNHCR (1996c) *Refugees and the Environment, Caring for the Future*, Geneva.

UNHCR (1997) *UNHCR Environmental News,* (II) June.

UNICEF (1975) *Aqua Plus Guidelist*. UNICEF Supply Division, Copenhagen.

UNICEF (1986) *Assisting in Emergencies. A Resource Handbook for UNICEF Field Staff*. UNICEF, New York, USA.

UNICEF (1995) *Water Engineering: Technical Supply Bulletin No8. Water Purification Unit*, UNICEF, Denmark.

UNICEF and All India Institute of Hygiene and Public Health (1996a) *A Manual on Water Quality Field Test Kit*. UNICEF, Calcutta Field Office and the All India Institute of Hygiene and Public Health.

UNICEF and All India Institute of Hygiene and Public Health (1996b) *Specification for Water Quality Field Test Kit for Testing 100 Samples*. UNICEF, Calcutta Field Office and the All India Institute of Hygiene and Public Health.

United Nations Department of Humanitarian Affairs (1996) *Mudflows; Experience and lessons learned from the Management of Major Disasters*, Prepared in support of the International Decade for Natural Disaster Reduction, United Nations Department of Humanitarian Affairs.

United States Environmental Protection Agency (1990) *Technologies for Upgrading Existing or Designing New Drinking Water Treatment Facilities*. United States Environmental Protection Agency, Washington.

United States Environmental Protection Agency, (1996) *Drinking Water Regulations and Health Advisories*, EPA 822-B-96-002. United States Environmental Protection Agency, Washington.

United States Environmental Protection Agency / Life Systems, Inc., (1994) *Emergency Spill Guidance Document for the Office of Water*, United States Environmental Protection Agency / Life Systems, Inc., Washington.

USAID, (1982a) *Water for the World: Methods of Developing Sources of Surface Water.* Technical Note No. RWS.1.M, USAID, USA.

USAID, (1982b) *Water for the World: Testing of the Yield Wells*. Technical note No. RWS.2.C.7.

USAID, (1982c) *Water for the World: Planning How to Use Ground Water Sources*. Technical note No. RWS.2.P.1.

USAID, (1982d) *Water for the World: Selecting a Well Site*. Technical note No. RWS.2.P.3.

WaterAid (1988), *Water Aid's Technical Handbook*, 2nd Edition. Water Aid, London.

Wegelin, M. (1995) 'Update on roughing filtration', *Sandec News* 1 pp22–3.

Whitton, D.G.A. and Brooks, J.R.V. (1975) *The Penguin Dictionary of Geology*. Penguin Books Ltd., UK.

WHO (1971) *International Standards for Drinking-Water*, 3rd Edition. WHO, Geneva.

WHO (1976) *Surveillance of Drinking Water Quality*. WHO, Geneva.

WHO (1984a) *Guidelines for Drinking-Water Quality Vol. 1 Recommendations*, 1st Edition. WHO, Geneva.

WHO (1984b) *Guidelines for Drinking-Water Quality Vol. 2 Health Criteria and Other Supporting Information*. WHO, Geneva.

WHO (1985) *Guidelines for Drinking Water Quality Vol. 3 Drinking-Water Quality Control in Small Community Supplies*. WHO, Geneva.

WHO (1993) *Guidelines for Drinking-Water Quality Vol. 1 Recommendations*, 2nd Edition. WHO, Geneva.

WHO (1996) *Guidelines for Drinking-Water Quality Vol. 2 Health Criteria and Other Supporting Information, 2nd edition*. WHO, Geneva.

WHO/Robens Institute, (1996) *Environmental Sanitation for Cholera Control* (draft), WHO/Robens Institute

Wilson, R., (1985) *Assessment of Present Water and Sanitation Situation and Recommendations for Improvement*. UNHCR, Geneva.

Youde, M. (1996) *Emergency Water Supply for Bujumbura Contingency Plan*, Oxfam (UK & Ireland).

WRC / WHO (1989) *Disinfection of Rural and Small Community Water Supplies: A Manual for*

Design and Operation. WRC, UK.

Zavaleta, J.O., Cantilli, R. and Ohanian, E.V. (1993) 'Drinking water health advisory program' *Ann. 1st. Super Sanita* 29(2) pp355–8.